Hierurgia Anglicana

'Ceremonies are advancements of order, decency, modesty, and gravity in the service of God; expressions of those heavenly desires and dispositions which we ought to bring along with us to God's house; adjuments of attention and devotion; furtherances of edification, visible instructors, helps of memory, exercises of faith; the shell that preserves the kernel of religion from contempt; the leaves that defend the blossoms and the fruit.'—ARCHBP. BRAMHALL.

Hierurgia Anglicana

DOCUMENTS AND EXTRACTS

ILLUSTRATIVE OF

The Ceremonial of the Anglican Church

AFTER THE REFORMATION

EDITED BY MEMBERS OF

THE ECCLESIOLOGICAL LATE CAMBRIDGE

CAMDEN SOCIETY, A.D. 1848

NEW EDITION

PART I

Revised and Considerably Enlarged by

VERNON STALEY

Author of 'The Ceremonial of the English Church,'
'Studies in Ceremonial,' etc.

WIPF & STOCK · Eugene, Oregon

Wipf and Stock Publishers
199 W 8th Ave, Suite 3
Eugene, OR 97401

Hierurgia Anglicana, Part 1
Documents and Extracts Illustrative of The Ceremonial of the Anglican Church After the Reformation
By Staley, Vernon
ISBN 13: 978-1-60608-359-8
Publication date 5/14/2009
Previously published by The de la More Press, 1902

EDITOR'S PREFACE
(1902)

THE *Hierurgia Anglicana*, which first appeared in one volume in the year 1848, was originally published in numbers, beginning in 1843 and finishing in 1848. A statement to this effect was made by the R--- John Fuller Russell, B.C.L., F.S.A., in the Jerusalem Chamber, Westminster, on November 28, 1867, in the course of his examination by the Archbishop of Canterbury before the Royal Commission on Ritual. Mr. Russell there described the *Hierurgia* as 'edited by myself.' On the title page of the original, the editing is attributed to 'Members of the Ecclesiological late Cambridge Camden Society.' From this we gather, that the book appeared under the auspices of that Society, and that Mr. Russell was the general editor.

At the conclusion of the Preface to the complete work, the fact that it appeared in parts, and at irregular intervals, as the extracts contained in it came to hand, is given as the explanation why its contents are not always arranged under particular heads and in chronological order. In the present edition an attempt has been made to remedy this defect, by classifying as far as possible

---

[1] *Second Report of the Royal Commission on Ritual*, E. 3, question 4.

the various quotations. This has proved by no means an easy task, as very many of the extracts treat of more than one subject or usage; and some slight repetition has been unavoidable. In order further to dispose of this difficulty, a copious index has been supplied to take the place of the confused table of contents given in the original edition of 1848.

In the original Preface we read, 'As we proceeded, our research was continually rewarded by the discovery of new facts and documents, and we doubt not, had we thought good to have delayed the completion of the *Hierurgia* till a future period, we might have increased it to double its size.' These words, written in the year 1848, are more specially true at the present time; a very large amount of additional evidence having, in recent years, been accumulated, some of which is incorporated in the present volume. The amount of material to hand is so large, as to necessitate the bringing out of the work in at least two volumes. The editor is preparing the second volume, which he hopes may be published early in 1903. Out of a total of five hundred extracts contained in this volume, some two hundred are new: the new extracts are marked with an asterisk. A considerable number of extracts contained in the first edition have been omitted, as superfluous and relatively unimportant. Special attention has been devoted to lessening the amount of Puritan evidence.

Eleven of the fourteen illustrations in this volume are new. For kind permission to use certain of these, the Editor's thanks are due to Messrs. Bemrose and Sons (plate v.), The St. Dunstan's Society (plates

EDITOR'S PREFACE

viii. x. xiii.), Messrs. Isbister and Co. (plates xi. xii.). The old plates are numbered vi. vii. and xiv.

Of the testimony contained in the following pages, too much as well as too little may be made. The extracts are 'illustrative' of post-Reformation usages. That, in certain particulars, they record universal or even widespread practice cannot be affirmed: for, historically considered, the facts recorded are in some cases obviously exceptional and abnormal. But it may be fairly maintained, that, broadly speaking, the extracts given bear witness to the continuance and survival of traditions, more or less strong, which have never been suffered to die out—traditions which happily are being recognised and invigorated on a considerable scale in our own day, as truer notions of liturgiology and ecclesi- ology prevail. It seems needful to add, that the exist- ence of ornaments at a given date does not necessarily imply that they were then in use: in some cases, we have positive evidence to the contrary.

As to the significance of the *Hierurgia Anglicana*, in its bearing on the continuity of English usages, nothing need be added to the admirable preface to the original edition which immediately follows. In the judgment of the present editor, the extracts from Puritan writers still remaining in the present edition should be read with caution; allowance being made for prejudice and ex- aggeration in statements drawn from such sources.

As far as possible, all extracts have been carefully collated with the originals, and minor defects remedied. In the case of the Preface, modern usage as to punctua- tion and the use of capitals has been followed, and a few evident though unimportant inaccuracies corrected. The annotations in the body of the book, signed 'ED. 1902,' have been made by the present Editor.

VERNON STALEY.

INVERNESS, N.B., *August* 1902.

PREFACE
(1848)

The following Introduction appeared in the first Part of the *Hierurgia Anglicana*.

Many causes have conspired to bring about not only the disuse, but the almost total ignorance, of the ritual and liturgical ceremonies of our Church in the first years after the Reformation.

The Great Rebellion of course violently interrupted the whole Church system, and many practices were found at the Restoration difficult to be re-established, while others probably, after so long a desuetude, had become extinct and forgotten. Still much more was preserved than we have now any idea of; the neglect and loss of which are to be attributed, partly to the immediate bad influence of the Revolution in making the Church little more than an *Establishment*, and partly to the increased laxity and coldness which characterised the last century. The whole was facilitated by the absence of any very exact Ritual or Pontifical in the Reformed Church.

It was never the intention of the compilers of our present Services that their work should be considered as a new fabric, but as a reformation of the existing system. Consequently many things then in actual use, and always intended to be retained, were not expressly commanded, any more than they were distinctly forbidden, in the new rubric. This general consideration will serve to explain why the existing rubrics do not mention many of the usages and ceremonies which the *Hierurgia Anglicana* will describe.

The design of the present work is to produce, in a collected form, the historical facts concerning the retention of certain rites and usages since the Reformation, which shall speak as it were for themselves, and set forth in the words of eye-witnesses the actual practice of the Church in points which are now viewed by many with suspicion and jealousy. Those who have laboured to bring back the ceremonial of the Church to what it was before the Great Rebellion have found, not only that they had much to learn concerning it which their own studies could scarcely compass, but that their motives were likely to be misunderstood and misrepresented by many who had no opportunity themselves of consulting the actual records of former times, and who could not be satisfied by references to rare books however numerous. To meet both these wants is the object of the Editors. They hope from the most authoritative sources to collect so great a number of illustrations of Anglican ceremonial as shall enable their readers to gain a much clearer idea of what the Anglican Church has allowed, and shall convince those who may have distrusted the late improved feeling on these points, that such ceremonial is entirely compatible with the most dutiful allegiance to our own Communion. They will also thus be able to deprive the advocates of modern laxity of the assumed shelter of the names of the Reformers, by shewing how very much which they retained, recommended, and practised, is now rejected by their pretended followers.

The Editors are members of the Cambridge Camden Society : which they mention to shew that they may be supposed at least to have paid some attention to ceremonial, not as in any way wishing to make that body answerable for anything herein to be put forward. Indeed it will be their object to abstain as much as possible from any expression of their own opinions, leaving each fact they may adduce to carry its own weight. But, once for all, they must acknowledge that they fully agree with the principles advocated by the Cambridge Camden Society, particularly in its publication the *Ecclesiologist*, believing that nothing has been there adduced which may not be fully borne out by satisfactory documentary evidence.

Between the publication of the foregoing remarks and the present time, nearly five years have passed away ; and, although this fact may be insufficient by itself to convince our readers that we have not accomplished our

PREFACE

undertaking in a superficial manner, we think it ought to do so when coupled with the statement, that during the above interval, amid all our other occupations and professional studies, we have constantly kept steadily in view the collecting of materials for the *Hierurgia*, and have, indeed, made it our business to consult, at great cost of time and labour, such books and pamphlets within our reach, however uncommon, obscure, or recondite, as seemed likely, in the slightest degree, to bear upon the subjects which that work is designed to illustrate. We confess that at the commencement of our investigation, we had little expectation of bringing together that amount of important and interesting matter which is contained in the following pages. As we proceeded, our research was continually rewarded by the discovery of new facts and documents, and we doubt not, had we thought good to have delayed the completion of the *Hierurgia* till a future period, we might have increased it to double its present size, and perhaps, even then, have not exhausted the evidence extant in proof that although Puritanical laxity, shabbiness, and irreverence may have been *in* the Reformed Church of England, they were never *of* her : nay that, in truth, she has authorised or allowed a very high degree of splendour in the decoration of her consecrated fabrics, and of rich and stately ceremonial in the celebration of her public worship.

A late writer has accused us of adducing ' evidence on the mere ceremonial side alone, instead of giving a true representation of the whole case.' Had this author referred to our original Introduction, he would have seen that our professed object was to examine how much English Churchmen are encouraged, not how little they are allowed, to aim at in things ceremonial : to vindicate for our Church that position to which, as a part of the

Church Catholic, she is well entitled, not to seek to lower her to a level with the platform of Geneva. To discover what was the very least of ceremonial ever required, or connived at, by our Holy Mother, is a work for which, we confess, we have no vocation. We are quite willing to surrender to others so ungrateful and undutiful a task.

The perusal of the *Hierurgia Anglicana* will shew that we have not merely achieved our main design of vindicating our Church from the charge of an undue neglect of the decent order of ceremonial worship, but have also collected a number of authorities peculiarly important, on several accounts, to all who, like ourselves, are striving to effect those ecclesiological restorations in our Communion, for which, in a less hopeful time, a king and an archbishop 'witnessed a good confession.' Such, for instance, are the extracts which relate to altar-lights, plate, hangings, and decorations; rood-lofts, vestments, processions, incense, crucifixes, mitres, waferbread, the mixed cup; the consecration of fonts, altars, chalices, &c.; and the reconciliation of churches.

How far the precedents contained in these and like citations, ought to *guide* or *rule* English Churchmen now, is a question upon which we would submit a few observations. We remarked in our Introduction, that it was never the intention of the compilers of our present Services, that their work should be considered as a new fabric, but merely as a reformation of the existing system; and that, consequently, many things then in actual use, and always intended to be retained, were not expressly commanded, any more than they were distinctly forbidden, in the new rubric.[1] On no other hypothesis can we

---

[1] For some excellent remarks on this subject see the *Christian Remembrancer*, XLVIII. pp. 505-508.

PREFACE

account for the observance by the Elizabethan and Caroline prelates and clergy, and in particular, by Andrewes, Laud, and Cosin, of many usages practised by the medieval Church, and about which the reformed office-book is wholly silent : but this, we think, is no argument for *the violation of the Church's existing written law* (especially since the violent and entire interruption and suspension of the traditional unwritten law of the Church's custom at the Great Rebellion) by the introduction, in these days, of any practices[1] unauthorised by rubric or canon into our public worship. Disobedience to the Church's written enactments by addition and excess, is, in our apprehension, as wrong as a refusal to act up to its requisitions. Every bishop, priest, and deacon is sworn to comply with those injunctions : 'to obey is better than sacrifice,' and were the prescribed English ceremonial carried out in all its fulness, there would then be, at least so far as mere externals go, little more to desire. Let us endeavour to restore everywhere amongst us the daily Prayers, and (at the least) weekly Communion ; the proper eucharistic vestments, lighted and vested altars, the ancient tones of prayer and praise, the meet celebration of fasts and festivals (all of which, and much more of a kindred nature, is required by our ecclesiastical statutes) : but let us be careful not to retard the general return of the clergy to rubrical regularity, by attempting as individuals, and by the adoption of isolated practices, to do more than our Church sanctions in the ceremonial departments of her services.

It is not, then, as giving a licence for illegal and uncanonical innovations, that the precedents above alluded

---

[1] To the pious gestures of adoration towards the altar and bowing at the Holy Name, the English Church gave her formal canonical sanction after they had been for a long time practised by her members only upon the authority of an unbroken tradition from the times antecedent to the Reformation.

to are of value and importance. They will be found so (I.) as illustrative and interpretative of the rubric in cases of doubt or difficulty, whether relative to the conduct of the divine offices, or to church arrangement and decoration: and further (II.) as directory in matters of the latter description, and in regard to those pious observances, *e.g.* processions and the like, where a certain degree of liberty is allowed by our Communion to its members and ministers. To elucidate our meaning by examples,—We shall seek in vain in the rubric for any distinct mention of the surplice, cope, or chasuble, altar-lights, fronts, and coverings;[1] the only allusion which it makes to these being comprised in the command that 'such Ornaments of the Church, and of the Ministers thereof at all times of their Ministration, shall be retained, and be in use, as were in this Church of England, by the authority of Parliament, in the second year of the reign of King Edward VI.' Those persons who are unacquainted with the 'ornaments' here intended, or are in quest of precedents for their complete resumption, will find in the *Hierurgia* copious information derived from authentic sources respecting them, and authorities in evidence of the almost uninterrupted 'use' of many[2] of them from the date of the Reformation until very recent times. Again, as regards the

---

[1] Perhaps we ought to except the order concerning the 'fair white linen cloth' in the Communion Service.

[2] *E.g.* of copes (in cathedrals, and on occasions of peculiar solemnity); and of altar-lights (in cathedrals and many parochial churches). In this volume will be found ample evidence that two lights on the altar (as distinct from the light or lamp attendant upon the pyx) were among the 'ornaments in this Church of England, by the authority of Parliament, in the second year of the reign of King Edward VI.,' and are therefore enjoined by the present rubric above quoted. The proof that the retention of these 'ornaments' is ordered by our Church, has been thus *succinctly* stated in a recent publication: '(1.) In the injunctions of Edward VI., set forth in 1547, the first year of his reign, it is ordered "that all deans, archdeacons, parsons, vicars, and other ecclesiastical persons, shall . . . suffer from henceforth no torches, nor candles, tapers or images of wax, to be set before any image or picture, but

PREFACE

garb of the preacher in the Morning Service—a point upon which the rubric is considered by some not explicit—the *Hierurgia* affords a body of evidence amply sufficient to determine the Church's intention upon this vexed question.[1] Again, in respect to the position of the celebrant at the Holy Communion (*i.e.* as to whether he ought to stand at the north end or in front of the altar, facing the east, during the solemn act of consecration), concerning which the mere force of the words of the rubric may not oblige a clergyman to turn from his congregation in such a way as to give the idea of his being engaged in any priestly function, the *Hierurgia* fixes their signification by proving, on the testimony of eye-witnesses, that the custom of the clergy of the

---

only two lights upon the high altar, before the sacrament, which, for the signification that Christ is the very true light of the world, they shall suffer to remain still." (2.) That such "lights" were "in this Church of England . . . in the second year of the reign of King Edward VI." appears from Archbp. Cranmer's "Articles to be enquired of in the Visitations in the Diocese of Canterbury" in that year (1548), in which he asks "whether they suffer any torches, candles, or tapers, or any other lights in their churches, but only two lights upon the high altar?" (3.) The act of 31 Henry VIII. c. 8, declared "that the king's proclamations, set forth by the advice of his privy council, were to be obeyed as though they had been made by authority of parliament." The aforesaid injunctions of King Edward were made "by the advice of his privy council;" and having been issued *before* the statute which gave to injunctions so set forth parliamentary authority was repealed, possessed such authority, and retained, of course, their original force *after* the repeal of that statute. This view of the subject is further confirmed by the internal evidence of the proclamations, etc., issued in the second year of Edward, in which the previous injunctions are still referred to as existing and obligatory; and by the fact that Cranmer's Articles (before cited), in the same year, were framed upon them in the very matter of lights, and that such articles are always framed upon the existing ecclesiastical law. Consequently two lights upon the altar were "in this Church of England, by the authority of Parliament, in the second year of the reign of King Edward VI.:" and (4.) are consequently enjoined by the rubric in the Prayer-book immediately preceding the "Order for Morning Prayer daily throughout the year," which stands thus: "And here is to be noted, That such Ornaments of the Church, and of the Ministers thereof at all times of their Ministration, shall be retained, and be in use, as were in this Church of England by the authority of Parliament, in the second year of the reign of King Edward the Sixth."'—*Obedience to the Church in Things Ritual*, 20, 21. 8vo. 1847.

[1] See the *Ecclesiologist*, vol. v. pp. 103-114.

reformed Anglican Church in her best days, was to stand at the broad-side of the Holy Table, with their faces to the east and their backs to the people, when consecrating the Eucharistic elements: and that when the Presbyterians, at the Savoy Conference, thought the rubric so much favoured the ancient catholic practice, as to petition for its alteration on the ground that it is fit and convenient for the minister to turn to the people throughout the whole ministration, the bishops of the Church and the latest revisers of the Offices then asserted and justified the principle, that it is convenient 'to turn another way' when the priest is acting for the people in 'things that pertain to God.' Again, the Book of Common Prayer says nothing, *totidem verbis*, of the distinctness and separation of the chancel from the nave, of rood-screens, stalls, etc.: in this case, the *Hierurgia* attests that, according to our best ritualists, the first rubric in the Prayer Book (*i.e.*, *the chancels shall remain as they have done in times past*), requires the retention of all these features of catholic arrangement, so dear to the lovers of primitive order and Christian symbolism. Such are a few examples of our first position respecting the worth of our hierurgical collections. We proceed to give two or three illustrations of our second. Is the church-restorer at a loss (in the absence of precise rubrical or canonical guidance), how suitably to decorate the eastern wall of his chancel, the *Hierurgia* will direct him to choose for that purpose hangings of costly material and appropriate colour, and prove by numerous documents that such ornaments have had the best and highest sanction in our Church since the Reformation: or, being a bishop, is he desirous of drawing up a satisfactory service for the consecration of altar-plate, or the reconciliation of desecrated sanctuaries, the *Hierurgia* will

PREFACE

refer him for precedents to the offices which Laud, Sancroft, and Hacket deemed suitable for similar occasions: or, being a parish priest, is he in doubt whether, *e.g.* dedication feasts; rogation and other processions; the separation of the sexes at public worship; the mixed chalice at the Holy Eucharist; the use of the credence-table; flowers, crosses, incense, pictures and imagery in churches; feretories, herses, banners, escutcheons, and the celebration of the Holy Communion at funerals; have the sanction of the Church of England, the *Hierurgia* will convince him that the maintenance of all these is perfectly compatible with her obedience, and has been so regarded by her staunchest and most dutiful sons.

We have now, we believe, said enough to exhibit the intention and value of the present volume: and we have said it not boastfully (because any persons with some little amount of reading, patience, and diligence, and with our means of access to public and private libraries, might have done as much as, and perhaps more than, we have effected in the *Hierurgia Anglicana*), but in order that our motives and labours may not be misrepresented or stigmatized as disloyal to our Church and papistical in tendency, by the apologists of rubrical irregularity, so long as it diverges on the side of Puritanism, in our Communion. We take our stand on the ground held by Andrewes, Bancroft, Laud, Wren, Montague, and their fellow confessors, and we claim, with them, for the English Church, the revival of all the vestments and ornaments to which, it can be proved, she is justly entitled. In reference to the Eucharistic vestments in particular, we are surprised that the ecclesiological movement of the last ten years has accomplished little or nothing towards their restoration. In the course of the above space of time, we have witnessed the revival amongst us of many usages concerning which the injunctions of the Church are not nearly so obvious and direct as in the matter in question. We have been privileged to walk in white-robed procession with gleaming banners (*vexilla Regis*),

'—— flourished fair
With the Redeemer's Name:'

we have assisted at High Communion, when jewelled cross and chalice, embroidered frontal and lighted tapers, have decorated the stone altar: we have seen, here and there, the re-edification of churches and chancels, 'all glorious within,' as before the overflowings of ultraprotestant sacrilege and impiety: but nowhere[1] have we witnessed one instance of compliance with the rubric, '*Upon the day, and at the time appointed for the ministration of the Holy Communion, the priest that shall execute the holy ministry, shall put upon him the vesture appointed for that ministration, that is to say, a white albe plain, with a vestment or cope. And where there be many priests or deacons, there so many shall be ready to help the priest in the ministration, as shall be requisite; and shall have upon them likewise the vestures appointed for their ministry, that is to say, albes with tunicles.*'[2] Much of late has been said and written about this rubric, to the effect that English Churchmen cannot much longer consent to its violation: why has all this brave talking and writing not developed into action? Why have none of our clergy and churchwardens determined, at all risks, to fulfil their official obligations in this behalf? Do they excuse themselves

---

[1] Since the above was written we have heard that a chasuble was worn by an English priest, at the celebration of the Holy Eucharist, on a recent festal occasion; and that a priest in the diocese of Exeter has, for some time past, officiated at the altar similarly apparelled.

[2] The editors of the original edition of the *Hierurgia* do not pause to explain their belief that, in the matter of ornaments, the Ornaments Rubric of 1662 refers back to the Rubric of 1549 quoted above.—ED. 1902.

by pleading that our Holy Mother is 'unworthy' of her beautiful garments? Be it remembered that this plea was first suggested by some who from dwelling too much upon, and, it may be, exaggerating, the blemishes of the Church of their baptism, proceeded ere long to renounce her for the obedience of—may it not be said without uncharitableness?—a less pure Communion. Are they deterred by apprehensions of popular clamour? Past events ought to have taught them that even this hydra-headed monster may be silenced by firmness and resolution. Are they afraid of episcopal interference or rebuke? In one diocese, at least, they will encounter neither, since its presiding bishop—the Cyprian of our time—has made known his determination to enforce the use of the cope and chasuble in all places under his jurisdiction, where the parochial authorities think proper to provide them.

Peradventure our warm expostulations on this and similar topics may expose us to the censure of caring more for the imaginative, than the severe side of religion: for the external garniture of the King's daughter, than her inward and spiritual comeliness. We think we cannot better vindicate ourselves from this charge, than by citing and adopting the language of one of the most earnest of our fellow-labourers.

'It is granted,' he remarks, 'that in themselves those "Ornaments of the Church, and the Ministers thereof," which it is now wished to re-introduce—copes, tapers, jewelled plate, rood-screens, deep chancels, sedilia, and the like,—can conduce nothing to holiness, and, in so far as they do not, cannot please God. But, in their effects, they may, with his blessing, do both. Those poor, to whom the Gospel is preached, are much influenced by these outward and visible signs. Is it not of the highest importance to lead them to look on the Holy Eucharist

CONTENTS

	PAGE
THE FONT,	1
CHANCELS and ROOD-SCREENS,	11
THE ALTAR,	25
Material and Position of the Altar,	27
Overthrow of Altars,	37
Consecration of an Altar,	39
Coverings of the Altar,	42
Ornaments and Furniture of the Altar,	46
Evidence as to Altar-lights,	113
Consecration of Altar-plate,	115
Censers, etc.,	122
The Houseling-cloth,	127
ECCLESIASTICAL VESTMENTS,	133
Copes at Coronations,	208
Copes at Funerals,	212
Clerical Outdoor Apparel,	215
The Churching-veil,	219
Mitres, Pastoral Staffs, etc.,	223
FABRICS, ORNAMENTS, ETC., *TEMP.* ELIZ.,	237
Cathedral and Parochial Churches,	239
Celebration of Divine Service,	242
Celebration of the Holy Communion,	244

CONTENTS

	PAGE
Position of the Officiating Minister,	245
Holy Days, and the Manner of their Celebration,	248
Lent religiously observed,	248
Holy Matrimony,	250
Penance,	251
Customs at Funerals,	253
Rogation Processions,	257
Plain Song enjoined,	257
'Points of Popery,'	258
Archbp. Parker's Visitation,	259
Canterbury Cathedral,	260
Queen Elizabeth's Maundy,	263
Varia,	264
NOTES,	270
INDEX,	277

LIST OF ILLUSTRATIONS

PLATE		AT PAGE

I. FONT: SWYMBRIDGE, DEVON. This font possesses an unusual form of cover, and canopy, . . . 5

II. FONT-COVER: UFFORD, SUFFOLK. This font-cover, which is one of the finest specimens in the kingdom, quite unaccountably escaped the fury of Dowsing, the destroyer, who visited and devastated the church on August 31, 1643, ... 9

III. SCREEN: SWYMBRIDGE, DEVON. A remarkably fine example of rood-screen, stretching across the whole width of the nave and aisles, ... 15

IV. MODERN CHALICE: SOUTH ASCOT, BERKS. A reproduction, with slight modification, of the famous Nettlecombe chalice, which belongs to the close of the fifteenth century; and which, through an ingenious device, was saved from theft at the hands of the Commissioners of Edward VI. in 1552, . . . 59

V. ELIZABETHAN COMMUNION-CUP AND COVER: ST. MARY'S, MONMOUTH. A beautiful example of Elizabethan work, ... 67

VI. PLAN OF BISHOP ANDREWES' CHAPEL, described in the text, ... 93

VII. OLD ALTAR-PIECE OF PETERBOROUGH CATHEDRAL. The altar is of the mediæval type, veiled in an ample frontal: two candlesticks with lighted tapers, and the alms bason, stand on the altar, without the intervention of a shelf, ... 100

LIST OF ILLUSTRATIONS

PLATE AT PAGE

VIII. PRIEST IN 'A VESTMENT,' *i.e.* in apparelled amice and albe, stole, maniple, and chasuble, . . . 145

IX. CANON IN CHOIR HABIT. This plate shows the long and full surplice with ample sleeves, and almuce. The square cap is also worn, in its proper shape, . . 151

X. PRIEST IN CHOIR HABIT. Emblematic frontispiece to *Comber's Discourses*, 1684; illustrating the hood before its elongation, ample surplice, and (apparently) tippet, 168

XI. COPE: made for the use of the Dean and Chapter of Westminster Abbey, at the coronation of King Charles II., ... 208

XII. COPE: made for the use of the Dean and Chapter of Westminster Abbey, at the coronation of King Edward VII. and Queen Alexandra, ... 212

XIII. PRIEST IN OUTDOOR HABIT: wearing the dress appointed by Canon 74;—cassock, M.A. gown ('as is used in the universities'), tippet, and square cap in its proper shape, ... 218

XIV. EDWARD VI., AND HIS COURT. Frontispiece to Cranmer's *Catechismus*, *c.* 1549. The bishops wear copes and mitres, and have pastoral staffs, . . . 223

REGNAL YEARS OF SOVEREIGNS SINCE THE REFORMATION [1]

EDWARD VI.,	January 28, 1547—July 6, 1553.
MARY,	July 6, 1553—November 17, 1558.
ELIZABETH,	November 17, 1558—March 24, 1603.
JAMES I.,	March 24, 1603—March 27, 1625.
CHARLES I.,	March 27, 1625—January 30, 1649.
[THE COMMONWEALTH,	January 30, 1649—May 29, 1660.]
CHARLES II.,	May 29, 1660—February 6, 1685.
JAMES II.,	February 6, 1685—December 11, 1688.
WILLIAM and MARY,	February 13, 1689—March 8, 1702.
ANNE,	March 8, 1702—August 1, 1714.
GEORGE I.,	August 1, 1714—June 11, 1727.
GEORGE II.,	June 11, 1727—October 25, 1760.
GEORGE III.,	October 25, 1760—January 29, 1820.
GEORGE IV.,	January 29, 1820—June 26, 1830.
WILLIAM IV.,	June 26, 1830—June 20, 1837.
VICTORIA,	June 20, 1837—January 22, 1901.

[1] This Table is given as a guide to the dates named in the following pages.—ED. 1902.

The Font

HIERURGIA ANGLICANA

The Font

A.D. 1552

* ST. JOHN, CAPELL.
  '*Item* one font clothe.'[1]

ST. NICHOLAS, COMPTON.
  '*Item* an old canype with a cloth for the fonte.'

ST. PETER, HAMBLEDON.
  '*Item* ij font clothes.'

ST. NICHOLAS, PYRFORD.
  '*Item* ij cloothes to kever the font.'

ST. MARY, SHALFORD.
  '*Item* ij font cloothes of lynnyn.'

—*Inventories of Goods and Ornaments in the Churches of Surrey in the Reign of K. Edward VI. by J. R. Daniel-Tyssen, Lond.*, 1869, pp. 12, 14, 34, 35.

1561

'*Item.* That the font be not removed from the accustomed place: and that in parish churches the curates take not upon them to confer baptism in basins, but in the font customably used.'—*Orders taken the* x *day of October, in the third year of the reign of our Sovereign Lady Elizabeth.*

---

[1] Cfer. the instructions to the first deacon at Coventry in 1460—'Ye sayd dekyn schall hyng a towell aboute ye Font at estur, and at wytsontyde.'—*The British Magazine*, vol. vi. p. 615 (1834). The purpose of the Font-cloth was to envelop the font after the cover was removed. See *sub* 1850, p. 10.—ED. 1902.

1563

The Font.

* '*Item* a canapie for the founte.'—*Inventories of Christchurch, Canterbury*, p. 212.

1565

* '*Item* an alb—whearof is made a coveringe for o^r font A.D. 1565.'

'A fonte clothe . . . Remanith in o^r pishe church A.D. 1565.'—*Peacock, English Church Furniture at the period of the Reformation*, pp. 54, 68.

1566

* '*Item* a painted cloth that covered the fonte sold sens the last visitacion.'

'*Item* ij albes—whearof wee haue made clothes for the coĩon table and the funt.'—*Ibid.* pp. 56, 136.

1569

'*Item.* Whether your curates or ministers, or any of them, do use to minister the Sacrament of Baptism in basins, or else in the font standing in the place accustomed. And whether the said font be decently kept?'—*Archbp. Parker's Visitation Articles.*

1571

* 'They shall take care that in every church there be a holy font, not a basin, wherein baptism may be ministered, and that it be kept comely and clean.'—*Canons of* 1571. *Cardwell, Synodalia*, i. 123.

1599

* 'A cover for the font, 1*s.* 8*d.*'—*Churchwardens' Accompts of Great Wigston: Nichols' Illustrations of the*

PLATE I.] [To face page 5.

Hier. 1.]

THE FONT

Manners and Expences of Antient Times in England in the
15th, 16th, and 17th Centuries, p. 148, 4to, 1797.

1601

'Whether your fonts or baptisteries be removed from the place where they were wont to stand: or whether any persons, leaving the use of them, do christen or baptize in basins, or other vessels not accustomably used in the Church beforetime, or do use any kind of laver with a removeable bason, or have taken down the old and usual font heretofore used in your parish?'—*Bp. Bancroft's Visitation Articles.*

1604

'According to a former constitution, too much neglected in many places, we appoint, That there shall be a font of stone in every church and chapel where Baptism is to be ministered; the same to be set up in the ancient usual places. In which only font the minister shall baptize publickly.'—*Canon* LXXXI.

1604

* 'Whether your children bee baptised in the time of morning and euening praier in the presence of the congregation, at the vsuall font in the Church?'—*Bp. Bridges' Visitation Articles.*

1616

* 'For makinge a Case about the ffont with pillors and a seate to the same.'—*Churchwardens' Accounts of Allhallows Staining, in the city of London.* Vide *The British Magazine,* iii. 654. 1833.

1619

* 'Whether your Fonts or Baptisteries be remooued

The Font. from the place where they were wont to stand? or whether any Parsons (leuing the vse of them) do christen in Basons, or other Vessels, or haue taken doune the old vsuall Font, heretofore vsed in your Parish?'—*Bp. Howson's Visitation Articles.*

1619-1629

* '*Item* for the cover for the font, vs.

'For a polley in iaron for the font coveringe, 2s. 6d.

'For the Funt covering and charges xxxs. ; for tow hands to the Funt coveryng, viijd.'—*Churchwardens' Accts. of Pittington and other parishes in the diocese of Durham,* pp. 91, 293, 298. *Surtees Soc.,* 1888.

1625-1649

'The christening and consecrating of churches and chapels, the consecrating fonts, pulpits, tables, chalices, churchyards, and many other things, and putting holiness in them ; yea, reconsecrating upon pretended pollution, as though every thing were unclean without their consecrating, and for want of this sundry churches have been interdicted and kept from use as polluted.'— *Nalson's Impartial Collection,* vol. i. p. 165, fol. 1682.

1627

'That part of the old font called the basin, then made use of in this place [St. Nicholas, Lynn], (before the erecting of that now standing, granted and consecrated by Samuel Harsenet, D.D. and Bishop of Norwich, in the year 1627, and which resembles that at St. Margaret's), I am apt to believe is the same which I observed to be upon the ground (with the pedestal some distance from it) among the rubbish and lumber in a certain place on the north side of the quire.'—*Mackerell's Account of King's Lynn, Norfolk,* p. 92. *Book of Fragments,* p. 46.

THE FONT

1627

'Have you a font of stone, with a comely cover, set in the ancient usual place?'—*Cosin's Articles of Inquiry in the Archdeaconry of the East Riding of York.*

1630

* '*Item.* A Font of Silver and gilt is to be provided ... and over the Font a fair bell canopy with a rich valence.

'*Item.* The Font is to be covered with a fine linen Cloath until the time of Baptism.'—*Sheppard's Memorials of St. James's Palace: Royal Baptisms,* ii. pp. 28, 29.

1631

'Whether have you in your church or chapel a font of stone set up in the ancient usual place?'—*Visitation Articles of Laud, Bp. of London.*

1635

'The Minster [Durham] is as neatly kept as any in England, built like unto Paul's; wherein are in the body of the church, on either side, eight great and stately pillars as great as Paul's; herein the daintiest font that I have seen in England, the body or font stone and foot of pure marble, over which is placed a cover or canopy folding of wood, curiously carved, wherein described the history of Christ's baptism.'—*Brereton's Travels, Chetham Soc.,* p. 83.

1636

* 'That for administering the Sacrament of Baptism, a font shall be prepared and fixed near the church-porch, according to ancient usage: That a fine linen cloth should likewise be provided for this purpose, and all decently kept.'—*Canons for the Scottish Church,* 1636. Vide *Collier's Eccles. Hist.* II. ix. 763, fol. 1714.

1636

The Font.

* 'Haue you a Font of stone set up in the ancient usuall place, with a hole in the bottome of it to convey away the water?'—*Visitation Articles of Pearson, Archdn. of Suffolk.*

1636

* 'Two surplisses, a font cloath, two tablecloths.'—*Inventory of Church Goods at Easingwold.* Vide *The Antiquary*, viii. 248.

1637

'Whether doth your minister baptize any children in any bason or other vessel than in the ordinary font, being placed in the church, or doth he put a basin in it?'—*Visitation Articles of Laud, Bp. of London.*

1638

'Is there in your church a font for the Sacrament of Baptism, fixed unto the Lord's freehold and not moveable? Of what materials is it made? where is it placed? whether near unto a church door, to signify our entrance into God's Church by Baptism? is it covered, well and cleanly kept? at time of Baptism is it filled with water clean and clear? or is some basin, bowl, or bucket, filled with water, set therein?'—*Bp. Montague's Visitation Articles.*

c. 1640

'In that cathedral [Canterbury] there hath been lately erected a superstitious font with three ascents to it, paled without with high gilded and painted iron bars, having under the cover of it a carved image of the Holy Ghost in the form of a dove, and round about it are placed carved images of the twelve Apostles and four Evangelists, and of angels, and over it a carved image

PLATE II.] [*To face page* 9.

Hier. 1.]

THE FONT

of Christ ... and that font was *consecrated* by the Lord Bishop of Oxford, as is testified by a Proctor of the Archbishop's Ecclesiastical Court of Canterbury.'—*Cathedral News from Canterbury, by Richard Culmer, Minister of God's Word*, p. 3, 4to, 1644.[1]

1643

* UFFORD. 'There is a glorious Cover over the Font, like a Pope's Tripple Crown, with a Pelican on the Top, picking its Breast, all gilt over with Gold.'[2]—*Dowsing's Journal, Ipswich*, 1885, p. 29.

1661

* 'The font usually stands, as it did in primitive times, at or near the church door, to signify that baptism was the entrance to the Church mystical.'—*Answer of the Bishops to the Puritans in* 1661, *Cardwell's Hist. of Conferences*, p. 355.

1662

'And the priest coming to the font (which is then to be filled with pure water), and standing there ...'—*The Book of Common Prayer*.

1662

* 'Is there a font of marble, or other stone, decently wrought and covered, set up at the lower part of your church?'—*Bp. Cosin's Visitation Articles*.

1689

* 'The font-cover of black oak is exceedingly elegant

---

[1] In the margin of the above extract occurs, 'consecrated by a Lord Bishop, who went round about it reading in a Booke, and went up the three steps, and put his head into the Font.'—EDD. 1848.

[2] *Vide* the accompanying illustration of the Ufford font-cover.—ED. 1902.

The Font. in design. It is ornamented with doves and wreaths of flowers, richly gilt, and on it the inscription records that "This font was the gift of William Bridgeman, 1689."'—*London Church Staves*, p. 29.

1803

* ST. BENEDICT'S, GRACECHURCH. 'The font stands under the gallery in the south west corner of the church. . . . The cover is crowded with emblematic carvings, and is suspended from an iron crane.'—*Malcolm's Londinium Redivivum*, i. 323.

1843

'Have you a decent fixed stone font with a cover? Does it stand near to the chief door? Is it well and cleanly kept? Is there space enough about it for the sponsors to kneel? Is it large enough for the immersion of infants? Is it, and none other, used for Baptisms? Has it a drain for the water to run off?'—*Articles of Inquiry by the Archdn. of Bristol*.

1847

* 'Fonts were ordered to be kept locked.[1] . . . In some churches, the remains of the ancient fastenings may still be seen.'—*Maskell, Monumenta Ritualia*, vol. iii. p. 374, 1847.

1850

* 'In 1889, the sexton at West Luccombe in Somerset told me that forty years ago he remembered the font being covered, just like the altar, with a large linen cloth, after the water was poured in for a baptism.'—*From a private letter*.

---

[1] Fonts were formerly ordered to be kept securely locked, for fear that weak and superstitious people should use the hallowed water for magical purposes.—ED. 1902.

'Fontes Baptismales sub Sera clausi teneantur propter Sortilegia.'—*Lyndw.*, lib. iii. tit. 25, p. 247, 1679.

Chancels and Rood=screens

A.D. 1551

'Paid for painting the rood-loft, 40s.'[1]—*Church-wardens' Accounts of the Parish of St. Martin's, Leicester.*

1551

* 'Paide for pulling downe the rowde lofte and setting up of the scriptures that is to saye the creacion of the worlde the comyng of our Saviour Christe the Beatytudes

---

[1] It has been generally but most hastily assumed, that rood-lofts are condemned by the Anglican Church. It must be borne in mind, that the injunctions for taking them down referred not to the lofts, *quoad* lofts, but to the crucifixes and figures which surmounted them. Indeed, the rood-loft and rood-screen not only had different origins, but in the Greek Church occupy different places. The rood-loft there stands in the singers' choir: it consists of either one or two pulpits; it occupies in the former case the middle of the choir; in the latter, one is placed on each side, near the *Stasidia* or stalls. The use of these is simply for the reading the Epistle and Gospel. The arrangement was at first the same in the Western Church, and is so in Seville Cathedral to the present day: but afterwards, the upper part of the rood-screen was found a convenient situation for the *analogia*, and in England this position was almost universally adopted. Now *this* use of the rood-loft is sanctioned even by Prelates of the Genevan school: Grindal (1571) orders that the Communion-service should be read at the altar, all except the Epistle and Gospel, which are to be read from the pulpit. In Rodney Stoke, Somersetshire, is a rood-loft of the date of 1625, probably used for this purpose; and in Weston-in-Gordano, in the same county, is a single *analogium* at the south-east end of the nave, entered by a flight of steps from the belfry, and fenced in with a baluster of seventeenth-century work, which answers the same end. Indeed Archbishop Grindal's injunction, that the pulpit should be also the *analogium*, has authority in ante-Reformation times. An elaborate stone pulpit, on the north side of the chancel-arch in Compton Martin, Somerset, evidently served also for rood-loft. And in many cases where the pulpit projects from the chancel wall, and there appears to have been no rood-staircase, its use was probably the same.—EDD. 1848.

Chancels and Rood-screens. the ten commaundments the xii articles of our belief and the Lordes Prayer the judgment of the world the kinges Majesties armes iij^{li} xij^{s} vj^{d}.'—*Daniel-Tyssen, Surrey Inventories*, p. 132.

1560

'We understanding, that furthermore in sundry churches and chapels, where divine service, as prayer, preaching, and ministration of the sacraments, be used, there is such negligence and lack of convenient reverence used towards the comely keeping and order of the said churches, and especially of the upper part, called the chancels, that it breedeth no small offence and slander to see and consider, on the one part, the curiosity and costs bestowed by all sorts of men upon their private houses, and the other part, the unclean or negligent order, or sparekeeping of the house of prayer, by permitting open decays and ruins of coverings, walls, and windows, and by appointing unmeet and unseemly tables, with foul cloths, for the communion of the sacraments, and generally leaving the place of prayers desolate of all cleanliness and of meet ornament for such a place, whereby it might be known a place provided for divine service; have thought good to require you our said commissioners . . . to consider, as becometh, the foresaid great disorders in the decays of churches and in the unseemly keeping and order of the chancels, and such like, and according to your discretions to determine upon some good and speedy means of reformation.'—*Queen Elizabeth's Letter about new Lessons in the Calendar before the Common Prayer-book.*[1] *Cardwell's Documentary Annals*, i. 295, 296.

1561

'Inprimis, for the avoiding of much strife and con-

---

[1] The Queen also ordered that 'the steps, which be as yet at this day remaining in any of our cathedral, collegiate, or parish churches, be not stirred nor altered, but be suffered to continue' (*L'Estrange's Alliance of Divine Offices*, third ed., pp. 72, 73).—EDD. 1848.

PLATE III.] [*To face page* 15.

CHANCELS AND ROOD-SCREENS

tention that hath heretofore risen among the Queen's subjects in divers parts of the realm, for the using or transposing of the rood-lofts, fonts, and steps, within the quires and chancels in every parish church. It is thus decreed and ordained that the rood-lofts, as yet, being at this day aforesaid, untransposed, shall be so altered that the upper part of the same with the soller be quite taken down, unto the upper parts of the vautes, and beam running in length over the said vautes, by putting some convenient crest upon the said beam towards the church, with leaving the situation of the seats (as well in the quire as in the church) as heretofore hath been used.

'Provided yet, that where any parish, of their own costs and charges by common consent, will pull down the whole frame, and reedifying again the same in joiner's work (as in divers churches within the city of London doth appear), that they may do as they think agreeable, so it be to the height of the upper beam aforesaid.

'Provided also, that where in any parish church the said rood-lofts be already transposed, so that there remain a comely partition between the chancel and the church, that no alteration be otherwise attempted in them, but be suffered in quiet. And where no partition is standing, there to be one appointed.

'Also, that the steps which be as yet at this day remaining in any cathedral, collegiate, or parish church, be not stirred nor altered, but be suffered to continue, with the tombs of any noble or worshipful personage, where it so chanceth to be, as well in chancel, church, or chapel.

'*Item.* That all chancels be clean kept and repaired within as without, in the windows and otherwise as appertaineth.'—*Orders taken the* x *day of October, in the third year of the reign of our Sovereign Lady Elizabeth.*

1562

'Whether your churches and chancels be well adorned,

Chancels and Rood-screens. and conveniently kept without waste, destruction, or abuse of any thing. Whether the rood-loft be pulled down, according to the order prescribed; and if the partition between the chancel and the church be kept.'—*Archbp. Parker's Visitation Articles.*

1566

'To John Sayght for makyn hyngs for the quyer dores and the tresoer dor, 2s. 10d.'—*Parish Accounts of St. Mary's, Shrewsbury.*

1571

* 'That the rood-lofts be taken down and altered, so that the upper boards and timber thereof, both behind and above where the rood lately did hang, and also the seller or loft be quite taken down unto the cross-beam, whereunto the partition between the choir and the body of the church is fastened.'—*Archbp. Grindal's Injunctions.*

1573

'The vigilant bishop of Norwich was informed that there was a popish rood-loft still remaining in St. George's church in Norwich, with the fashion and order as was in the time of popery. This, many good people, and especially one Morley of that parish, complained of. Others of the said parish . . . were as fond of it.'—*Strype's Life and Acts of Archbp. Parker*, ii. 337, 8vo, Oxford, 1821.

1578

'There is in every church, for the most part, a distinction of places betwixt the Clergy and the laity. We term one place the chancel, and another the body of the church: which manner of distinction doth greatly offend the tender consciences (forsooth) of the purer part of the Reformers. Insomuch as Mr. Gilby, a chief man in his

CHANCELS AND ROOD-SCREENS 17

time among them, doth term the quire *a cage*, and reckoneth that separation of the ministers from the congregation one of the hundred points of Popery, which, he affirmeth, do yet remain in the Church of England. The book from which he quotes is "A View of Antichrist, his Laws and Ceremonies in our English Church unreformed."'—*Circ.* 1578, *Strype, Ann.* II. ii. 215. *Note on the above in Keble's edition of Hooker*, ii. 67, 8vo, 1836.

<small>Chancels and Rood-screens.</small>

1597

'The like unto this [the objection to the names whereby we distinguish our churches] is a fancy which they have against the fashion of our churches, as being framed according to the pattern of the Jewish temple. A fault no less grievous, if so be it were true, than if some king should build his mansion-house by the model of Solomon's palace. So far forth as our churches and their temple have one end, what should let but that they may lawfully have one form? The temple was for sacrifice, and therefore had rooms to that purpose such as ours have none. Our churches are places provided that the people may there assemble themselves in due and decent manner, according to their several degrees and order. Which thing being common unto us with Jews, we have in this respect our churches divided by certain partitions, though not so many in number as theirs. They had their several for heathen nations, their several for the people of their own nation, their several for men, their several for women, their several for their priests, and for the high-priest alone their several. There being in ours for local distinction between the clergy and the rest (which yet we do not with any great strictness or curiosity observe neither) but one partition, the cause whereof at the first (as it seemeth) was, that as many as were capable of the holy mysteries might there assemble themselves, and no other creep amongst them: this is now made a matter so heinous, as

B

18   HIERURGIA ANGLICANA

Chancels and Rood-screens.

if our religion thereby were become even plain Judaism; and as though we retained a most holy place whereinto there might not any but the high-priest alone enter, according to the custom of the Jews.'—*Hooker's Eccles. Polity*, v. 14.

1610-1634

'Wimborne Minster (St. Cuthberga), Dorsetshire. The choir of this church is very interesting, containing a rich and complete set of double stalls, with rood-screen, holy doors, returns, and miserere-seats, put up in 1610, and consequently (like the rood-screen in the chapel of Sackville College) before the Laudian reaction in favour of Catholick arrangement.'

'The chapel of Low Ham, Somerset, built about 1620, as a domestick chapel, has chancel, aisles, clerestory, and a rood-screen; a groined ceiling and arches, all pointed.'

'The chancel of St. Guthlac, Passenham, Northamptonshire, rebuilt 1623, in a mixed style, fitted with a rood-screen and stalls.'

'Post-Reformation rood-lofts; such as that in Rodney Stoke, Somersetshire, (1625).'

'St. Mary, Ditcheat, Somersetshire. There is a perfect rood-screen of two bays on each side of the holy doors, which are perfect. The date of this wordwork is 1630.'

'St. John, Leeds, built 1634, has one aisle divided by a pointed arcade, a rood-screen, and square-headed windows.'[1]—*The Ecclesiologist*, vi. 183; vii. 44, 45; iii. 51; vi. 184.

1625-1649

'The church being finished (which is a goodly fabrick), that the inside of it might correspond with that which

---

[1] To the above examples may be added the rood-screen in St. Hugh, Harlow, erected at the beginning of the last century. There is another of about the same date in St.———, Great Dunmow, Essex.—EDD. 1848.

CHANCELS AND ROOD-SCREENS

is without, she gave hangings of watched taffeta to cover the upper end of the chancel, and those bordered with a silk and silver fringe. Also she gave a beautiful screen of carved wood, which was placed where the former one in the old church stood.'—*Funeral Sermon of the Duchess of Dudley*, p. 23. *Some Account of the Hospital and Parish of St. Giles's-in-the-Fields*, p. 201 *n*.

1627

' First, whether is the body of your church or chapel, or the chancel thereof, in good reparation, decently kept as well within as without, etc. ?

' Is there a partition between the body of the church and the chancel ? and if not, when, and by whom, and by what authority was it taken down ?'—*Cosin's Articles of Inquiry in the Archdeaconry of the East Riding of York.*

1634

' SS. Peter and Paul, Catstock, Devon. Inscription on rood-screen :
   Tempus edax rerum, ligno non marmore sculptum,
   Dicito non genitis hoc pietatis opus.
   Ric. Bishop Hol. struxisse, 1634.'—*Hutchins' Dorsetshire.*

1634

' He [the Bishop of Landaff] certifies that one William Newport, Rector of Langua, in Monmouthshire, hath pulled down the partition between the chancel and the church, and sold part, and disposed the rest to his own use, with some other violences, to the great profanation of that place, for which the Bishop desires leave to bring him into the High Commission.'—*Archbp. Laud's Troubles, etc.*, p. 533.

1638

' Is your chancel divided from the nave or body of

Chancels and Rood-screens. your church, with a partition of stone, boards, wainscot, grates, or otherwise? Wherein is there a decent strong door to open and shut (as occasion serveth), with lock and key, to keep out boys, girls, or irreverent men and women?'—*Bp. Montague's Visitation Articles.*

1638

'He (Bp. Montague) caused a meeting of the clergy to be held at Ipswich, for the parts adjoining, where he prescribed these following orders: that is to say, First, After the words or exhortation pronounced by the minister (standing at the Communion-table, the parishioners as yet standing in the body of the church) "Draw near," etc., all which intend to communicate should come out of the church into the chancel: Secondly, That all being come in, the chancel door should be shut, and not opened till the Communion be done,' etc.—*Heylyn's Cyprianus Anglicus*, II. iv. 75, 76, fol. 1719.

1638

'More churches have been built and adorned in the reign of King Charles than in the reign of many kings before. . . . The chancel being divided from the church by grates of wood curiously carved, or of iron, or of brass cast into comely works, is not only very graceful, but according to the laws and orders of building observed by the primitive Christians. . . . Of all parts of the chancel, that where the Communion Table stands has ever been accounted most sacred: in the adorning that no cost ought to be thought too much. . . . Hither bring your stateliest hangings to adorn the walls; hither your richest carpets and bespread the ground; hither the most precious silks and finest linen to cover the Holy Table.'—*De Templis: a Treatise of Temples*, by N. T., pp. 184-201. *Lond.* 1638.

1639

'Sir Paul Pinder—having at his own charge first repaired the decays of that goodly partition made at the west end of the quire, adorning the front thereof outwards with fair pillars of black marble and statues of those Saxon kings which had been founders or benefactors to the church—beautified the inner part thereof with figures of angels, and all the wainscot work of the quire with excellent carving, viz. of cherubims and other imagery richly gilded; adding costly suits of hangings for the upper end thereof: and afterwards bestowed £4,000 in repairing of the south cross.'—*Dugdale's History of St. Paul's Cathedral.*

1640

'In 1640, we learn from the diary of Dr. Dillingham, a new rood-screen was erected (in Great St. Mary's, Cambridge) under the authority of Cosin, who was then Vice-chancellor. . . . Very stately and magnificent . . . his erection seems to have been, from the pictures drawn of it in the *Querela Cantabrigiensis* and other contemporaneous notices.'—*Transactions of the Cambridge Camden Society*, part iii. p. 280, 4to, 1845.

1640

'Do the chancels remain as they have done in times past, that is to say, in the convenient situation of the seats, and in the ascent or steps unto the place appointed anciently for the standing of the holy Table? Is the chancel of your church or chapel clean kept, and repaired within and without, in the windows and otherwise as appertaineth? And is there a comely partition betwixt your chancel and the body of the church or chapel, as is required by the law?'—*Articles to be enquired of within the Diocese of London,* by Bp. Law, 4to, 1640.

1640

Chancels and Rood-screens.

'The said church is divided into three parts: the *sanctum sanctorum* being one of them, is separated from the chancel by a large screen, in the figure of a beautiful gate, in which is carved two large pillars and three large statues: on the one side is Paul with his sword; on the other, Barnabus with his book; and over them, Peter with his keys. They are all set above with winged cherubims, and beneath supported with lions. Seven or eight feet within this holy place is a raising by three steps; and from thence a long rail from one wall to the other, into which place none must enter but the priests and subdeacons. This place is covered before the altar with a fair wrought carpet; the altar doth stand close up to the wall on the east side, and a desk raised upon that with degrees of advancement [projecting steps]. This desk is overlaid with a covering of purple velvet, which hath a great gold and silver fringe round about; and on this desk is placed two great books, wrought with needle-work, in which are made the pictures of Christ, and the Virgin Mary with Christ in her arms; and these are placed on each side the desk: and on this altar a double covering, one of tapestry, and upon that a fine long lawn cloth with a very rich bone lace.[1] The walls are hanged round within the rail with blue silk taffeta curtains.'—*Petition by the Puritans to Parliament against the Rector, Dr. Heywood*, 1640. *Some Account of the Hospital and Parish of St. Giles-in-the-Fields*, p. 201.

---

[1] Bone lace was netting of very elaborate and delicate work, made of variously-coloured silks, and gold and silver twist, as well as of white thread or black silk. See Strickland's *Queens of England*, vol. vi. p. 444 *n*.—EDD. 1848.

Although lace was occasionally used in the seventeenth century, it never really obtained hold in England. Ornament partly composed of drawn thread work was sometimes used towards the end of the middle ages; but never lace sewed on as we know it now. Fringe and embroidery were common.—ED. 1902.

CHANCELS AND ROOD-SCREENS 23

c. 1650[1]

'*And the chancels shall remain as they have done in times past.* That is, distinguished from the body of the church by a frame of open-work, and furnished with a row of chairs or stools on either side ; and if there were formerly any steps up to the place where the altar or table stood, that they should be suffered to continue so still, and not to be taken down and laid level with the lower ground, as lately they have been by violence and disorder, contrary to law and custom.'—*Bp. Cosin's Notes on the Book of Common Prayer, Second Series, Works,* v. 228. *Lib. Anglo-Cath. Theol.*

1681

'The Sacrament of the Lord's Supper being the highest mystery in all our religion, as representing the death of the Son of God to us, hence that place where this Sacrament is administered was always made and reputed the highest place in the church. And therefore, also, it was wont to be separated from the rest of the church by a screen or partition of network, in Latin *cancelli*, and that so generally, that from thence the place itself is called the 'Chancel.' That this was anciently observed in the building of all considerable churches within a few centuries after the Apostles themselves, even in the days of Constantine the Great, as well as in all ages since ; I could easily demonstrate from the records of those times. But having purposely waived antiquity

---

[1] The year in which Bp. Cosin's Notes on the Book of Common Prayer were written cannot accurately be ascertained. According to Mr. Perry's opinion, the Second Series is to be placed '*c.* 1638 to 1656,' and the Third Series '*prob.* most before 1640.' (See *Notes on the Purchas Judgment,* pp. 94-96 *nn.*). In revising this work I have set down quotations from the Second Series '*c.* 1650 '; and those from the Third Series '*c.* 1640.' There are no quotations, in the original *Hierurgia*, from the First Series, which almost certainly is not Cosin's work.

It is to be observed that the 'Notes' are to be read with caution; for we cannot assert that they express Cosin's rule of practice under the existing Prayer Book of his time. They may be merely his suggestions for the improvement of that book, or of the nature of memoranda.—ED. 1902.

Chancels and Rood-screens.

hitherto, I am loth to trouble you with it now. But I mention it at present, only because some perhaps may wonder why this should be observed in our church [St. Peter's, Cornhill, London [1]] rather than in all the other churches which have lately been built in this city. Whereas they should rather wonder, why it was not observed in all others as well as this. For, besides our obligations to conform, as much as may be, to the practice of the universal Church, and to avoid novelty and singularity in all things relating to the worship of God, it cannot be easily imagined that the Catholick Church, in all ages and places, for thirteen or fourteen hundred years together, should observe such a custom as this, except there were great reasons for it.

'What they were, it is not necessary for us to enquire now. It may be sufficient to observe at present, that the chancel in our Christian churches was always looked upon as answerable to the Holy of Holies in the Temple; which, you know, was separated from the sanctuary or body of the Temple, by the command of God Himself. And that this place being appropriated to the Sacrament of the Lord's Supper, it ought to be contrived, as may be most convenient for those who are to partake of that blessed ordinance. But it must needs be more convenient for those who are to enjoy communion with Christ, and in Him with one another, in this holy Sacrament, to meet together as one body, in one place separated for that purpose, than to be dispersed, as otherwise they would be, some in one and some in another part of the church: or, in short, it is much better for the place to be separate than the people.'—*Bp. Beveridge's Sermon preached at the Opening of St. Peter's, Cornhill. Works*, vi. 388. *Lib. Anglo-Cath. Theol.*

---

[1] This church, built by Wren, and that of All-hallows-the-Great, Thames-street, have real and *bona fide* chancel-screens; and we know but one of the churches built at that period, St. Andrew-by-the-Wardrobe, which is destitute of a low partition, answering the same purpose. See *Ecclesiologist*, vol. ii. p. 140.—EDD. 1848. All-hallows-the-Great is now pulled down, and the screen set up in St. Margaret's, Lothbury.—ED. 1902.

The Altar

The Altar

Material and Position of the Altar[1]

A.D. 1559

'Whereas her majesty understandeth, that in many and sundry parts of the realm the altars of the churches be removed, and tables placed for the administration of the Holy Sacrament, according to the form of the law therefore provided ; and in some places, the altars be not yet removed, upon opinion conceived of some other order therein to be taken by her majesty's visitors ; in the order whereof, saving for an uniformity, there seemeth no matter of great moment, so that the Sacrament be duly and reverently ministered ; yet for observation of one uniformity through the whole realm, and for the better imitation of the law in that behalf, it is ordered,

---

[1] It has been recently asserted by persons of undoubted orthodoxy, that stone altars are forbidden by the Church of England. This statement however appears to be destitute of proof. The injunction of Elizabeth above cited *permits*, but does not enjoin, the removal of stone altars : such altars remained in Bishop Overall's time in the Chapels Royal and many of the Cathedrals, and they were in very many places restored by the Caroline Bishops and Confessors. The rubrick directs that 'the chancels shall remain as they have done in *times past*,' i.e. anterior to Edward the Sixth's second Prayer-book, and the removal of the ancient altars ; and on the supposition that the altar is an 'ornament of the church' (as affirmed by Bishop Cosins), it ought to be of stone in obedience to the rubrick, which directs that 'such ornaments of the church shall be retained and be in use as were in this Church of England, by authority of Parliament, in the second year of the reign of King Edward VI.' —EDD. 1848.

'The real contest in the seventeenth century was not about the material so much as the position of the altar, and that was finally set at rest in 1662. Stone or marble altars of the eighteenth and the first half of the nineteenth century are not uncommon.'—*Micklethwaite, St. Paul's Eccles. Soc. Trans.* vol. ii. p. 313 *n*.

The Altar. that no altar be taken down, but by the oversight of the curate of the church, and the churchwardens, or one of them at least, wherein no riotous or disordered manner to be used. And that the Holy Table in every church be decently made, and set in the place, where the altar stood, and there commonly covered, as thereto belongeth.'—*Injunctions of Queen Elizabeth. Cardwell, Doc. Ann.* i. 233, 234.

c. 1563

* 'The Comunion prayer daily through the yeare though there be no Comunion, is songe at the comunion table standing northe and southe, wheare the high aulter did stande. . . . The holie Comunyon is mynistred ordinarylie ye fyrste Sondaie of euerie moneth, thorough the yeare, at what tyme the Table is sett Easte and weaste.'—*The Certificat of the Vice Deane of the Cathedrall churche of Christe in Canterburye.* Vide *Inventories of Christchurch, Canterbury, transcribed and edited by J. Wickham Legg, and W. H. St. John Hope*, p. 209. Archibald Constable, Westminster, 1902.

c. 1619[1]

'In King Edward's first Service-book, the word *Altar* was permitted to stand, as being the name that Christians for many hundred years had been acquainted withal. Therefore, when there was such pulling down of altars, and setting up of tables, at the beginning of Queen Elizabeth's reign, she was fain to make an injunction, to restrain such ungodly fury—(for which St. Chrysostom says, the Christians in his time would have stoned a man to death, that should but have laid his hands on an altar to destroy it)—and appointed decent and comely tables

---

[1] Overall's Notes in Nicholls' *Commentary on the Book of Common Prayer* were originally written in an interleaved Prayer Book printed in 1619, the year of the bishop's death. It is possible, however, that they are of an earlier date. Nicholls supposes the Notes 'to be made from the Collections of Bp. Overall, by a friend or chaplain of his.'—ED. 1902.

covered, to be set up again, in the same place where the altars stood; thereby giving an interpretation of this clause [*The Table at the Communion-time shall stand in the body of the church, or in the chancel*] in our Communion-book. For the word *table* here stands not exclusively, as if it might not be called an altar, but to shew the indifferency and liberty of the name; as of old it was called *Mensa Domini*, the one having reference to the participation, the other to the oblation of the Eucharist. There are who contend now, it was the intent and purpose of our Church at this Reformation, to pull down and wholly extinguish the very name of an altar; but all their reason being only the matter of fact, that altars were then pulled down, and this place of the Liturgy, that here it is called a table: We answer, that the matter of fact proves nothing, being rather the zeal of the people, that were newly come out of the tyranny that was used in Queen Mary's time. But if this were not by order of the Church, or according to the intent and meaning of the Church and State at the Reformation: How came it to pass then, that from that day to this, *the altars have continued in the King's and Queen's households after the same manner as they did before?* They never dreamt there, of setting up any tables instead of them: And likewise in *most cathedral churches, how was it that all things remained as they did before?* And it will be worthy the noting, that *no cathedral church had any pulling down, removing, or changing the altar into a table, no more than in the court*; but in such places only, where deans, and bishops and prebends were preferred, that suffered themselves more to be led by the fashions of what they had seen at Strasburg in Germany, and Geneva in France, and Zurich in Switzerland, than by the orders of the Church of England established, and continued in her Majesty's family; the likeliest to understand the meaning of the Church and State of any other place. Therefore they that will not either endure we should have, or they who will not believe we have, any altar allowed or continued

The Altar.

in our Church (howsoever as it is here, and as it is in most of the Fathers, sometimes called a table), let them go to the King's court, and to most of our cathedral churches, and enquire how long they have stood there, and kept that name only, as being indeed the most eminent, and the most usual among Christians.'—*Bp. Overall's Notes in Nicholls' Commentary*, p. 37, fol. 1710.

1626

'In the years 1626 and 1627, Master John Cosins, a great acquaintance and comrade of this Archbishop's [Laud], set up a goodly stone altar (railed in altarwise, adorned with pictures, candlesticks, tapers, basins, altar-cloths having superstitious images upon them) instead of a Communion-table, and bowed constantly to it . . . in that cathedral.'—*Canterbury's Doom*, p. 78. Lond. 1646.

1635

'An altar stone of marble erected and set upon four columns.'—*Ibid.* p. 81. *An account given of what service the Dean of Worcester did at his Majesty's cathedral there, what time he first came thither, in November last,* 1634.

1636

'Is the Communion-table placed conveniently so as the minister may best be heard in his administration, and the greatest number may reverently communicate? to that end, doth it ordinarily stand up at the east end of the chancel, where the altar in former times stood, the ends thereof being placed north and south?'— *Bp. Wren's Visitation Articles*, qu. *Canterbury's Doom*, p. 96.

1636

'My Lord [Bishop of Lincoln] in his certificate mentions two particulars fit for your Majesty's notice:

THE ALTAR

the first is, that one of his clergy in Bedfordshire, a learned and pious man (as he saith), set up a stone upon pillars of brick for his Communion-table, believing it to have been the altar-stone. And because this appeared to be but a grave-stone, and for avoiding further rumours in that country among the preciser sort, his Lordship caused it to be quietly removed, and the ancient Communion-table placed in the room of it.'

[*The King's marginal note.*] 'This may prove a bold part in the Bishop, and the poor Priest in no fault.'— *Archbp. Laud's Annual Accounts of his Province to the King. Laud's Troubles*, etc., pp. 542, 543.

1637

'The thirteenth innovation is, "the placing of the Holy Table altarwise, at the upper end of the chancel," that is, "the setting of it north and south, and placing a rail before it" to keep it from profanation, which, Mr. Burton says, "is done to advance and usher in popery." To this I answer, that 'tis no popery to set a rail to keep profanation from the Holy Table; nor is it any innovation to place it at the upper end of the chancel, as the altar stood. And this appears both by the *practice* and by the *command* and *canon* of the Church of England. First, by the practice of the Church of England: for in the King's royal chapels and divers cathedrals, the Holy Table hath ever since the Reformation stood at the upper end of the quire, with the large or full side towards the people: And though it stood in most parish churches the other way, yet whether there be not more reason the parish churches should be made conformable to the cathedral and mother churches, than the cathedrals to them, I leave to any reasonable man to judge. But, howsoever, I would fain know how any discreet moderate man dares say, that the placing of the Holy Table altarwise (since they will needs call it so) is done either to advance or usher in popery?

The Altar.

For, did Queen Elizabeth banish popery, and yet did she all along her reign, from first to last, leave the Communion-table so standing in her own Chapel Royal, in St. Paul's and Westminster, and other places; and all this of purpose to advance or usher in that popery which she had driven out? And since her death have two gracious kings kept out popery all their times, and yet left the Holy Table standing as it did in the Queen's time, and all of purpose to advance or usher in popery, which they kept out? Or what's the matter? May the Holy Table stand this way in the King's chapel, or cathedrals, or Bishops' chapels, and not elsewhere? Surely, if it be decent and fit for GOD's service, it may stand so (if authority please) in any church. But if it advance or usher in any superstition and popery, it ought to stand so in none. Nor hath any King's chapel any prerogative (if that may be called one) above any ordinary church to disserve GOD in, by any superstitious rites . . . Secondly, this appears by the canon or rule of the Church of England too, for 'tis plain by the last injunction of the Queen, that the Holy Table ought to stand at the upper end of the quire, north and south, or altarwise. For the words of the Queen's injunctions are these: *The Holy Table in every church* (mark it, I pray, not in the royal chapel or cathedrals only, but in *every* church) *shall be decently made, and set in the place where the altar stood.* Now, the altar stood at the upper end of the quire, north and south, as appears before by the practice of the Church. . . . So you see, here's neither popery nor innovation in all the practice of Queen Elizabeth or since. These words of the injunction are so plain, as that they can admit of no shift.'—*Archbp. Laud's Speech in the Star Chamber. Laud's Works*, VI. i. 59, 60. *Lib. Anglo-Cath. Theol.*

1637

'For the remaining passage in this first paragraph, where it is said "that altars were removed by law, and

THE ALTAR

tables placed in their stead, in all or the most churches in England"; and for the proof thereof the Queen's injunctions cited as if they did affirm as much, it is plain that there is no such thing in the said injunction. The Queen's injunctions, an. 1559, tell us of neither all nor most, as it is alleged, but only say, that "in many and sundry parts of this realm the altars in the churches were removed, and tables placed for the administration of the Holy Sacrament," &c. Sundry and many are not all nor most in my poor conceit: and it is plain by that which follows, not only that in other places the altars were not taken down upon opinion of some further order to be taken in it by the Queen's Commissioners; but it is ordered "that no altar shall be taken down without the oversight of the Curate and one of the churchwardens at the least," and that too with great care and caution, as before is said. Nay, the Commissioners were contented well enough that the altars formerly erected might have still continued, declaring, as it doth appear by the said injunction, that the removing of the altar seemed to be a matter of no great moment; and so it is acknowledged by this Epistoler in the following paragraph, where he confesseth it in these words: "It seems the Queen's Commissioners were content that they [the altars] should stand, as we may guess by the injunction 1559, in which we have that great advantage which Tully speaks of—confitentem reum." The Queen's Commissioners, as they had good authority for what they did, so we may warrantably think that they were men of special note and able judgments; and therefore, if they were contented that the altars formerly erected should continue standing, (as the Epistoler confesseth,) it is a good argument that in the first project of the Reformation neither the Queen nor her Commissioners disallowed of altars, or thought them any way unserviceable to a Church reformed. So that, for ought appears unto the contrary, neither the Article, nor the Homily, nor the

Queen's injunctions, nor the Canons of 1572, have determined anything; but that as the Lord's Supper may be called a sacrifice, so may the Holy Table be called an altar, and consequently set up in the place where the altar stood.'—*Heylyn's Coal from the Altar.* 1637.

1637

'That a rail about the Communion-table is one of the ingredients to make up an high altar or a popish altar . . . may appear by all the cathedral churches, in which only high altars have been continued since times of Reformation, all which also have been railed in, and all the communicants made to receive kneeling at the rails, and nowhere else.'—*Retractation of Mr. Chancy, formerly Minister of Ware, in Hertfordshire; written with his own hand before his going to New England, in the year* 1637, *etc.,* pp. 6, 7, 4to, 1641.

1638

'Is your Communion-table, or Altar, of stone, wainscot, joyner's work, strong, fair and decent? What is it worth in your opinion, were it to be sold?'

'Is the Communion-table fixedly set, in such convenient sort and place within the chancel, as hath been appointed by authority, according to the practice of the ancient Church, that is, at the east-end of the chancel, close unto the wall, upon an ascent or higher ground, that the officiating Priest may be best seen and heard of the communicants, in that sacred action?'—*Bp. Montague's Visitation Articles.*

1640

'It was ordered by the injunction and advertisements of Queen Elizabeth of blessed memory, that the Holy Tables should stand in the place where the altars stood, and accordingly have been continued in the royal chapels of three famous and pious princes, and in most cathedral and some parochial churches, which doth sufficiently acquit the manner of placing the said tables from any illegality or just suspicion of popish superstition or innovation. And therefore we judge it fit and convenient that all churches and chapels do conform themselves in this particular to the example of the cathedral or mother churches, saving always the general liberty left to the bishop by law, during the time of administration of the Holy Communion. And we declare that this situation of the Holy Table, doth not imply that it is, or ought to be esteemed a true and proper altar, whereon Christ is again really sacrificed: but it is, and may be called an altar by us, in that sense in which the primitive Church called it an altar, and no other.'—*Canon* VII. *Cardwell's Synodalia*, i. 404.

1643

'Sir Robert Harlow . . . breaking into Henry the Seventh's chapel, brake down the altar-stone which stood before that goodly monument of Henry the Seventh: the stone was touch-stone, all of one piece, a rarity not to be matched that we know of in any part of the world.'—*Mercurius Rusticus*, p. 238.

1644

'The Sacrament of the Lord's Supper they [the first Reformers] called the Sacrament of the Altar, as appears plainly by the statute, 1 Edward VI., entituled "An Act against such as Speak unreverently against the Sacrament of the Body and Blood of Christ, commonly called the Sacrament of the Altar," for which consult the body of the Act itself. Or, secondly, by Bishop Ridley (one of the chief compilers of the Common Prayer-book), who doth not only call it the "Sacrament of the Altar," affirming thus, "that in the Sacrament of the Altar is

The Altar. the natural Body and Blood of Christ," &c. But in his reply to an argument of the Bishop of Lincoln's, taken out of St. Cyril, he doth resolve it thus, viz. "The word *altar* in the Scripture signifieth as well the altar whereon the Jews were wont to offer their burnt-sacrifice, as the Table of the Lord's Supper ; and that St. Cyril meaneth by this word *altar*, not the Jewish altar, but the Table of the Lord," &c. (*Acts and Mon.* part iii. pp. 492, 497). Thirdly, by Bishop Latimer, his fellow-martyr, who plainly grants "that the Lord's Table may be called an altar, and that the doctors called it so in many places, though there be no propitiatory sacrifice, but only Christ." (Part ii. p. 85.) Fourthly, by the several affirmations of John Lambert, and John Philpot, two learned and religious men, whereof the one suffered death for religion under Henry VIII., the other in the fiery time of Queen Mary ; this Sacrament being called by both the Sacrament of the Altar in their several times ; for which consult the *Acts and Monuments*, commonly called the *Book of Martyrs*. And that this Sacrament might the longer preserve that name, and the Lord's Supper be administered with the more solemnity, it was ordained in the Injunctions of Queen Elizabeth, that no altar should be taken down, but by oversight of the Curate of the church and churchwardens, or one of them at least ; and that the Holy Table in every church be decently made and set up in the place where the altar stood, and there commonly covered as thereto belongeth. It is besides declared in the Book of Orders, anno 1561, published about two years after the said injunction, "That in the place where the steps were, the Communion-table should stand ; and that there shall be fixed on the wall over the Communion-board the tables of God's precepts imprinted for the same purpose." The like occurs in the advertisements published by the Metropolitan and others the High Commissioners, 1565, in which it is ordered "that the parish shall provide a decent Table, standing on a frame for the Communion-table, which they shall decently cover with a carpet of silk, or other decent covering, and with a white linen cloth in the time of the administration, and shall set the Ten Commandments upon the east-wall over the said Table." All which being laid together, amounts to this, that the Communion-table was to stand above the steps and under the Commandments, therefore all along the wall on which the Ten Commandments were appointed to be placed, which was directly where the altar had stood before.'—*Heylyn's Cyprianus Anglicus, Introd.* xxii, xxiii.

1666

* 'Then the bishop and clergy shall go towards the Chancel, the doors of which being shut, he shall stand there, and with the priests recite this hymn alternately, "Open to me the gates of righteousness. . . ." Then the doors being open'd, the bishop with his clergy shall enter and ascend to the Communion Table.'—*Irish Form of Consecration of Churches*, 1666. S.P.C.K. 1893, pp. 17, 18.

Overthrow of Altars by Edward VIth's Nobles and the Zuinglian Gospellers

1550-1553

'John a Lasco, bringing with him a mixed multitude of Poles and Germans, obtained the privilege of a church for himself and his, distinct in government and forms of worship from the Church of England. This gave a powerful animation to the Zuinglian Gospellers (as they are called by Bishop Hooper, and some other writers) to practise first upon the Church of England; who, being countenanced, if not headed, by the Earl of Warwick, (who then began to undermine the Lord Protector,) first quarrelled with the episcopal habit, and after-

Overthrow of Altars. wards inveighed against caps and surplices, against gowns and tippets; but fell at last upon the altars, which were left standing in all churches by the rules of the Liturgy. The touching on this string made excellent music to most of the grandees of the court, who had before cast many an envious eye on those costly hangings, that massy plate, and other rich and precious utensils which adorned those altars. And *What need all this waste?* said Judas; when one poor chalice only, and perhaps not that, might have served the turn. Besides, there was no small spoil to be made of copes, in which the priest officiated at the Holy Sacrament; some of them being made of cloth of tissue, of cloth of gold and silver, or embroidered velvet; the meanest being made of silk or satin, with some decent trimming. And might not these be handsomely converted into private uses, to serve as carpets for their tables, coverlids to their beds, or cushions to their chairs or windows? Hereupon some rude people are encouraged underhand to beat down some altars, which makes way for an order of the council-table, to take down the rest, and set up tables in their places; followed by a commission, to be executed in all parts of the kingdom, for seizing on the premises to the use of the king. But, as the grandees of the court intended to defraud the king of so great a booty, and the commissioners to put a cheat upon the court lords who employed them in it; so they were both prevented in some places by the lords and gentry of the country, who thought the altar-cloths, together with the copes and plate of their several churches, to be as necessary for themselves as for any others. This change drew on the alteration of the former Liturgy, reviewed by certain godly prelates, and confirmed by Parliament in the 5th and 6th years of this king; but almost as displeasing to the Zuinglian faction as the former was. In which conjuncture of affairs died King Edward the Sixth.'—*Heylyn's History of the Reformation,* ed. *Eccles. Hist. Soc.* 1849, vol. I., *To the Reader,* vii, viii.

THE ALTAR

Consecration of an Altar at Wolverhampton

1635

'Upon Saturday, being the 10th of October, 1635, Master Edward Latham, one of the Proctors of Lichfield, and surrogate of Wolverhampton, accompanied with some twenty or thirty persons, men, women, and choristers, came to the town, many of the inhabitants, but chiefly the clergy, going to meet him. Consecration of an Altar.

'The intent of his and their coming was to perform the solemnity of *Dedicating the Communion Table to be an altar*, and of consecrating certain altar-cloths (as they said) "to the glory of God."

'The Table was made new for this purpose, being about a yard and a half in length, exquisitely wrought and inlaid, a fair wall of wainscot being at the back of it; and the rail before it was made to open in the middle, and not at one side, the middle where the ministers tread being matted with a very fair mat.

'Upon the Table was placed a fair Communion Book, covered with cloth-of-gold, and bossed with great silver bosses, together with a fair cushion of damask with a carpet of the same; both particoloured of sky colour and purple, the fringe of the carpet being blue and white.

'On each side of the Table hangs two pieces of white calico, and betwixt them the Ten Commandments, written in a fair table with gilded letters, the foresaid cushion standing just below it.

'But on the north end where the Minister stands to consecrate, and in that piece of white calico, is represented at the top, the picture of angels with faces, clouds, and birds flying; about the middle, the picture of Peter on the cross; at the bottom, George on horseback treading on the dragon; leaves and grass, with some trees, being beneath all, almost at the end of it.

'In the other piece of white calico on the west end is

Consecration of an Altar. the same as on the north end, only the picture in the middle differs, being the picture of Paul with his sword in his hand; all this being the curious work of some needlewoman.

'Now the mystery why the pictures of Peter and Paul and George on horseback, and more other are in this work, is imagined because the church is dedicated to the memory of Peter and Paul, and it is under the jurisdiction of St. George's chapel at Windsor.

'The next day, being the Lord's Day, as soon as the priests (for so they would be called, to suit the better with the altar,) came to the church; each of them made a low congie apiece at their very first entering in at the great church door, and another congie apiece at the aisle door, and after that, three congies apiece towards the altar (before its dedication); and so they went into the chancel, where a basin of water and a towel was provided for the priests to wash in, where was incense burned which perfumed the whole church; and then they returned back making three congies apiece, and went to service, which was solemnly performed, the organs blowing, great singing not heard of in this church before, which kind of service lasted two hours at least.

'Service being finished, there was a sermon preached by one Master Jeffery, Archdeacon of Salop, in the county of Salop, whom the surrogate brought with him.

'His text was John x. 22, 23. "And it was at Jerusalem the feast of the Dedication, and it was winter, and Jesus walked in the temple in Solomon's porch."

'All this whole sermon was to prove the truth of the altar. He had not one place of Canonical Scripture, as we remember; and but one place in all, which was out of the Maccabees. His sermon lasted an hour.

'After sermon they went to the *Dedication*, or rather, as the preacher styled it, *Renovation* of the Altar: and in the bell-house four of them put on the rich broidered copes, and every one of them had a paper in his hand, which they termed a censer,[1] and so they went up to the altar reading it as they went, for they looked often on it.   *Consecration of an Altar.*

'As they went they made three congies apiece, and when they came to the altar, they kneeled down and prayed over the cloth and the other consecrated things, the organs blowing all the while; this solemnity lasted almost half-an-hour.

'After all this was performed there was a Communion, and one was appointed to stand with a basin to receive the Offertory: divers gave money, and it was thought it had been given to the poor, but the man that held the basin gave it to the surrogate (the sum gathered being reputed about forty shillings); he calling the churchwardens gave them, as he said, ten shillings; the remainder, he told them, he would bestow on other pious uses, but the ten shillings being counted, proved to want six of the just sum he said he had delivered them. None gave the Communion but the four that had copes.

'This finished they washed their hands and returned, making three congies apiece as before.

'These copes and the silver basins were brought from Lichfield.

'The Communion and Dedication ended, they went to dinner, and in the afternoon they come to church again, where was a sermon preached by one Master Usual, a Minister, and his text was 2 Sam. vii. 2, "And David said to Nathan the prophet, See now, I dwell in a house of cedar, and the ark of GOD abideth under curtains."

'This sermon did justify and magnify the altar, and lasted more than an hour: which being finished, they went to prayer, which was very solemnly performed, the organs blowing, and divers anthems and responds being

---

[1] The 'censer' named above was obviously not a thurible, but a book. Probably the Puritan who wrote the account meant to use the word 'processioner.' In Peacock's *English Church Furniture*, p. 71, occurs the curious entry, 'an Antifoner a pressioner with ij portis, solde to Chrofer Hawksworth whose folke made sensors of against Christemas.' This entry is followed immediately by 'Sensors ij crewetes and ij handbells sold to a metle man.'—ED. 1902.

sung at that time: which done, they departed from the church to their lodging, where they were very merry.... Thus ended this late Dedication, with which I here conclude my rude discourse and Quench-Coal.'—*The manner of Altaring the Communion Table of the Collegiate Church of Wolverhampton in the County of Stafford, and consecrating it for an Altar, the 11th day of October*, A.D. 1635.— *A Quench-Coal*, pp. 196-199, 4to, 1637.

1635

'In the Collegiate church of Wolverhampton, in the county of Stafford, the altar and cloths thereof were consecrated 11 October, 1635. As soon as the priests come to the church, each of them made a low congie at their first entering in at the church door, and after that three congies apiece towards the altar, so they went into the chancel where a basin with water and a towel was provided for the priests to wash in, where also was incense burning; after, they returned making three congies apiece. After the sermon every one of them had a paper in his hand which they termed a censer, and so they went up again to the altar: as they went they made three congies apiece. The Communion being ended they washed their hands, and returned giving congies as before.'—*A Large Supplement of the Canterburian's Self-Conviction*, p. 87 n., 4to, 1641.[1]

Coverings of the Altar

A.D. 1549

* ST. LAWRENCE, CATERHAM.
'*Item* a ffrond above the aulter of lynnyn cloth steynyd.

---

[1] This is the second edition of Bailie's infamous *Canterburian's Self-Conviction*, lauded by Prynne.—EDD. 1848.

THE ALTAR

'*Item* another bynethe the aulter of blewe and grene clothe. Coverings of the Altar.

'*Item* a coverlett to lye before the aulter.'—*Daniel-Tyssen, Surrey Inventories*, p. 107.

1551

* 'Whether the Table for the Communion be decked and apparelled behind and before, as the altars were wont to be decked?'—*Bp. Hooper's Later Writings*, p. 142, § xxiii. *Parker Soc.*

1552

* ST. PETER, CHALDON.

'*Item* ij frountes for thaulter one lynnen thother silk.

'*Item* vij aulter clothes of lynnen.

'*Item* a frount for thaulter of whit and grene dornix.'

ST. MARY, EAST MOLSEY.

'*Item* a clothe to hang before the aulter off sarcenet paned yelow and redd.

'*Item* an other cloth of redd sylke with yelow braunched flowers for the table off the aulter.

'*Item* one other gold cloth off sylke wrought with images and flowers.'—*Daniel-Tyssen, Surrey Inventories*, pp. 62, 78.

1552-1553

* ST. JOHN, CROYDON.

'*Item* a quyssion to the communyon table for the bokis.

'*Item* a canapie of blew damaske for the table.

'*Item* ij copis grene velvit for the communyon table.[1]

---

[1] As a result of the visitation of the Commissioners of Ed. VI. in the year 1552-1553, we find many instances recorded in *The Surrey Inventories* of copes, chasubles, and hearse-cloths, being turned into altar-coverings: *e.g.* 'an other table cloth made of a cope'; 'a cope of blew bawdekin for the communyon

44 HIERURGIA ANGLICANA

Coverings of the Altar.

'*Item* an alter cloth embroderid sett with small perles for the communyon table.'—*Church goods delivered by Ed. VIths Commissioners for use in the parish church. Daniel-Tyssen, Surrey Inventories,* p. 144.

1553

'A Turkey carpet for the Communion-table.'—*Appendix to Dugdale's Hist. of St. Paul's,* p. 58, fol. 1715.

1554-1555

* 'P^d more ffor the altar clothes and the front that was beffore the hy altar, xxxiii*s*. iiii*d*.'

'*Item*. The best ffront of the hyghe altar of sylke and golde. *Item*. The best alter clothes of twesshewe (tissue). *Item*. iiij alter clothes.'—*Inventory of Church-goods at Holy Trinity, Bristol.*

1559

* 'That the Holy Table in every church be decently made, and set in the place, where the altar stood, and there commonly (usually) covered, as thereto belongeth.' —*Queen Elizabeth's Injunctions, Cardwell's Doc. Ann.* i. 234.

1559

* 'The Table necessary for celebrating the Holy Mysteries was decorated with a carpet and a cushion, and was

---

table'; 'a white vestment and a herce cloth of bawdkin for the communyon table'; 'a vestment and a sepulcre cloth for the communion table'; 'ij chesables for the communyon table'; 'iij old vestmentes to make a communion table cloth.'—*Surrey Inventories,* pp. 148, 151, 156, 162, 171, 176. Even in this time of shameful robbery, when the bare necessities of church ornaments were hardly left, amongst these we invariably find an altar-cloth for the holy table. As an illustration of the conversion of vestments to altar-coverings, the following is of interest:—'After the Restoration, we hear of an almost incredible amount of vestments as having then belonged to the College. At present, a few fragments, representing pelicans, pieced together in the cover for a Puritan Communion Table, are the only representatives of this large collection.'—(*Fowler's Hist. of Corpus Christi Coll. Oxford,* p. 99). See also *sub* 1566.—ED. 1902.

THE ALTAR

placed towards the east.'—*Account of Archbp. Parker's Consecration, Cardwell's Doc. Ann.* i. 276.

Coverings of the Altar.

1559

'The carpet of velvet for the communion table' in St. Paul's at the obsequies of Henry II. of France, cost £16, 13s. 4d. 'The hangings, covering the ground in the Chancel, £48, 4s. 4d.'—*Strype's Annals of the Reformation,* vol. I. pt. i. p. 188, 8vo, Oxford, 1824.

1562

'*Item.* One altar-cloth of crimson velvet and gold, and two other altar-cloths of blue and russet velvet with flowers of gold.'—*Accounts of St. Margaret's, Westminster; Malcolm's Londinium Redivivum,* iv. 137.

1564

'They shall decently cover with carpet, silk, or other decent covering, and with a fair linen cloth, at the time of the ministration, the Communion-table.'—*Queen Elizabeth's instructions to Archbp. Parker. Strype's Life of Parker,* iii. 88.

1565

* 'An alter clothe wythe rede and grene and damaske. A nother alter clothe of grene and rede sylke.'—*Inventory of Church-goods at Holy Trinity, Bristol.*

1565

'Over the Communion-table was fastened a front of rich cloth of gold set with pelicans; before the said table hung, reaching to the ground, another front of the same suit.'—*Leland's Collectanea,* ii. 692, 8vo, 1770.

1566

Coverings of the Altar.

* '*Item*, v albes two alter clothes a sarcenett clothe defaced and coveringes made for õr coion table and for the funte.

'*Item*, . . . the vestment y^s mad a cavarying ffor the comvnyon tabell.

'*Item*, one other vestment of silk cut in peces and a clothe made therof for õr comunion table.'—*Peacock, English Church Furniture*, pp. 129, 137, 143.

1571

* 'They shall see that there be a joined handsome Table, which may serve for the administration of the Holy Communion, and a clean carpet to cover it.'— *Canons of* 1571. *Cardwell, Synodalia*, i. 123.

1596

* '*Item* a grene carpett of Carsey frenged.'—*Inventory of Church-goods at St. Ewen's, Bristol*, 1596.

1604

'The same tables shall . . . be covered, in time of divine service, with a carpet of silk or other decent stuff, thought meet by the ordinary of the place, if any question be made of it, and with a fair linen cloth at the time of the ministration, as becometh that table.'— *Canon* LXXXII.

1608

'*Item*. Bought a cloth of gold and a cushion for the Communion-table.'—*Accounts of St. Margaret's, Westminster; Malcolm's Londinium Redivivum*, iv. 141.

1613

* 'One greene Kersy Carpett for the Communion-

THE ALTAR 47

table.'—*Accompte Book of the Parish of St. Ewen's, Bristol*, Coverings of
1548-1632. the Altar.

1615

* 'New carpet-cloth for the Communion-table, 7s. 6d.'
—*Extracts from the Churchwardens' Accounts of Great
Wigston, Leicestershire; Nichols' Illustrations of the Manners
and Expences of Antient Times in England*, 1797, p. 149.

1622

'That the said room (in Prince Charles' apartment at
Madrid) be decently adorned chapel-wise, with an altar,
fronts, palls, linen coverings. . . .'—*Collier's Eccles.
Hist.* ii. 726.

1625

'Mrs. Ferrar provided two new suits of furniture for
the reading-desk, pulpit, and Communion-table, one for
the weekdays, the other for Sundays and other festivals.
The furniture for weekdays was of green cloth, with
suitable cushions and carpets. That for festivals was of
rich blue cloth, with cushions of the same. . . .'—*MS. of
Nicholas Ferrar, cited in Trans. of the Cambridge Camden
Soc.* i. 41.

1628

* 'Have you a decent table for the Communion,
covered with silk, or other decent stuff in time of divine
service, and with a fair linen cloth over that, at the
administration of the Communion?'—*Bp. Neile's Visitation Articles.*

1630

* 'Have you a convenient and decent Communion-
table, with a carpet of silke or some other decent stuff,

and a fair linen cloth to lay thereon at the Communion-time?'—*Bp. Curle's Visitation Articles.*

1631

'The country parson hath a special care of his church, . . . that there be a fitting and sightly communion-cloth of fine linen, with a handsome and seemly carpet of good and costly stuff or cloth, and all kept sweet and clean in a strong and decent chest; with a chalice and cover, and a stoop or flagon; and a bason for alms and offerings: besides which he hath a poor man's box conveniently seated to receive the charity of well-minded people, and to lay up treasure for the sick and needy.'—*Herbert's Country Parson*, ch. xiv.

1634

* DURHAM CATHEDRAL. 'A high altar-cloth of crimson velvet to cover the Table; another of purple velvet to hang above.'—*A Topographical Excursion in the Year* 1634; *Graphic and Historical Educator*, p. 127.

1634

* LICHFIELD CATHEDRAL. 'A fair Communion-cloth of cloth-of-gold for the high altar.'—*Ibid.* p. 208.

1634

* 'Upon that half-pace stood the Communion-table, with a rich carpet, hanging very large upon the half-pace, and some plate, as chalice and candlesticks with wax candles.'—*Letter from Edward Lenton describing a visit to Gidding in* 1634. Vide *Nicholas Ferrar*, ed. T. T. Carter, p. 112 *n.*

c. 1634

* 'There were two "communion tables," one new,

THE ALTAR 49

the other old; the latter had a silk carpet, the expression used in the canons of 1603 for the frontal. And there were others: "a new purple velvet cloth with gold fringe for the communion table and one with a less fringe," also "three carpettes of red silke and golde, one for the communion table and two other for Mr. Deane and Vicedeane's seat on solemne dayes." Thus altogether there were three carpets for the holy table, besides the one on the old. The new purple one was probably made of one suit with the back cloth of purple which excited so much indignation in the puritan mind.'—*Inventories of Christchurch, Canterbury*, p. 251.

Coverings of the Altar.

1635

'According to the example of their Lord and Chancellor, the principal Colleges in Oxford beautified their chapels, transposed their tables, fenced them with rails, and furnished them with hangings, palls, plate, and all other necessaries.'—*Cyprianus Anglicus*, II. iv. 31.

1635

'When the Communion is here [Durham Cathedral] administered, there is laid upon the altar, or rather Communion-table, a stately cloth of gold.'—*Brereton's Travels, published by the Chetham Soc.*, p. 83.

1636

'Have you a convenient and decent Communion-table, with a carpet of silk or some other decent stuff continually laid upon the table at the time of divine service, and a fair linen cloth thereon laid at the time of administering the Communion?'—*Bp. Wren's Visitation Articles.*

1636

* 'That at the time of divine service the Table shall

Coverings of the Altar.

be covered with a handsome stuff carpet; and when the Holy Eucharist is administered with a white linen cloth.'
—*Canons for the Scottish Church,* 1636; *Collier's Eccles. Hist.* II. ix. 764.

1637

* 'The Holy Table having at the Communion-time a carpet, and a faire white linen cloth upon it. . . .'—*The Booke of Common Prayer for the use of the Church of Scotland, Edinburgh,* 1637.

1638

'Have you a covering or carpet of silk, satten, damask, or some more than ordinary stuff, to cover the Table with at all times, and a fair, clean, and fine linen covering, at time of administering the Sacrament?'
—*Bp. Montague's Visitation Articles.*

1638

* '*Item,* one velvet cover for the Communion Table with silke fringe of the gift of Mrs. Saunders, price 8*l.*'
—*Kerry, St. Laurence's, Reading,* p. 28.

1661

	£	s.	d.
* 'For diaper for a table cloth for the Communion table,	1	8	0
For damask linnen for two table cloths for the Communion table,	4	10	0[1]
For the worke about the Three table cloths,	0	5	0'

—*Inventories of Christchurch, Canterbury,* p. 271.

---

[1] 'The amount spent upon the linen seems considerable even for those days; the damask and diaper must have been handsome and large, for no doubt the ancient custom was followed of enveloping the whole of the Lord's Table in linen at the time of the celebration of the Eucharist.'—J. W. L. *in loco.*

THE ALTAR

1664

ST. MARTIN'S, LUDGATE. 'In 1664 Sir Francis Bridgen gave the pulpit a crimson velvet hanging, and a border of the same, both fringed with gold, and a cushion; to which he added an altar-cloth of velvet and cushion, the former fringed with gold, and a prayer-book bound and embroidered in velvet and gold. It is barely necessary to mention that the altar now [1807] has a redundancy of rich vessels of massy silver.'— *Malcolm's Londinium Redivivum*, iv. 363.

<small>Coverings of the Altar.</small>

1667

'For the Holy Table there are two fronts (the upper and the nether), both of cloth-of-gold interpaned with like breadths of a brown velvet and well fringed.'—*Bp. Wren's Will, proved* 1667.

1689

* 'One communion Table with a veluet cloth.'— *Inventories of Christchurch, Canterbury*, p. 284.

c. 1692

* 'The Queen (Mary II.) sent for Dr. Hooper (Dean of Canterbury, 1691-1703), and carried him into her drawing-room, and showed him some pieces of silver stuff and purple flowered velvets, which her Majesty told him, if he approved of, she intended to give to the Cathedral at Canterbury, as she had observed the furniture to be dirty when she was there; that as there was not enough of the figured velvet, she had sent into Holland to match it, but could not. Her majesty sent down a page of her back stairs, who understood those things, to see it done. The altar was furnished with a pane of the figured velvet, and a pane of gold stuff, flowered with silver, and the Archbishop's throne with plain velvet. The figure for both was a ruffted one, of gold, silver, and purple, which alone cost £500.'—G. S. *Chronological History of Canterbury Cathedral*, Canterbury, 1883, p. 330.

1727

* 'In all the churches the altars are covered with a velvet or damask silk cloth; candlesticks are placed upon them, and pictures are frequently hung above as ornaments.'—*Letter of M. de Saussure, describing the English churches in* 1727.

1735

* 'The Altar Hanging and Table Cloth of Crimson Velvet Laced with Gold and Two Cushions with Four Gold Tassels each.'—*Inventories of Christchurch, Canterbury*, p. 294.

1738

* ST. JAMES', WESTMINSTER. 'Magnificent draperies of crimson velvet embroidered with gold, and trimmed with gold fringe, were presented to the vestry for the altar . . . by the Prince of Wales, in 1738; and valued at £700.'—*Malcolm's Londinium Redivivum*, iv. 226.

1745 and 1752

* '*Item* One Communion Table with a Red Velvet Covering.'—*Inventories of Christchurch, Canterbury*, pp. 300, 306.

1807

WESTMINSTER ABBEY. 'The altar-table is of oak, apparently almost coeval with the Reformation, massy and strong. It is covered with dark purple cloth, fringed and tasseled with a lighter purple. The eastern side of it

THE ALTAR

is raised,[1] for supporting the great candlesticks and their wax candles.'—*Malcolm's Londinium Redivivum*, i. 87.

Coverings of the Altar.

Royal Gifts of Altar-Palls

1553

* [Mary I.] 'And then her Grace was brought unto the said throne again, and immediately removed into a rich chair by the gentleman ushers before the high altar, upon which altar her Grace offered her pall of baudekin and xx s., verifying the words of Scripture, " Thou shalt not appear void before the Lord God."'—*MS. in Herald's College*, qu. *Planché, Regal Records.*

1603

* [James I.] 'There he maketh his first Oblation, which is, *Pallium unum et una libra auri.*'—Prynne, *Signal Loyalty*, Lond. 1660, ii. 263-302, qu. Chr. Wordsworth, *Appen.* vi., *The Manner of the Coronation of K. Charles I.* H. Bradshaw Soc. Lond. 1892.

1626

* [Charles I.] ' The ArchBp. being ready at the Altar, the King supported by the two Bps. as before, and attended on by the Deane of Westminster, goeth downe from his Chaire of Estate, to the Steppes of ye Altar, where vppon Carpetts and Quishions, the King maketh his first oblation, *Pallium vnum, et vnam Libram auri*,

---

[1] Altar-shelves were occasionally used in London churches in the 17th and 18th centuries; but they appear to have been uncommon until some time after the commencement of the Oxford Movement. Before the 17th century, they were seldom, if ever, used either in England or abroad; the cross and candlesticks standing directly on the altar. The shelf or *halpas*, sometimes mentioned in mediaeval documents, meant the top of the reredos, upon which reliquaries and plate were often set, but not candlesticks.—ED. 1902.

Coverings of the Altar.

Eius complendo praeceptum, qui dixit. "Non appareas vacuus in conspectu Domini Dej tui." '—*Coronation Order of Charles I., MS. Brit. Mus. Harl.* 5, 222, ed. L. G. Wickham Legg, *English Coronation Records,* p. 250.

1661

* [Charles II.] 'The Master of the Great Wardrobe did also provide the Pall of Cloath of Gold for the King to Offer.'—*MS. Heralds' College C.G.Y.* 369, *by Sir Edward Walker, entitled A circumstantial Account of the Preparations for the Coronation of His Majesty K. Charles II.,* qu. L. G. Wickham Legg, *E.C.R.* p. 279.

1685

* [James II.] '¶ This being done ; ye King supported by ye two Bishops, attended (as allwaies) by ye Dean of Westminster, (ye Lords, y^t carry y^e *Regalia* going before him) goeth down to ye Steps of the Altar, and there kneeling down makes his first Oblation ; wch is 1) a pall of Cloth of Gold ; deliverd by ye M^r of ye great Wardrobe to ye great Chamberlain, and by him to ye King ; and 2) an Ingot. . . .'—*Coronation Order of James II., MS. St. John's Coll., Cambridge, L.* 14, ed. L. G. Wickham Legg, *E.C.R.* p. 294.

1689

* [William III. and Mary II.] '¶ This being done, the King and Queen each of them supported by two Bishops, attended (as allwaies) by the Dean of Westm^r. and the Lords, that carry the Regalia, going before them, go down to ye Altar, and kneeling down upon the Steps there, make each of them their first Oblation : Which is, each of them a Pall (or Altar Cloth) of Cloth of gold ; delivered by the Master of the Great Wardrobe to the Lord great Chamberlain, and by him to their Majesties ; and each of them an Ingot or Wedge of gold . . . to

THE ALTAR 55

be received by the ArchBishop standing, (in which posture he is also to receive all other Oblations) the Palls to be reverently laid upon the Altar, and the gold to be received into the Basin, and with like reverence put upon the Altar.'—*Coronation Order of William and Mary, MS. Heralds' College*, L. 19, ed. J. Wickham Legg, *Three Coronation Orders*, H. Bradshaw Soc. pp. 16, 17.

<small>Coverings of the Altar.</small>

This rubric remained the same until Victoria so far as the Altar-cloth is concerned, except that in the cases of George II., George III., and William IV., the following addition was made to it:—

'Then the Queen ariseth from Her Chair, and being likewise supported by two bishops, and the Lords which carry Her *Regalia* going before Her, goeth down to the Altar, and kneeling upon the Cushions there layd for Her, on the left Hand of the King's, maketh Her *Oblation*, which is a *Pall*, to be received also by the Archbishop, and layd upon the Altar.'—*Ibid*. p. 137.

1838

* [Victoria.] 'The Queen, supported by the two Bishops, of Durham and Bath and Wells, and attended by the Dean of Westminster, the Great Officers, and the Lords that carry the Regalia going before Her, goes down to the Altar, and kneeling upon the Steps of it, makes her *First Oblation*; Which is a *Pall* or *Altar-cloth of Gold*, delivered by an Officer of the Wardrobe to the Lord Great Chamberlain, and by Him, kneeling, to Her Majesty, and an Ingot or Wedge of Gold of a pound weight, which the Treasurer of the Household delivers to the Lord Great Chamberlain, and He to Her Majesty, kneeling: Who delivers them to the Archbishop, and the Archbishop standing (in which posture he is to receive all other Oblations) receives from Her, one after another, the Pall to be reverently laid upon the Altar, and the Gold to be received into the Bason, and with the like

Coverings of the Altar.

Reverence put upon the Altar.'—*The Form and Order of the Service that is to be performed, and of the Ceremonies that are to be observed, in the Coronation of Her Majesty Queen Victoria, in the Abbey Church of St. Peter, Westminster, on Thursday, the* 28*th of June,* 1838. *Lond. Eyre and Spottiswoode,* 1838.

1902

* [Edward VII.] 'Then the King kneeling, as before, makes his Oblation, offering a *Pall* or *Altar-Cloth* delivered by the Officer of the Great Wardrobe to the Lord Great Chamberlain, and by him, kneeling, to his Majesty, and an *Ingot* or *Wedge of Gold* of a pound weight, which the Treasurer of the Household delivers to the Lord Great Chamberlain, and he to his Majesty; And the Archbishop coming to him, receiveth and placeth them upon the Altar.

'The Queen also at the same time maketh her Oblation of a *Pall* or *Altar-Cloth*, and a *Mark* weight of Gold, in like manner as the King.'—*The Form and Order of the Service that is to be performed and of the ceremonies that are to be observed in the Coronation of their Majesties King Edward VII. and Queen Alexandra in the Abbey Church of St. Peter, Westminster, on Thursday, the* 26*th day of June* 1902.¹ *Lond. Eyre and Spottiswoode,* 1902.

Ornaments and Furniture of the Altar

A.D. 1547

Ornaments and Furniture of the Altar.

'And shall suffer from henceforth no torches nor candles, tapers or images of wax to be set afore any

---

¹ This was the Form and Order prepared for June 26, 1902. The Coronation was postponed to Aug. 9, 1902. In this Order, the First Oblation has been transferred to the place of the Second Oblation, viz. after the Offertory.—ED. 1902.

image or picture, but only two lights upon the high altar, before the Sacrament, which, for the signification that Christ is the very true light of the world, they shall suffer to remain still.'—*Injunctions of Edward VI. Cardwell, Doc. Ann.* i. 7.

Ornaments and Furniture of the Altar.

1547

'*Item*, whether they suffer any torches, candles, tapers, or any other lights to be in your churches, but only two lights upon the high altar.'—*Articles to be enquired of in the Diocese of Canterbury. Ibid.* i. 51.

1547

'They reduced candles, formerly sans number in churches, to two, upon the high altar, before the Sacrament; these being termed lights, shews they were not lumina cæca, but burning.'—*Fuller's Church History*, p. 374, fol. 1655.

1549

* '*Item* ij kandyllstykks for the hey altar of laten and a crewett of pewther.'

'*Item* ij hanggyngs for the alter for lent of lynnen clothe with redde crossys.

'*Item* a lenten clothe hanggyng in the quere.'— *Inventory of goods*, etc., *Sandal Magna, Hist. MSS. Com.* 11*th Report. Appen.* vii. 119, qu. *Antiquary*, xxxiii. 356.

1550

* '*Item*, for ij tapers weyinge iij pound for the first mas, ij s.'—*Churchwardens' Accounts of Ludlow*, p. 43. Camden Soc., 1869.

1552

* '*Item*. ij great candelstyckes of latten;

Ornaments and Furniture of the Altar.

Item. ij other candelstyckes to stand on the aulter.'—*Inventory of Ornaments of Wyford Church, qu.* Parker, *The Ornaments Rubric,* p. 39.

1552

* ST. PAUL'S CATHEDRAL, LONDON.

'The Inventarie of the Plate, Jewells, Coopes, Vestements, Tunacles, Albes, Bells, and other Ornaments appertayninge to the Cathedrall Churche of Sayncte Paule in London 1552.

In primis a longe pix silver and all gilte standinge upon a foote and upon the over parte a greate rounde ball or pomill with a great flower upon the same.	xlij. unc.
Item, a rownde pounsedd pix used to reserve the sacremente, silver and all gilte.	xiij. unc. di.
Item, an ymage of our Ladie and her Sonn in her arme, with a spone in his hande, silver and all gilte.	C. xiiij. unc.
Item, an ymage of Saincte Pawle with a swearde in his hande and a booke in thother hand sylver and gilte.	C. viij. unc.
Item, a precious crosse of cristall set in silver and all gilte with many precious stones aboughte hym on both sides with three stones in the corners with a foote and iiij. divers armes in it enamelled and a crowne of silver and gilte sett with many divers precious stones finelie wrought with perles and iiij. heddes or faces in the over parte.	C. unc.
Item, a faire crosse with a crucifix and Marie and John with a foote and a vice. the bosse VI. square with ij. anngelles upon the foote and iiij. Evangelistes enamelled with iiij. floure de luces in the iiij. corners and a lamb on the backe side.	C. xx. unc.
Item, a greate large crosse with the crucifix with Marie and John and iiij. Evangelists enamelled at the iiij. corners the bosse vj. square with vj. ymages enamelled in everie pane one, with a greate pomell and sockett, silver and all gilte.	lxvij. unc. di.
Item, a crosse with the crucifix onlie with iiij. ymages and iiij. floure de luces adjoyning, silver and gilte.	xxxvij. unc.
Item, a plaine crosse platedd with silver and gilte with iiij. redd stones in the iiij. corners sett throughlie with perels and stones.	

PLATE IV.] [*To face page* 59.

Hier. I.]

THE ALTAR

Item, ij. cristall crosses with plates of silver at everie joynte ordeinedd for processions.

Item, a greate chalice silver and gilte, the foote round with leaves and branches graven. The Paten having an hande blessinge, a spone in the chalice, and with a knoppe of cristall at the end of the spone. — xxij. unc. di.

Item, a chalice silver and gilte, the foote vj. square with a crucifix Marie and John in the foote and Jesus Christus graven alsoe in the foote the paten having the ymage of the Trinitie and this scripture graven aboughte the paten, Benedicamus patrem et filium, etc. — xxx. unc. di.

Item, a chalice plaine with a rounde foote silver and gilte, the ymage of the crucifix graven in the foote of the same and a hande blessing with a crosse upon the paten. — xx. unc. iij. q^{tr}.

Item, a faire antique chalice of silver and gilte with a rounde foote and with muche curyous workmanship and flowers, the paten having graven upon it this worde, Ihus, enameled. — xxviij. unc. di.

Item, a chalice used dailie for the Communyon and kept in the utter vesterie silver and all gilte graven both aboughte the cuppe and upon the paten, Calicem salutaris accipiam et nomen domini invocabo. — xxviij. unc.

Item, iij. greate Ampulles or cruetts silver and gilte with covers. The greatest of them having a silver spone in hitt. — xx. unc.

Item, ij. cruetts silver and percell gilte without handells or pipes straked with iiij. rowes of leaves gilte. — xvi. unc. di.

Item, ij. ampules silver and parcell gilte plaine having ij. silver spones in eche ampull one. — xvij. unc. iii. q^{rs}.

Item, iij. ampulles silver and parcell gilte with stoppells in them and silver spones in each of them occupied with oyles and enclosedd in a case of lethere. — xxi. unc.

Item, ij. cruetts of silver ij. w. upon eche of them . on w. usedd dailie. — viij. unc.

Item, ij. faire Censoures of silver and gilte with high covers with vj. windows and batillments in the myddes of them with iiij. chaynes of silver a peece. — cx. unc.

Item, one Censoure of silver and parcell gilte with iij. libardes heddes on the cover with vj. windows and pinnacles and iiij. chaynes of silver thereunto apperteynynge. — xxxv. unc.

Item, on little Sensoure of silver and gilte, the cover is the forme of an oled churche with wyndows and pinacles with v. shorte chaynes of sylver wyre. — xii. unc. iii. qrs.

Ornaments and Furniture of the Altar.

60 HIERURGIA ANGLICANA

Ornaments and Furniture of the Altar.

Item, a greate large Sensoure all silver with many windowes and batillments usedd to sense withall in the Penticoste weeke in the bodie of the Chirche of Pawles at the Procession tyme. — clviii. unc. iii. qrs.

Item, ij. greatte candellsticks silver and parcell gylte, the shafte and powmells of them be all gylte with ij. vices in the botomes, one in eche of them. — lxviij. unc.

Item, ij. candellsticks silver and parcell gilte the shafte whereof plaine withought gyltynge and withoughte vices in ye botomes. — lxiiij. unc.

Item, ij. candelsticks of silver the shafte whereof be crystall joynted with silver plate. — lvj. unc.

Item, a sconse of sylver percell gylte vj. square with an handell alsoe of silver. — xxxiiij. unc.

Item, two basons silver and all gilte with the Rose and Crown graved and straked in them with armes enamelled with Egles and flowers de luce in the myddes. — lxxxiiij. unc.

Item, ij. basons of sylver and parcell gilte with ij. roses graven and gylte in the myddes with these letters: T. L. and O. D. — lij. unc.

Item, one holye water stocke of sylver and parcell gylte viij. square ij. libardes heddes at the socketts of the handle with a sprinkle allsoe of sylver and percell gylte. — xlv. unc.

Item, on shyppe of silver all whight with a spone in it to take out frankensence withall. — xviij. unc. di.

Item, a pontificall of golde with a blewe stone in the myddes with perles and many little stones of divers colors. — j. unc.

Item, a pontificall of golde with a great saphyer in it of playne worke. — q^t of an unc.

Item, a great pontificall of silver and gylte with a border of perells sett with viij. stones whereof on lackethe and enamelled in the myddes. — j. unc. di.

Item, a paire of gloves with broches sowedde upon eche of them with perles and stones.

Item, a principall myter all the ground worke whereof is sett with saphires and other stones in the middes.

Item, a new myter the groundwork whereof is clothe of silver sett full with perles with iiij. broches silver and gylte lynedd with crymosin velvett and ij. labells with v. bells at eche lable silver andd gylte.

[Then follows, though in a different handwriting, an estimate of the entire weight of the Church plate appropriated by the Commissioners not only from St. Paul's, but apparently from other London churches. This MS.

THE ALTAR

<small>Ornaments and Furniture of the Altar.</small>

has been pasted in between leaves 2 and 3 of the St. Paul's Inventory.]

From Powles by the Lord Maire	In gilte plate ... M . vj. oz. In parcell gilte . ccclxxvij. oz. In white plate . ccclxiiij. oz.	l. c. m. vij. xlvij. oz.
Rec^{d.} oute of London	c. *Item*, in gilte plate mmvijxvj. oz. c. In parcell gilte mmvjxxxviij. oz. In white plate mccclxxxv. oz. di.	m. c. vi. ix. xxxix. oz. di.

m. c.
Totalis. viij. vj. lxxxvi oz. di.

Item, one Ryng of golde with a stone therein sett, called } di. oz. di.
a topeas, weing } q^{rt.}
Item, two myters garnished with silver and gilte and } lxj. oz.
with course stones or glasses, weing altogethur }

[The inventory then continues in the original handwriting.]

Item, iiij. myters with perles and stones sett and wroughte with goldsmith worke.

Item, a myter the grounde whereof is sett with perles and stones and wrought with goldsmyth worke, havinge manye silver plates about it gylte and manye things befallen from it.

Item, a staffe silver and all gylte with ij. bosses : in thover } lxxxxvii.
bosse are vi. apostels and divers pinnacles are lacking } unc.
thereof. This staffe hath iiij. partes. }

Item, a staffe all silver and parcell gylte with muche fyne } lxxxix.
worke; in the hedd whereof ar th ymages of ower } unc.
Ladie and Pawle. This staff hath iiij. partes to be }
joynedd together with vices. }

Item, a staffe of timber with a picke and iij. bosses with a } xxxviij.
hedd silver and all gylte having in the hedd ij. } unc. di.
ymages and a dragon under them. }

Item, a staffe of yverie for the chaunter of the queere with a hedd and a crosse of birall wrought with goldesmith worke with vij. joyntes silver and gylte beside the picke and the bosse.

Item, a pax with the ymage of the Crucifix and of Marie and John all gylte with the Sonn alsoe and the Moone, the backsyde whereof crymosin velvett.

Item, a pax with the ymage of our Ladie sett aboughte with x. greate stones the backside whereof is grene velvett.

Item, a greate text of the Gospels for the yeare with the ymage of the Crucifix and of Marie and John all gylte with iiij. ymages at the iiij. corners.

Ornaments and Furniture of the Altar.

Item, a less texte of the Gospells with the ymages alsoe of the Crucifix Marie and John and iiij. ymages at the iiij. corners.

Item, a texte of the Gospells platedd with silver and gylte with the ymages of the Trinitie graven upon the one syde and v. bosses of silver upon thother syde.

Item, a greate texte of the Gospels, one syde thereof is platedd with silver and parcell gilte and graven with th ymage of the doome.

Item, a texte of the Epistells one syde whereof is partlie platedd with silver and gylte with a crosse and an ymage therein and thother syde hath iiij. bosses of silver.

Item, iij. longe staves usedd to carie the crosses upon in processions all throughlye platedd with silver except one which is not throughoughtlye platedd with silver but to the myddes onlye.

Item, a large Maser with a bande of silver and gylte haveing alsoe a standinge foote of silver and gylte.'[1]

—*Exchequer Q. R. Church Goods*, ₄/₇₁ *Public Record Office.*

1552

* In the sixth year of Edward VI., there were remaining in the church of St. Mary, Colechurch, London, amongst other goods:

'A cross of silver and gilt.
A Communion cup with a paten.
Two small Communion cups with patens.
A chalice of silver with a paten all gilt, and in the foot a crucifix.
A chalice of silver with a paten all gilt, in the paten a lion.
A chalice with a paten all gilt, and in the paten a lamb.
Two cruets of silver.
Two basons of silver, parcel gilt.
Two silver candlesticks, parcel gilt.
Two silver censers with chains, parcel gilt.
A ship of silver with a spoon.
A chrismatory of silver.
Two cross-staves garnished with copper.
A latten cross with a foot of copper.'

—*Milbourn's History of St. Mildred's Church, Poultry*, etc., p. 44, *Lond.* 1872.

1552

* ST. OLAVE'S, SOUTHWARK. '*Item*, one gospeller

---

[1] This Inventory is continued *sub* Ecclesiastical Vestments, 1552.

THE ALTAR

booke garnyshed with sylver and parcell gylte with Mary and John weynge cxx ounces.'

'*Item,* one pisteler booke with Peter and Palle garnished with sylver and parcell gylte weynge c ounces.'—*Surrey Inventories,* p. 79.

1555

* 'Those aulters to be orderly alway covered with two aulter clothes, and garnished with the crosse of Christe, or some little cofre of reliques. At eche ende a candelsticke, and a booke towarde the middes.'—*Fardle of Facions, printed* A.D. 1555.

1558

'Provided always, and be it enacted, that such ornaments of the church . . . shall be retained, and be in use, as was in this church of England by authority of Parliament in the second year of the reign of King Edward VI. until other order shall be therein taken, by the authority of the Queen's Majesty, with the advice of her Commissioners appointed and authorized under the great seal of England, for causes ecclesiastical or of the Metropolitan of this realm.'—*Act of Uniformity, primo Eliz.*

1558 etc.

* 1558. 'At the head of the Hearse, without the rayle, there was made an altar . . . covered with purple velvet, which was richly garnished with ornaments of the Church.' —(*Funeral of Q. Mary*).[1]

---

[1] The custom of exposing church plate by way of decorating the altar, is by no means a post-Reformation invention, but rather an usage which can claim respectable antiquity: *e.g.,* in 1449, Sir W. Bruges bequeathed to St. George's Church, Stamford, 'for their solemne fest dayes, to stande upon the high awter ij grete basyne of sylver.'—*Nichols' Illustrations,* p. 132. In 1537, Prince Edward, son of Henry VIII., was baptized at Hampton Court, when 'the High Altar was richly garnished with Stuffe and Plate.'—*Leland's Collectanea,* ii. 671.

For evidence of this usage at the present day in the Spanish churches, see *Transactions of St. Paul's Eccles. Soc.* iv. pp. 122-5.'—ED. 1902.

Ornaments and Furniture of the Altar.

1840. 'The Communion Table was covered with a rich profusion of gold plate.'—(*Marriage of Q. Victoria*).

1891. 'The massive gold Sacramental Plate belonging to the Chapel was displayed upon the Communion Table.'—(*Baptism of the first daughter of the Duke and Duchess of Fife*).

1893. 'Upon the altar, which had a white silk frontal, was placed the magnificent altar plate belonging to the Chapel Royal.'—(*Marriage of the Duke and Duchess of York*).—*Sheppard's Memorials of St. James's Palace*, ii. 146, 110, 62, 129.

1559

'But beside the habits, this divine (whether it was Grindal, or Parkhurst, or some one else) had made his observation of other things which he disliked in that degree, as to doubt the undertaking of the episcopal office upon him, lest in so doing he might seem to approve, and uphold, and countenance those things. And they were these. . . . III. The enjoining unleavened bread to be used in the sacrament. . . . IV. The processions in Rogation week. . . . V. The image of the crucifix on the communion table in the administration of the supper. . . . Concerning the use of the crucifix to be still retained in the churches, the divine before mentioned was so offended at it, that in his letter to Dr. Martyr, he desired him and Bullinger and Bernardin to write to the Queen against it. But Martyr excused himself by reason of his great business. . . . The Queen indeed being used to these things, that is, crosses and saints' images in churches, where she and her nobles that resorted thither used to give honour to them, had them at first in her own chapel. But she seemed to have laid them aside. . . . But it seems not long after the Queen resumed burning lights and the image of the crucifix again upon the altar in her oratory.'—*Strype's Annals*, I. i. 258 ff.

1560

'She [Queen Elizabeth] was known still to be favourable to the use of crosses and crucifixes, and they continued to be exhibited not merely in her own chapel, but also in many of the churches. Bishop Cox, in writing to P. Martyr in August 1559, says, 'crucis crucifixique imaginem in templis tolerare cogimur, cum magno animorum nostrorum cruciatu.' (*Hess, Cat.* vol. ii. p. 122. *Zurich Letters*, 38.) Sampson to the same in the following January, asks, 'si princeps ita injungat omnibus episcopis et pastoribus ut vel admittant in suas ecclesias imaginem cum candelis, vel ministerio verbi cedant, quid hic faciendum sit?' (*Hess, Cat.* vol. ii. p. 131. *Zurich Letters*, 36.) And Bishop Jewel, in February 1560, says to the same, 'Nunc ardet lis illa crucularia. . . . Eo enim jam res pervenit ut aut cruces argenteæ et stanneæ, quas nos ubique confregimus, restituendæ sunt, aut episcopatus relinquendi.' (*Hess, Cat.* vol. ii. p. 133. *Zurich Letters*, 39.) It appears from the same letter that a disputation was to be held on the subject, and that Parker and Cox had undertaken to defend the use of crosses, against Grindal and Jewel, who were most earnest in opposing them.'—*Cardwell's Doc. Ann.*, i. 268 *n*.

[margin: Ornaments and Furniture of the Altar.]

1560

'The Altar [in the Queen's Chapel] furnished with rich plate, two fair gilt candlesticks with tapers in them, and a massy crucifix of silver in the midst thereof.'—*Heylyn's History of the Reformation*, ii. 315.

1560

'March 6th, Dr. Bill, dean of Westminster, preached in the queen's chapel: where on the table, standing altarwise, was placed a cross and two candlesticks, with two tapers in them burning.'

Ornaments and Furniture of the Altar.

'The same day [the 24th], in the afternoon, bishop Barlow, one of king Edward's bishops, now bishop of Chichester, preached in his habit before the queen. His sermon ended at five of the clock: and presently after, her chapel went to evening song; the cross, as before, standing on the altar, and two candlesticks, and two tapers burning in them: and, service concluded, a good anthem sung.'—*Strype's Annals*, 1. i. 297, 298.

1560

'What can I hope, when three of our lately appointed bishops are to officiate at the table of the Lord, one as priest, another as deacon, and a third as subdeacon, before the image of the crucifix, or at least not far from it, with candles, and habited in the golden vestments of the papacy; and are thus to celebrate the Lord's Supper without any sermon?'—*Letter of Sampson to Peter Martyr, Jan.* 6, 1560. *Zurich Letters*, p. 63, *Parker Soc.*

1561

'Paid for four pound of candles upon Christmas in the morning for the mass, 1s.'—*Churchwardens' Accounts of St. Helen's, Abingdon, Berkshire. Nichols' Illustrations of the Manners and Expenses of Antient Times in England*, 142.

1565

'The Queen still to this year kept the crucifix in her chapel, as appears by a letter written to Secretary Cecil by a zealous gentleman, earnestly persuading him to use his interest with her majesty to have it removed, as tending too much to idolatry.'—*Strype's Annals*, 1. ii. 198.

1565

* WITHAM. '*Item*, on lynnen clothe a velvet quussin and a chalice—w̃ch nowe remaine in the churche and

PLATE V.] [*To face page* 67.

Hier. 1.]
From "LLANDAFF CHURCH PLATE."

THE ALTAR

ar occupied aboute the coĩon table there.'—*Peacock's Church Furniture*, 166.

<small>Ornaments and Furniture of the Altar.</small>

1565

'*Item.* The said chapel, both before and behind the stalls to the ground, was hanged with rich arras, and the upper part, from the table of administration to the stalls, hanged with like stuff, which said table was richly garnished with plate and jewels, as followeth. First, to the wall was set in a row, five gilt basons, and afore them another row, and in the middle a gilt cross between two great gilt cups covered, garnished with stone, a ship or ark likewise garnished, a fountain of mother-of-pearl, and a pair of gilt candlesticks; afore that, another row, in the middle whereof was set a rich bason and ewer, gilt railed over with gold, between two great maudlin cups with covers, two great lavers, two cruets, and a pax, all gilt; and over the said table on the wall upon the arras was fastened a front of cloth of silver, embroidered with angels of gold, and before the said table to the ground, a front of the same suit.

'The order and manner of furnishing the chapel at the Queen's Palace of Westminster, against Thursday, the 24th of January 1565, anno 8 Eliz. Reginæ, that the Duke of Norfolk and Earl of Leicester received the order of S. Michael there.'—*Ashmole's Institution, etc., of the Order of the Garter*, p. 369, fol. 1672.

1565

'The back part of the stalls in the royal chapel wherein the gentlemen of the chapel do sing, was hanged with rich tapestry, representing the twelve months, and the front of the said stalls was also covered with rich arras. The upper part of the chapel, from the table of administration to the stalls, was hanged with cloth of gold, and on the south side was a rich traverse for the

Ornaments and Furniture of the Altar.

Queen. The Communion-table was richly furnished with plate and jewels, viz. a fountain and basin of mother-of-pearl, a basin and a fountain gilt, railed with gold; a rich basin garnished with stones and pearls; a ship or ark garnished with stones; two great leires garnished with stones, and two lesser leires garnished with stones and pearls; a bird of agate furnished with stones; a cup of agate furnished with stones and pearls: a bowl of coral garnished with pearls; a bowl of crystal with a cover; two candlesticks of crystal; two ships of mother-of-pearl; one tablet of gold set with diamonds; another ship of mother-of-pearl: two pair of candlesticks of gold; two great candlesticks, double gilt, with lights of virgin wax, and a cross. . . . Also there was let down from the roof of the said chapel ten candlesticks in manner of lamps of silver and gilt, with great chains, every one having three great wax lights. Over the aforesaid table was set on a shelf as high as the window, twenty-one candlesticks of gold and silver double gilt with twenty-four lights. On the north side of the quire between the organs and the upper windows, stood seventeen candlesticks, double gilt, with seventeen lights; and on the tops of the stalls were fastened certain candlesticks with twelve lights, so that the whole lights[1] set there were eighty-three.'—*Christening of the child of Lady Cecile, at the Palace, Westminster, Sept.* 30, 1565.—*Leland's Collectanea*, ii. 691, 692, 8vo. 1770.

---

[1] The arrangement of lights may here be noticed. Only two lighted candles were actually placed on the altar, although other pairs of candlesticks are included amongst the plate. The numerous additional lights were set round the walls of the chapel, above the altar as well as elsewhere, besides those hanging from the roof. The placing of a row of six lights upon the altar, or the similar use of small candles in branches, was unknown in this country till quite recently. If more than two lights actually upon the altar were used, they were set in some position round about the altar. At the same time, we have record of two or three occasions of special magnificence (the Field of the Cloth of Gold, the Christening of Lady Cecile's child, and the Coronation of William and Mary), on which a number of lights were used on or behind the altar—not a row of six, nor yet branches—but several pairs of large candlesticks of various sizes, which were always used in connection with an extensive display of plate.—ED. 1902.

THE ALTAR

1566

* In a letter from Beza to Bullinger of Sept. 3, 1566, the former complains—'ac tandem etiam pileis quadratis, collipendiis, superpelliciis, casulis[1] et ceteris id genus sacerdotes Baalis referant.'—*Zurich Letters*, 2nd *series*, *Epistolæ Tigurinæ*, p. 77. *Parker Soc.*

Ornaments and Furniture of the Altar.

1570

'The crucifix, which had been before removed out of the Queen's chapel, was now of late brought in again.' —*Strype's Life of Archbp. Parker*, ii. 35.

'A rich and massy crucifix was kept for many years together, on the Table or Altar of the Chapel Royal in Whitehall, till it was broke in pieces by Pach, the Queen's fool (when no wiser man could be got to do it), upon the secret instigation of Sir Francis Knollis.' *Cyprianus Anglicus, Introd.*, xv.

1584

* 'One lytle cussion for the Communion table.'— *Inventories of Christchurch, Canterbury*, p. 241.

1603-1625

'I would not be understood to condemn all use of candles by day, in Divine service, nor all churches that have or do use them; for so I might condemn even the Primitive Church in her pure and innocent estate. And therefore, that which Lactantius, almost three hundred years after Christ, says of those lights, and that which Tertullian, almost a hundred years before Lactantius, says in reprehension thereof, must necessarily be understood of the abuse and imitation of the Gentiles therein:

---

[1] Possibly by 'casulis' is meant long gowns or cassocks.—ED. 1902.

Ornaments and Furniture of the Altar.

for, that the thing itself was in use before either of these times, I think admits little question. About Lactantius' time fell the Eliberitan Council; and then the use and the abuse was evident: for in the 34th Canon of that Council it is forbidden to set up candles in the church yard; and the reason that is added declares the abuse . . . that the souls of the faithful departed should not be troubled. Now the setting up of lights could not trouble them, but these lights were accompanied with superstitious invocations, with magical incantations, and with howlings and ejaculations which they had learned from the Gentiles, and with these the souls of the dead were, in those times, thought to be affected and disquieted. It is in this ceremony of lights as it is in other ceremonies. They may be good in their institution, and grow ill in their practice. So did many things which the Christian Church received from the Gentiles in a harmless innocency, degenerate after into as pestilent superstition there, as amongst the Gentiles themselves. For ceremonies which were received but for the instruction and edification of the weaker sort of people, were made real parts of the service of God and meritorious sacrifices. To those ceremonies, which were received as helps to excite and awaken devotion, was attributed an operation and an effectual power, even to the ceremony itself; and they were not practised, as they should, *significativè*, but *effectivè*; not as things which should signify to the people higher mysteries, but as things as powerful and effectual in themselves as the greatest mysteries of all, the Sacraments themselves. So lights were received in the Primitive Church, to signify to the people that God the Father of lights was otherwise present in that place than in any other: and then men came to offer lights by way of sacrifice to God; and so, that which was providently intended for man, who indeed needed such helps, was turned upon God, as though He were to be supplied by us. But what then? Because things good in their institution may be depraved in

THE ALTAR

their practice . . . shall therefore the people be denied all ceremonies for the assistance of their weakness? . . . We must not be hasty in condemning particular ceremonies, for in so doing, in this ceremony of lights, we may condemn the Primitive Church that did use them, and we condemn a great and noble part of the reformed Church, which doth use them at this day.'—*Dr. Donne's Sermons*, p. 80, fol. 1640.

Ornaments and Furniture of the Altar.

1622

'That a face of the Church of England might appear, and the worship be kept up in the Prince's apartment at Madrid, the King gave the chaplains above mentioned the following instructions:

'1. That there be one convenient room appointed for prayer; the said room to be employed, during their abode, to no other use.

'2. That it be decently adorned chapelwise, with an altar, fronts, palls, linen-coverings, demy-carpets, four surplices, candlesticks, tapers, chalices, patens, a fine towel for the Prince, other towels for the household, a traverse of waters for the Communion, a bason and flaggon, two copes.'—*Collier's Eccl. Hist.* ii. 726.

1622

'Chapels he [Bp. Laud] found none at his Episcopal house of Aberguilly, and one he was resolved to bestow upon it . . . which being finished, he provided it of rich furniture, and costly utensils, and whatsoever else was necessary or convenient for the service of God; the very plate designed for the celebrating of the Holy Supper amounting to one hundred fifty-five pounds, eighteen shillings, four pence. Insomuch that, if Felix the Proconsul had been still alive, he might have cried out now, as he did in the time of Julian the Apostate, viz. "Behold in what rich vessels they minister to the Son of Mary!" But this unhappy age hath

Ornaments and Furniture of the Altar. given us Felixes enough to reckon this amongst his crimes, and so they do his solemn consecration of it, performed by himself in person according to an order firmly drawn up by the most learned Bishop Andrews, than whom there could not be a greater enemy to the errors, superstitions, and corruptions of the See of Rome.'

'When he was Bishop of St. David's, he built a new chapel in his house of Aberguilly, and furnished both the chapel and the altar in it, with hangings, palls, fronts, plate, and other utensils, to a very great value.'—*Cyprianus Anglicus,* II. i. 61 ; IV. ii. 31.

1625

'Many workmen having been employed near two years, both the house and church were in tolerable repair, yet with respect to the church Mrs. Ferrar was not well satisfied, she therefore new floored and wainscotted it throughout; she also provided two new suits of furniture for the reading-desk, pulpit, and Communion-table, one for the week-days, the other for Sundays and other festivals. The furniture for week-days was of green cloth, with suitable cushions and carpets. That for festivals was of rich blue cloth, with cushions of the same, decorated with lace and fringe of silver. The pulpit was fixed on the north, and the reading-desk over against it on the south side of the church, and both on the same level, it being thought improper that a higher place should be appointed for preaching than that which was allotted for prayer. A new font was also provided, the leg, laver, and cover all of brass, handsomely and expensively wrought and carved, with a large brass lectern, a pillar and eagle of brass for the Bible. The font was placed by the pulpit, and the lectern by the reading-desk.

'The half-pace or elevated floor on which the Communion-table stood at the end of the chancel, with the stalls on each side, was covered with blue taffety and

THE ALTAR

cushions of the finest tapestry and blue silk. The space behind the Communion-table under the east window, was elegantly wainscotted and adorned with the Ten Commandments, the Lord's Prayer, and the Apostles' Creed, engraved on four beautiful tablets of brass, gilt.

Ornaments and Furniture of the Altar.

'The Communion-table itself was furnished with a silver paten, silver chalice, and silver candlesticks with large wax candles in them; many other candles of the same sort were set up in every part of the church, and on all the pillars of the stalls. And these were not for the purposes of superstition, but for real use, which for a great part of the year the fixed hours of prayer made necessary both for morning and evening service. Mrs. Ferrar also, taking great delight in church music, built a gallery at the bottom of the church for the organ. Thus was the church decently furnished, and ever after kept elegantly neat and clean.'—*MS. of Nicholas Ferrar*, cited in *Trans. of the Cambridge Camden Soc.* part i. pp. 41, 42.

'Within her [Mrs. Ferrar's] chapel was a rich altar, crucifix, and wax candles, and before the reading of prayers they bowed thrice to the altar as they went up and came down.'—*Fosbrooke's Monachism*, p. 398.

1625

'Finding the *Old Crucifix* among the *Regalia*, Laud caused it to be placed on the Altar, as in former times.' —(*Coronation of Charles I.*). *Cyprianus Anglicus*, II. i. 92.

1625-1649

'Now what an Arminian and popish innovator this prelate [Wren] was in all particulars, the popish furniture of whose chapel, with basins, candlesticks, corporals,

Ornaments and Furniture of the Altar. altar-cloths, a chalice with a cross upon it, and other popish trinkets, as appears by his own book of accounts, costing him £159, 4s. 1d., and how great a persecutor, silencer, suppressor of godly ministers, people, the world experimentally knows.'—*Canterbury's Doom*, p. 353.

1625-1649

'Upon this new altar Laud had much superstitious Romish furniture, never used in his predecessor's days, as namely, two great silver candlesticks with tapers in them, besides basons and other silver vessels (with a costly Common Prayer-book standing on the altar, which, as some say, had a crucifix on the bosses), with the picture of Christ receiving his last supper with his disciples in a piece of arras, hanging just behind the midst of the altar, and a crucifix in the window directly over it. . . . This new altar furniture of his was proved and attested upon oath by Sir Nathaniel Brent, Dr. Featly, Dr. Haywood (his own popish chaplain), who justified his lord, that he did it in imitation of the king's chapel at Whitehall, where he had seen not only tapers and candlesticks standing, but likewise burning in the day-time on the altar.'—*Ibid.* p. 62.

1625-1649

'The great conformity and likeness, both continued and increased, in our Church to the Church of Rome, in vestures, postures, ceremonies, and administrations, namely, as the Bishops' rochets and the lawn sleeves, the four-cornered cap, the cope and surplice, the tippet, the hood, and the canonical coat; the pulpits clothed, especially now of late, with the Jesuits' badge [IHS] upon them every way; the standing up at *Gloria Patri* and at the reading of the Gospel; praying towards the east; the bowing at the name of Jesus; the bowing

THE ALTAR 75

to the altar, towards the east; the cross in baptism; the kneeling at the Communion; the turning of the Communion-tables altarwise; setting images, crucifixes, and conceits over them, and tapers and books upon them, and bowing and adoring to or before them; the reading of the second service at the altar, and forcing people to come up thither to receive, or else denying the Sacrament to them; terming the altar to be the mercy-seat, or the place of God almighty in the church, which is a plain device to usher in the Mass.'—*Nalson's Impartial Collection*, i. 165, fol. 1683.

Ornaments and Furniture of the Altar.

1628

DURHAM CATHEDRAL. 'But the mass coming in, brings in with it an inundation of ceremonies, crosses, and crucifixes, and chalices, and images, copes, and candlesticks, and tapers, and basins, and a thousand fresh trinkets which attend upon the mass; all which we have seen in this church since the Communion-table was turned into an altar. . . . Before, we had ministers, as the Scripture calls them, we had Communion-tables, we had sacraments; but now we have priests, and sacrifices, and altars, with much altar furniture, and many massing implements. . . . If religion consist in altar decking, cope wearing, organ playing, piping, and singing, crossing of cushions and kissing of clouts, oft starting up and squatting down, nodding of heads, and whirling about till their noses stand eastward, setting basins on the altar, candlesticks, and crucifixes, burning wax candles in excessive number when and where there is no use of lights; and what is worst of all, gilding of angels and garnishing of images, and setting them aloft . . . if, I say, religion consist in these and such like superstitious vanities, ceremonial fooleries, apish toys, and popish trinkets, we had never more religion than now.'—*Sermon by Peter Smart*, pp. 11, 23, 24, 4to, 1628.

1633

<small>Ornaments and Furniture of the Altar.</small>

CORONATION OF CHARLES THE MARTYR AT EDINBURGH. 'The archibishop of Sanctandroiss, the bischopis of Morray, Dunkell, Ross, Dumblane, and Brechyn, servit about the coronatioun (whiche wes done be the said bischop of Brechyn) with white rotchetis, and white sleives, and koopis of gold, haueing blew silk to thair foot. . . . Now it is markit that thair wes ane four noikit taffill maner of ane altar standing within the kirk, haueing standing thairvpone tua bookis at leist resembling claspit bookis, callit blynd bookis, with tua chandleris and tua wax candles, quhilkis war on lichtit, and ane bassein whairin thair wes nothing. At the bak of this altar (coverit with tapestrie) thair wes ane ritche tapestrie, quhairin the crucifix wes curiouslie wrocht; and as thir bischopis who wes in seruice past by this crucifix, thay war sein to bow thair knie and bek, whiche with thair habit wes nottit, and bred gryt feir of inbringing of poperie. . . .'—*John Spalding, Memorials of the Troubles in Scotland and England*, 1624-1645, vol. i. p. 36. *Aberdeen Spalding Club*, 1850.

1633

* 'Christ-tide, 1633, was the first day of the high altar, and candlesticks on it, and candles in them, and other dressings very brave, in Christ-Church, Canterbury.'—*Culmer's Cathedrall Newes from Canterbury*, 1644, p. 8.

1634

* 'At York, the candlesticks in 1634 were kept with the communion plate and the bible and common prayer book covered with crimson velvet and embossed with silver double gilt, which apparently took the place of the ancient textus.'—*Inventories of Christchurch, Canterbury*, p. 250.

c. 1634

* 'Two greate Candlestickes[1] and a greate siluer bason all guilt.'—*Inventories of Christchurch, Canterbury*, p. 260.

<small>Ornaments and Furniture of the Altar.</small>

1635

'Our parish churches and chapels, all of which Laud miserably defiled, corrupted with popish superstitious crucifixes, altars, bowings, ceremonies, tapers, copes, and other innovations.'—*Canterbury's Doom*, p. 59.

1635

'Abp. Laud began first with Canterbury, his own cathedral, where he found the Table placed at the east end of the choir by the Dean and Chapter, and adoration used towards it by their appointment . . . which having found in so good order, he recommended to them the providing of candlesticks, basons, carpet, and other furniture for the adorning of the altar, and the more solemn celebrating of the blessed Sacrament.'

'As for the Communion Table, which he found standing in the middle of the chapel of Croydon Palace, a very sorry one in itself, he ordered it to be removed to some other room, and caused a new one to be made, placed where the Altar sometimes stood, shadowed overhead with a very fair frieze, and fenced with a decent and costly rail: the gilding of the one, and the curious workmanship of the other, together with the Table itself, amounting to thirty-three pounds and upwards; copes, altar-cloths, plate, and other necessaries which belonged to the adorning of it, he had been master of before, in his other chapels, and therefore was at the less charge in completing this.'—*Cyprianus Anglicus*, IV. ii. 29, 31.

---

[1] These two candlesticks for the altar can be traced in the Canterbury Inventories of 1689, 1735, 1749, 1752, 1761.—ED. 1902.

1635

Ornaments and Furniture of the Altar.

'To make the adoration [towards the altar] more significant, the altars in Cathedrals were adorned with the most pompous furniture, and all the vessels underwent a solemn consecration. The Cathedral of Canterbury was furnished, according to Bishop Andrews' model[1] . . . with two candlesticks and tapers, a bason for oblations, a cushion for the service-book, a silver-gilt canister for the wafers, like a wicker basket lined with cambric lace, the tonne on a cradle; a chalice with the image of Christ and of the lost sheep, and of the wise men and star, engraven on the sides and on the cover. The chalice was covered with a linen napkin, called the aire, embroidered with coloured silk; two patens, the tricanale, being a round ball with a screw cover, out of which issued three pipes, for the water of mixture; a credentia or side-table, with a bason and ewer on napkins, and a towel to wash before the consecration; three kneeling stools covered and stuffed, the foot-pace, with three ascents, covered with a turkey carpet; three chairs used at ordinations, and the septum or rail with two ascents. Upon some altars there was a pot called the incense-pot, and a knife to cut the sacramental bread.'

'At Worcester, Manwaring, who succeeded Juxon in that Deanery . . . having erected a fair table of marble, standing on four well-fashioned columns, he covered the wall behind the same with hangings of azure-coloured stuff, having a white silk lace upon every seam, and furnished it with palls and fronts, as he had observed in his Majesty's and some bishops' chapels; and ordered

---

[1] Neal's description of the furniture at Canterbury Cathedral cannot be regarded as trustworthy. It is just as improbable that the chapter at Canterbury followed 'Bishop Andrewes' model,' as that Bishop Andrewes took his from the 'Roman Ceremonial, Missal, and Pontifical.'—ED. 1902.

THE ALTAR

the King's scholars, being forty in number, who used formerly to throng tumultuously into the choir, to go in rank by two and two, and make their due obeisances at their coming in.'—*Neal's History of the Puritans*, ii. 223, 224, 292. 8vo, 1822.

Ornaments and Furniture of the Altar.

c. 1635

* 'About this time the chapter appear to have bought an embroidered purple velvet cloth to go behind the altar.'—*Inventories of Christchurch, Canterbury*, p. 245.

c. 1635

* 'Their *Cathedrall-Altar-Glory-Cloth*, which is the shame of their Cathedrall, is made of very rich Imbroydery of Gold and Silver, the name *Jehovah* on the top in Gold upon a cloth of Silver, and below it a *semicircle of Gold, and from thence glorious rayes and clouds, and gleames and points of rayes, direct and waved, streame downewards upon the Altar*, as if *Jehovah* (*God himselfe*) were there present in glory, in that Cathedrall at the Altar; and all this to draw the people to looke and worship towards the Altar.'—*Culmer's Cathedrall Newes from Canterbury*, 1644, p. 6.

1637

ST. GEORGE'S CHAPEL, WINDSOR. 'And now, at length, (a considerable sum having been collected) the work began to be set on foot, and the workman made choice of was one Christian Van Vianan of Utrect, a man excellently well skilled in chasing of plate . . . and before the month of June 1637, he had finished and made ready for the use of the altar nine pieces of

Ornaments and Furniture of the Altar.

plate, the particulars whereof with their weight here follow:—

	oz.	dwt.
Two little candlesticks, chased and gilt, for wax candles,	92	6
Two chalices with four patens,	113	1
Two great candlesticks neat, for tapers,	553	15
Two little basons, containing the whole history of Christ in chased work,	251	15
One great bason,	210	0
	1220	17

The value, at 12s. the ounce, came to £742.

All this plate was treble gilt, and thereon were the Scripture histories rarely well designed and chased; and especially the great bason, and the covers of two books, hereafter mentioned. ... At a Chapter held the 2nd of October, in the year aforesaid, the said plate was ordered to be offered the next morning at the altar, and there to be consecrated to God and his service for ever, by the Prelate of the Order. And because the whole ceremony was performed with great veneration and all due reverence, his late Majesty being a high promoter of ecclesiastical decency and holy discipline, we think fit to present it here at large. On the 3rd day of the said month of October, being the Feast day (held by prorogation at Windsor Castle) in the time of the second service, at the versicle *Let your light so shine before men, etc.*, Walter, Bishop of Winchester, then Prelate, standing before the middle of the altar, read certain select verses out of the Old Testament, concerning the dedication of Solomon's Temple, and the riches thereof, the first of which was taken from the 35th chapter of Exodus, verse 4; the second being the 21st verse of the same chapter; and the third taken out of the 2nd chapter of St. Matthew's Gospel, verse 11; and afterwards fitted himself for the offering. At which time the Sovereign descended from his throne, as in the manner of offering, and thrice bowed towards the altar,

THE ALTAR

worshipping and adoring God in the middle of the choir, and so passed to the degrees of the altar; where, humbly kneeling [he] did present and offer to God the before-mentioned great bason, devoutly saying, "Part of Thy bounty to us, O Lord Almighty, I offer to Thee and to Thy service." The offering was forthwith received by the Prelate, and set upon the altar; which done, every one of the knights companions present, (after the example of this holy king) in their due ranks and single, did offer his piece of dedicated plate, with the same words, and in like manner. And that their ordinary offerings of gold and silver might not be interrupted or omitted, all the knights companions, at the time of offering the plate, made the same in another bason held by one of the Prebends. Every of these holy vessels being thus offered, and decently placed upon the altar, the Prelate with his hand touched every piece severally, as on God's part receiving them; and after made the following prayers of Consecration and Benediction: Ornaments and Furniture of the Altar.

'O Lord God, Heavenly Father, we Thy most humble servants do earnestly entreat Thee that Thou wilt graciously vouchsafe to accept these sacred offerings, by the hands of our most gracious Sovereign Lord King Charles, and the most honourable companions which are here present, dedicated to Thee. Grant, we beseech Thee, and cause, that whatsoever is this day offered unto Thee may be preserved from all profane use, and may for ever abide consecrated to Thy service, through Jesus Christ our Lord. Amen.

'Let us bless Thee, our most glorious Lord God, for that it hath pleased Thee to put into the heart of our most gracious Lord Charles, and of these Princes, to dedicate these oblations to Thy service. Regard, we beseech Thee, from the highest heavens, and pour out Thy blessings upon the head of his gracious Majesty: bless him in his royal person, in his most gracious Queen Mary, in the most illustrious Prince Charles, and in all the rest of the branches of the royal stock. Bless, we pray Thee, all those whose donations offered to Thee we have here this day received. Let Thy blessing fall down (as the dew of heaven) upon them, and upon their posterities, and upon all things which they have from Thee; and grant that by the holy and devout use of these things which are here offered, the glory of Thy Name may ever be proclaimed, and Thy Majesty may by these our due observances be exalted, through Jesus Christ our Lord. Amen.

Ornaments and Furniture of the Altar.

'These sacred ceremonies being completed, the Sovereign and knights companions marched to the great hall to dinner. But to make some further addition to the glory of this altar, his Majesty that now is [Charles II.], at the time of his installation into this most noble order (being the 22nd of May 1638), offered two large gilt water-pots, chased with histories also, weighing 387 ounces, 10 pennyweight . . . amounting (at 12*s.* the ounce) to the sum of £232, 10*s.* . . . These sacred vessels were afterwards delivered to be kept for the service of the altar. And yet the bounty of this pious Sovereign, King Charles the Martyr, rested not here. He thought the altar was not with all these sufficiently furnished, and therefore finding by an account delivered by the Chancellor in Chapter, the 23rd of May 1628, that there had been collected £137, 4*s.* more . . . the said money was by Sir Philip Palmer, then deputy Chancellor, immediately given to the said Christian Van Vianan, for furnishing this additional plate, bespoken by the Sovereign, as aforesaid. . . . The plate made upon the last advance was two great candlesticks, weighing together 471 ounces: on the foot of the one was excellently chased the histories of Christ's preaching on the Mount; and on the other, those of the lost groat and sheep. Two covers for books, both weighing 233 ounces: the one for a Bible contained the histories of Moses and the Tables, David and the Ark on the one side, and on the other Christ's preaching on the Mount, the sending of the Holy Ghost, and St. Paul falling from his horse. The other cover[1] was for the Common Prayer, having the Angel of incense on the one side, and the King healing the evil, the manner of our preaching and

---

[1] As an example of pre-Reformation use of costly covers for the *Textus*, and the placing of the same upon the altar at the celebration of the Eucharist, the following may suffice. At Durham, before the Suppression, 'the Gospeller did carrye a marvelous FAIRE BOOKE, which had the Epistles and Gospells in it, and did lay it on the Altar, the which booke had on the outside of the coveringe the picture of our Saviour Christ, all of silver, of goldsmith's worke, all parcell gilt, verye fine to behould: which booke did

THE ALTAR 83

christening on the other: and two great flagons, whereon were the histories of Christ's Agony and Passion, weighing 268 ounces; all being silver-gilt. And now, if we sum up the number, weight, and value of all the before-mentioned parcels of plate, wrought by the said Van Vianan for the service of the altar, we shall find them to be 17 pieces, weighing 3580 ounces, 7 penny-weights, and amounting (with some other small charges) to the sum of £1564, 6s. These last-mentioned parcels were finished against the feast of St. George, held at Windsor the 8th, 9th, and 10th days of October 1639, upon the last day of which feast, at the second service, the knights companions descended from their stalls and offered the same at the altar; and thereupon, after the usual manner and with the accustomed words, were they consecrated by the Prelate of the Order, and the 19th of November following delivered to the custody of the Dean and Canons of Windsor.'—*Ashmole's Institution of the Order of the Garter*, pp. 492-496.

Ornaments and Furniture of the Altar.

1637

ST. MARY AT AXE.—'Their Communion-plate in the year 1637 was,—One silver wine-cup gilt, weight 25 oz. 9 dwt., and one bread plate gilt; one other wine-cup gilt, weight 34 oz. 12 dwt., and one other bread-plate, being both the gift of Mrs. Jone Cartwright, 1609. Two fair large livery stoops or flagons of silver white, weighing 153 oz., being both the gift of Mr. Alderman Abdy, 1637. One small livery stoop or flagon of silver white, weighing 48½ oz., being the gift of Mr. Thomas Langton and Mr. Henry Boone, 1637. One bread-plate of silver white, weighing 15 oz. 2 dwt., being the

---

serve for the PAX in the masse. The Epistoler, when he had sung the Epistle, did lay by the booke againe on the Altar, and, after, when the Gospell was sunge, the Gospeller did lay it downe on the Altar untill the masse was done; and, the masse beinge ended, they went all three into the Revestrie, from whence they came, and caryed the booke with them.'—(*The Rites of Durham*, p. 7. Surtees Soc. 1842.)—ED. 1902.

Ornaments and Furniture of the Altar.

gift of Mr. John Steward, 1637. Which silver flagons and bread-plate mentioned, were by the churchwardens brought up from the body of the church to the Communion-table, and there offered unto Jesus Christ in the donor's name, 7th of May, 1637; and were then received and consecrated by Mr. Henry Mason, rector of the said parish, (leave being first obtained in that behalf from the Right Reverend Father in God, the Lord Bishop of London,) in form following:

'"To the honour of Jesus Christ, and for the more reverence of His blessed Sacrament, Mr. Alderman Abdy hath given these two silver pots or flagons, and doth here offer them up to God, to be dedicated to the service of this Holy Table. And I do receive them from him, for the use of my Lord and Master Jesus Christ, and do put them into His possession, beseeching God that He will bless these gifts, and that their use may serve for setting forth of His praise, and for the increasing of piety in the minds of His people. And I pray God bless the donor with the blessings of this life, and the blessedness of the life to come. And let the curse of this sacred altar, and the curse of my Lord and Master Jesus Christ, be upon that man, or that woman, that shall purloin them away, alienate them, or either of them, from their sacred use; in the name of the Father, Son, and Holy Ghost." At the saying of these words, *and do put them into His possession*, the flagons were set on the Communion-table.'—*Malcolm's Londinium Redivivum*, i. 62, 63.

1637

'But see the practice of these times. They will have priests, not ministers; altars, not communion-tables; sacrifices, not sacraments: they will bow and cringe to and before their altars; yea, they will not endure any man to enquire after what manner Christ is in the Sacrament, whether by way of consubstantiation, or transubstantiation, or in a spiritual manner; yea, they will have tapers, and books never used, empty basons and chalices there: what is this but the mass itself, for here is all the furniture of it?'—*The Retraction of Mr. Charles Chancy*, p. 6.

<small>Ornaments and Furniture of the Altar.</small>

1638

* 'One velvet quisheon and a booke of Common Prayer gilt for the Communion Table of the gift of James Read and Mrs. Henry, 3 *l.*'—Kerry, *History of St. Lawrence's, Reading*, p. 28.

1640

'For organs, candlesticks, a picture of a History at the back of the Altar, and copes at communions and consecrations, all which Dr. Featly named. First, these things have been in use ever since the Reformation. And, secondly, Dr. Featly himself did twice acknowledge that it was in my chapel as it was at Whitehall—no difference: and it is not to be thought, that Queen Elizabeth and King James would have endured them in their time in their own chapel, had they been introductions for popery. And for copes, they are allowed at times of communion by the Canons of the Church.'

'The third witness for this charge [against his chapel] was one Mr. Boreman, who came into my chapel at prayers time, when I had some new plate to consecrate for use at the Communion . . . This man says first, he then saw me bow and wear a cope . . . Secondly, that he saw me consecrate some plate; that in that consecration, I used some part of Solomon's prayer at the dedication of the Temple, and that in my prayer I did desire God to accept those vessels. No fault in any of the three. For in all ages of the Church, especially since Constantine's time, that religion hath had public allowance, there have been consecrations of sacred vessels, as well as of churches themselves. And these inanimate things are holy, in that they are deputed and dedicated

Ornaments and Furniture of the Altar.

to the service of God . . . And this being so, I hope my use of a part of Solomon's prayer, or the words of my own prayer, " that God would be pleased to accept them," shall not be reputed faults. But here stepped in Mr. Prynn, and said " this was according to the form in *Missali Parvo*." But 'tis well known I borrowed nothing thence. All that I used was according to the copy of the late Reverend Bishop of Winchester, Bishop Andrews, which I have by me to be seen, and which himself used all his time.'—*Archbp. Laud's Answer to the Articles of Accusation. Troubles and Trial*, p. 313, fol. 1695.

1640

'The consecration . . . was after this manner: the Archbishop in his cope, attended by two chaplains in their surplices, having bowed several times towards the altar, read a portion of Scripture ; then the vessels to be consecrated were delivered into the hands of the Archbishop, who, after he had placed them upon the altar, read a form of prayer, desiring God to bless and accept these vessels, which he severally touched and elevated, offering them up to God, after which they were not to be put to common use.'—*Neal's History of the Puritans*, ii. 224.

c. 1640

'Amongst other ornaments of the church also then in use, in the second year of Edward VI., there were two lights appointed by the injunctions (which the Parliament had authorized him to make, and whereof otherwhiles they make mention, as acknowledging them to be binding) to be set upon the High Altar, as a significant ceremony of the light which Christ's Gospel brought into the world ; and this at the same time when all other lights and tapers superstitiously set before images were by the very same injunctions, with many other abused ceremonies and superfluities, taken away. These lights were (by virtue of the present Rubrick referring to what was the use in the 2nd of Edward VI.) afterwards continued in all the Queen's chapels, during her whole reign ; and so are they in all the King's, and in many cathedral churches, besides the chapels of divers noblemen, bishops, and colleges, to this day. It was well known that the Lord Treasurer Burleigh (who was no friend to superstition or popery) used them constantly in his chapel, with other ornaments of fronts, palls, and books upon the Altar. The like did Bishop Andrews, who was a man who knew well what he did, and as free from Popish superstition as any in the kingdom besides. In the latter end of King Edward's time they used them in Scotland itself, as appears from Calvin's Epistle to Knox, and his fellow-reformers there, anno 1554, (Ep. 206), where he takes exception against them for following the custom of England. To this head we refer the organ, the font, the altar, the communion-table, and pulpit, with the coverings and ornaments of them all ; together with the paten, chalice, and corporas, which were all in use in the 2nd of Edward VI. by the authority of the Acts of Parliament then made.'—*Bp. Cosin's Notes on the Book of Common Prayer, Third Series, Works*, vol. v. pp. 440, 441. *Lib. Anglo-Cath. Theol.*

1640

'The Communion-plate of all sorts, in silver and gilt, for that sacred use, and which is as large and rich as any in the city or suburbs, was also her gift. And she also gave, among others, the following church ornaments, viz. for the back of the altar, a rich green velvet cloth, with three letters in gold I H S, embroidered on it. *Item.* Two service-books in folio, embossed with gold, a green velvet cloth with a rich deep gold fringe, to cover the altar over with on Sundays. *Item.* A cambric altar-cloth with a deep bone lace[1] round about. Another fine damask altar-cloth, two cushions for the altar, richly

---

[1] See p. 22 *n.*

<small>Ornaments and Furniture of the Altar.</small>
embroidered with gold; a large turkey carpet to be spread on week days over it, and likewise very costly rails to guard the altar or Lord's Table from profane uses.'—*Funeral Sermon of the Duchess of Dudley, preached by Dr. Boreham*, p. 23. *Some Account of the Hospital and Parish of St. Giles's in the Fields*, p. 199 *n.*, 4to, 1822.

1641

'Placing candlesticks on altars in parochial churches in the day-time, and making canopies over them with curtains, in imitation of the veil of the Temple, advancing crucifixes and images upon the parafront[1] or altar-cloth, and compelling all communicants to come up before the rails.'—*Neal's History of the Puritans*, ii. 397.

1641

'When the deacon hath lifted the text of the Gospel from the altar, he gives it to the sub-deacon to carry at his back; two wax candles are lifted from the altar by two acolytes, to be carried burning before him so long as the Gospel is in reading; the cross or crucifix is also on festival days carried before the Gospel, and also a censer with fire and incense; the book is crossed and perfumed, and when the lesson is ended the book by the deacon is kissed . . . From none of these superstitions we can be long secured: our deacons are begun already to be consecrate; the chief part of their office is their service at the Sacrament and their reading of Scripture; the orders of sub-deacons and acolytes are proclaimed to be convenient, if the church had maintenance for them, by Andrewes: the wax candles are standing on the altar already; the silver crucifix is avowed by Pocklington to have a mete standing upon the same altar; the crossings, and perfumings, and lights are maintained by Andrewes,

---

[1] This shows that 'altar-cloth' often meant 'frontal.'—ED. 1902.

THE ALTAR 89

as Canterbury sets him forth ; the kissing of the book is now daily practised.'   *Ornaments and Furniture of the Altar.*

'It remains that we should parallel with our Book the accidental parts of the Mass, so to call them. The most of these we have actually—their vestments, hoods, surplices, rochets, mitres, copes of all colours filled with numbers of images, palls, corporals, chalices, patens, offertory basins, wax candles, veils, rails, stalls, lavatories, repositories, reclinatories ["for confessions within the chancel," p. 81], bowings, duckings, crosses, kissings, coursings, perfumings. These we have already; and what of the ceremonies we want, it were easy to fetch testimonies from our party's writs for their lawfulness, or at least to show the necessity of taking them, whenever they shall be imposed by our Bishops, upon as good grounds as we have taken the rest.'—*A parallel or Brief Comparison of the Liturgy with the Mass-Book*, p. 84.

1641

'The ornaments of the Holy Table, the silk curtains, carpet, covering, books, and much plate, were all the pious gift of the same honourable lady which bestowed the screen : and being for the decency of God's service, and well accepted of by the parishioners, the Doctor had no reason to refuse them. As for the crucifix, organs, and church music mentioned in the petition, they were long before Dr. Haywood's coming. There is no desk upon the Lord's Table, only a little stay to hold up the plate, nor any such pictures on the books as the petitioners speak of.—*An Answer to a lawless Pamphlet entitled 'The Petition and Articles exhibited in Parliament against Dr. Haywood, etc.,'* by R. R. M., pp. 14, 15, 4to, 1641.

1641

'And as he was . . . most eager, keen, and active to innovate, change, alter, and deform what he pleased in or concerning the Church, to erect altars, to remove tables,

Ornaments and Furniture of the Altar.

to make rails, to set up tapers and candlesticks, golden plate on altars, embroidered and carved images, crucifixes, saints' pictures, and such Babylonical idolatries, so was he most fervently zealous, and most wonderfully careful, to introduce a ministry that should yield to all things, to bring in such as he knew most certainly to be for all turns, for all purposes, for all matters whatsoever should be put upon them, etc.'—*Wren's Anatomy*, pp. 10, 11, 4to, 1641.

1641

'There are divers high altars, solemnly dedicated of late in divers Colleges of Cambridge and Oxford, adorned with tapers, candlesticks, crucifixes, basins, crosses, rich altar-cloths, crimson cushions, rich hangings.'—*A Large Supplement, etc.*, p. 87 n.

1641

'It is this day ordered by the Commons in Parliament assembled, that the churchwardens of every parish church and chapel respectively do forthwith remove the Communion-table from the east end of the church, chapel, or chancel, into some other convenient place; and that they take away the rails, and level the chancels, as heretofore they were before the late innovations. That all crucifixes, scandalous pictures of any one or more Persons of the Trinity, and all images of the Virgin Mary, shall be taken away and abolished, and that all tapers, candlesticks, and basins[1] be removed from the Communion-table. That all corporal bowing at the name (Jesus), or towards the east end of the church, chapel, or chancel, or towards the Communion-table, be henceforth forborne.' A Declaration of the Commons in Parliament, made September the ninth, 1641 [without the consent of the House of Lords].—*Nalson's Impartial Collection*, ii. 481, 482.

---

[1] From the above we learn, that decking the altar with plate was regarded as 'popish' by the Puritans.—ED. 1902.

THE ALTAR

1603-1649

THE KING'S CHAPEL, WHITEHALL. 'He [Sir Henry Mildmay] further says, "There was a fair crucifix in a piece of hangings hung up behind the altar, which he thinks was not used before my time." But that *he thinks so* is no proof. If this were scandalous to any, it must be offensive in regard of the workmanship; or *quatenus tale*, as it was a crucifix. Not in regard of the work certainly, for that was very exact. And then, if it were because it was a crucifix, why did not the old one offend Sir Henry's conscience as much as the new? For the piece of hangings which hung constantly all the year at the back of the altar, thirty years together upon my own knowledge, and somewhat above, long before, (as I offered proof by the vestry-men), and so all the time of Sir Henry's being in court, had a crucifix wrought in it, and yet his conscience never troubled at it.'—*Archbishop Laud's Answer. Troubles, etc.*, p. 315.

Ornaments and Furniture of the Altar.

1641

'They [the managers of Laud's prosecution] objected likewise to his furnishing the altar in his own chapel, and the King's at Whitehall, with basins, candlesticks, tapers, and other silver vessels, not used in his predecessor's time; and to the *credentia* or side table . . . on which the elements were to be placed on a clean linen cloth before they were brought to the altar to be consecrated; and to the hanging over the altar a piece of arras with a large crucifix.'—*Neal's History of the Puritans*, iii. 169.

1641

'The walls about the altar or Communion-table were hanged with very rich cloth of gold bawdkin; the septum or rail about the altar was covered with the like, and

Ornaments and Furniture of the Altar. the floor within the septum or rail with a fair large turkey carpet. Upon the altar or Communion-table, the old English Bible, printed in 1541, and the Liturgy or Common Prayer-Book, both with silver and gilt covers, together with a gilt basin, two chalices, one paten, two candlesticks, &c., the whole weighing two thousand two hundred ounces. The doors of the septum were opened and turned back close to the rest of the rail; and a rich carpet of silk and gold was spread from the step where the door stood, before the altar or Communion-table, and thereon two rich long cushions were laid just without the rail for the bride and bridegroom to kneel on.' Marriage of William, only son of Frederic Henry, Prince of Orange, and Mary, eldest daughter of King Charles I., May 2, 1641.—*Leland's Collectanea,* v. 339.

1642

'The rebels, under the conduct of Sir William Waller, entering the city of Chichester on Innocents' Day 1642, the next day their first business was to plunder the cathedral church; the marshal, therefore, and some other officers, having entered the church, went into the vestry; there they seized upon the vestments and ornaments of the church, together with the consecrated plate serving for the altar and administration of the Lord's Supper: they left not so much as a cushion for the pulpit, nor a chalice for the Blessed Sacrament.'—*Mercurius Rusticus,* p. 223, 12mo, 1646.

1642

WINCHESTER CATHEDRAL. 'They seized upon all the Communion plate, the Bibles and service-books, rich hangings, large cushions of velvet, all the pulpit-cloths, some whereof were of cloth of silver, some of cloth of gold.'—*Ibid.* p. 234.

PLATE VI.] [*To face page* 93.

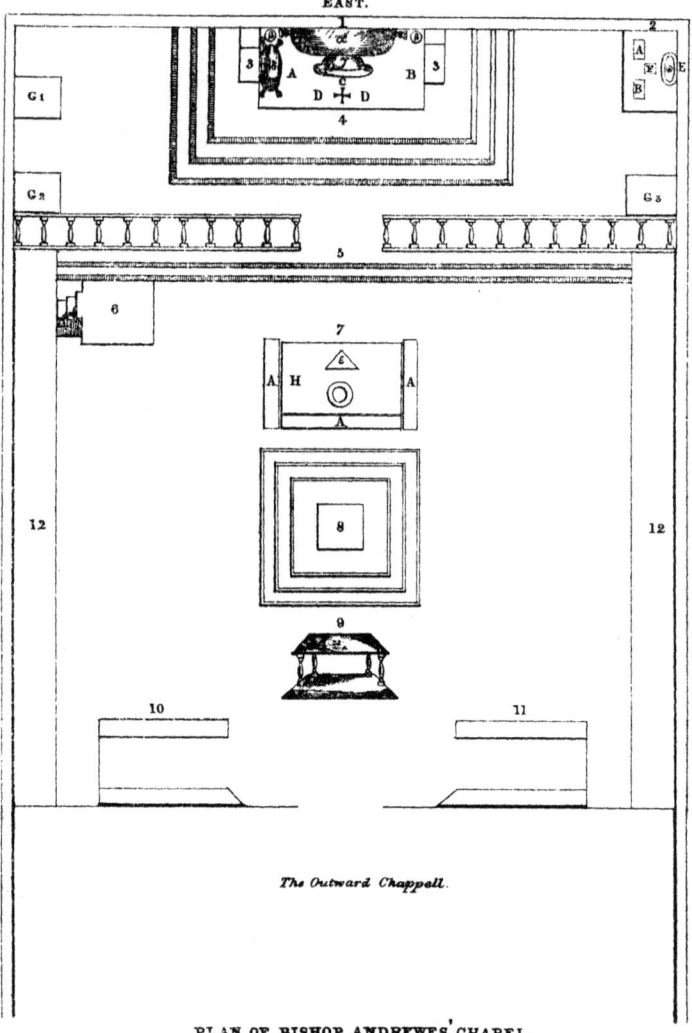

PLAN OF BISHOP ANDREWES' CHAPEL.

THE ALTAR

1643

'Mr. Prynn deposed, that he found in the Arch- <small>Ornaments and Furniture of the Altar.</small>
bishop's [Laud] study this paper indorsed and corrected
with his own hand, concerning the consecration of this
his chapel [at Aberguilly]. . . . With this instrument,
he likewise found a note of the dimensions of this chapel,
written with the Bishop's own hand : " My chapel at
Aberguilly is five yards and a half broad at the east end.
My altar-frame, besides the thickness of the table, is a
yard and three inches high. And the table is a yard
and three quarters long ;[1] and in breadth it wants three
inches of a yard ; the foot-pace is two yards broad."
This note was inclosed and wrapped up within these two
following papers found together with it, thus endorsed
with the Archbishop's own hand :—

'*Chapel and furniture as it was in use by the Right
Reverend Father in God, Lancelot Andrews, Lord Bishop
then of Winton:* from whom the Archbishop confessed at
the bar, he took his pattern of consecrating and furnishing churches, chapels, and altars. By which two papers
publicly read and shewed in the Lord's house, the Popish
furniture both of Bishop Andrews' and this Archbishop's
chapels at Aberguilly, London-house, and Lambeth, will
most evidently appear to all the world. The portraiture
of the first of these two papers, with the Popish furniture
of the altar in the Archbishop's and Bishop Andrews'
chapels, is expressed to the life in the following copper
piece.[2]

1. The Altar, 1 yard $\frac{1}{4}$ high, 1 yard $\frac{3}{4}$ long, 1 yard broad.
    α. A cushion.
    ββ. Two candlesticks, with tapers. ⎫ The daily furniture
    γ. The bason for oblations. ⎬ for the Altar.
    δ. A cushion for the service-book. ⎭

---

[1] Observe this example of a short altar. These short altars, which came into fashion in England in the seventeenth century, are a curious approximation to the square altars of the East.—ED. 1902.

[2] The reader is referred to the 'Plan of Bishop Andrewes' Chapel,' which is an accurate copy of the 'copper piece' above mentioned.—EDD. 1848.

Ornaments and Furniture of the Altar.

A. The silver and gilt canister for the wafers, like a wicker basket and lined with cambric laced. B. The Tonne, upon a cradle. C. The chalice, having on the outside of the bowl Christ with the lost sheep on his shoulders ; on the top of the cover, the wisemen's star, both engraven ; it is covered with a linen napkin (called the Aire) embroidered with coloured silks. DD. Two patens. ✠. The Tricanale, being a round ball with a screw cover, whereout issue 3 pipes, and is for the water of mixture.

2. A sier [side ?] table on which, before the Communion, stand A and B, upon two napkins. E. A bason and ewer, to wash before consecration. F. The towel appertaining.

3.3. The kneeling-stools covered and stuffed.

4. The foot-pace, with three ascents covered with a Turkey carpet, of fir boards. GGG. Three chairs used at Ordinations, or [by] prelates communicant.

5. The septum, with two ascents.

6. The pulpit.

7. The music table with (AAA) three forms. ϵ. A Triquertral censer wherein the clerk putteth frankencense at the reading of the first lesson. H. The Navicula, like the keel of a boat, with a half cover and a foot out of which the frankincense is poured.

8. A foot-pace with three ascents, on which the lectern standeth covered, and thereon the great Bible.

9. The faldstory whereat they kneel to read the Litany.

10. The chaplain's seat where he readeth service.

11. A seat with a canopy over it for the Bishop ; but at the Communion time he sits on G3.

12. 12. Two long forms for the family.

'Lo here in this piece and chapel, you have first an altar ; secondly, strange Popish furniture on this altar ; viz. two silver candlesticks with tapers in them, (expressly prohibited by Queen Elizabeth's Injunctions, anno 1559, Injunct. 3, 23, which prohibit setting up of candles ; ordering all candlesticks, trindals, and rolls of wax to be taken away and extinct, as monuments of superstition and idolatry ; by the Homily against the peril of idolatry, part 3, pp. 50, 51, which condemns the use of tapers and candle religion, as foolish, superstitious, ethnical, and idolatrous ; and generally censured by all our orthodox writers, as popish and heathenish). A bason for oblations. A silver and gilt canister[1] for wafers. A chalice,

---

[1] 'Candlesticke' in the original.—ED. 1902.

with the picture of Christ engraven on it. An aire. A tricanale or pot with three pipes for the water of mixture (that is, for water to mix with the wine, and for holy-water). A credentia or side table. A bason and ewer (for the polluted priests and prelates to wash in before consecration), and a towel to wipe their unhallowed fingers. A censer, to burn incense in, at the reading of the first lesson, as in the Popish mass and churches. A little boat out of which the frankincense is poured, &c. (which Dr. Cosins had made use of in Peter-house, where he burned incense). Furniture directly borrowed from the Roman Ceremonial, Missal, and Pontifical, nowhere to be found but in Popish chapels and churches. You may judge of this prelate's chapel and Popish inclination, by this Romish furniture thereto belonging; and that mentioned in the next ensuing, being an inventory of his chapel furniture and plate, found with the former, attested by Master Prynn.

Ornaments and Furniture of the Altar.

Furniture belonging to the Chapel.

Behind the Altar: a piece of hangings 11 feet deep, and 5 yards $\frac{3}{4}$ long. Another piece of hangings. The story of Abraham and Melchisedec; part of the story of David.

A Table, with a frame of deal, used for the Altar, 1 yard $\frac{1}{4}$ high, 1 yard $\frac{3}{4}$ long, 1 yard broad. A back-piece of crimson and violet damask paned, 1 yard $\frac{1}{2}$ deep, 3 yards long.[1]

A front-piece of the like, 1 yard $\frac{1}{4}$ deep, 3 yards long.[2]

A pall of violet damask, 1 yard $\frac{1}{4}$ broad, 3 yards $\frac{1}{4}$ long.

A cushion of violet and crimson damask, $\frac{1}{2}$ yard broad, 1 yard long.

A rail of wainscot banisters before the Altar.

Two traverses of taffeta crimson and velvet paned, 3 yards $\frac{1}{4}$ deep, 4 yards $\frac{3}{4}$ broad.

A foot-pace with two ascents of deal, underneath the Altar, 3 yards $\frac{3}{4}$ long, 1 yard $\frac{31}{48}$ broad.

A Turkey carpet to it 4 yards $\frac{3}{4}$ long, 2 yards $\frac{11}{48}$ wide.

Two low stools to kneel on at each end of the Altar, stuffed and covered with purple baise.

---

[1] The upper frontal, or dorsal.—ED. 1902.
[2] The nether frontal.—ED. 1902.

Ornaments and Furniture of the Altar.

A square pulpit of wainscot, 1 yard ¾ high, 1 yard square.
A pulpit cloth of crimson and violet damask paned, 1 yard ¼ deep, 3 yards long.
A music table of deal.
Three forms to it, covered with purple baise.
A carpet of purple broad-cloth, 3 yards long.
A carpet of purple baise, 3 yards long and ¾ broad.
A foot-pace of three ascents, 2 yards ½ square, and thereupon a lectern with the great Bible.
A cloth to the lectern of purple broad-cloth, 3 yards long.
Another of purple baise, 3 yards long, 1 yard ¾ broad.
A faldstory of wainscot, 1 yard 1 nail high, 1 yard lacking a nail broad at top: 1 yard lacking two nails breadth below.
A cloth to it of purple broad-cloth, 2 yards ¾ long, 1 yard ½ broad.
Another of purple baise, 2 yards ¾ long, 1 yard ¼ broad.

Over the Bishop's seat.

A canopy of crimson and violet damask paned, 2 yards $\frac{11}{48}$ long, 2 breadth.
The valence to it, 3 yards compass, $\frac{11}{48}$ deep.
A cushion to it of violet damask, 1 yard long, $\frac{11}{28}$ yards broad.
A folding table of wainscot near the Altar.
A carpet of baise on it, 1 yard ½ wide, 1 yard ½ long.
Four folding chairs of leather.

Plate for the Chapel.

		s.	d.	
Two candlesticks, gilt, for tapers,	60 oz. at	5	6	the oz.
A round bason for offerings, gilt and chased,	31½ „	6	8	„
A round bason for alms, gilt and chased,	30 „	6	0	„
An oval bason and ewer, gilt and chased,	51 „	6	0	„
Two patens, gilt,	36 „	10	0	„
For cutting the figure, 13s. 4d.				
A chalice and cover, gilt,	43 „	10	0	„
For making the star on the chalice, 3s.				
A tun, gilt,	47 oz. 3 dwt.	6	11	„
A cradle to it, gilt,	18¾ oz. at	6	11	„
A funnel to it, gilt,	3 „	6	11	„
A canister, gilt,	5¾ „	10	0	„
A triquertral censer,	85 lack 6 dwt.	7	0	„
For gilding it, at 16d. the ounce.				
A laten pan for it,		5	0	„
For making the knob of it,		2	0	„

THE ALTAR

A crewet, gilt, with three spouts,   10 oz. $\tfrac{11}{28}$ dwt. 7   9 the oz.
Another, gilt, with a bird's bill, .   . 4 less 5 ,,   6   8 ,,
Five copes.
Five surplices.
Two Altar-cloths.
Two towels thereto.
A cloth to lay over the chalice, wrought with coloured silk, called the Aire.'

Ornaments and Furniture of the Altar.

—*Canterbury's Doom*, pp. 120-124, fol. 1646.

1643

ST. GEORGE'S CHAPEL, WINDSOR. '*Item.* The hangings of the head of the choir, 12 feet deep, of crimson velvet and gold.

Item. The great Bible ruled, covered with purple velvet, with thick silver bosses, double gilt, strung with blue riband, fringed with gold.

Item. Another large Bible embossed.

Item. Thirteen rich copes, embroidered and wrought in gold.

Item. Two rich copes of wire gold.

Item. A pulpit-cloth and long cushion of crimson tufted velvet, interwoven with gold.

Item. Another large pulpit-cloth, crimson damask, interwoven thick with flowers-de-lis, portcullises, roses, and crowns of gold.

Item. A large carpet of wire gold, for the Communion-table.

Item. A large cushion of the same suit.

Item. Two fair standing brass candlesticks, double gilt.

Item. The great brass desk in the middle of the chapel, with the Bible in two volumes, on each side fairly bound and embossed.'—*A Memorial of the Goods and Monuments belonging to the King's Majesty's Free Chapel and Treasury at Windsor.*[1]

'We see in the foregoing inventory, taken 1643, that

---

[1] Nearly all the plate had been carried away in the preceding October, by one Captain Fog (*Ashmole*, p. 496).—EDD. 1848.

98 HIERURGIA ANGLICANA

Ornaments and Furniture of the Altar.

formerly there was belonging to the altar a large carpet of wire gold: this we find mentioned in the inventories taken the 4th of February, an. 43 Eliz. the 9th of November, an. 17 Jac. R., and the 12th of December 1638, an. 14 Car. I.; and being seized on by Colonel Ven, as aforesaid, is now [1670] supplied in a covering, given by the present Sovereign [Charles II.], consisting of seven panes of cloth of gold and purple velvet, with a fair broad gold fringe towards the front, and a narrow gold fringe on the two sides. There is now also two diaper table-cloths, diamond work, made to lie upon the altar, and two fine Holland cloths with great buttons and red crosses in the middle, to cover the consecrated elements in the time of the Communion. . . . The east wall of the Chapel is now adorned with twenty-two panes of cloth of gold and purple damask, the gift of the present Sovereign: but those in the late Sovereign's reign were of crimson velvet and gold. In the middle of these hangings over the altar, have been heretofore placed very rich altar-cloths, concerning some of which, we have met with a memorial which informs us, that it pleased the late Sovereign, in a chapter held at Windsor the 6th of November, an. 9 Car. I., to give command that two little pieces of arras-hangings, the hanging over the altar (in one of which was wrought the picture of St. George on horseback, and on the other the Assumption of the Blessed Virgin) should be preserved in such places where the Dean and his Lieutenant should think best, for the use of the said altar at the Grand Feast, and other festivals of the Order. Hereupon they were fetched from Windsor, to set over the altar in the Chapel at Whitehall, an. 11 Car. I., the feast of St. George being then celebrated. There are now two other pieces of arras, which are appointed to that use: the one hath the pictures of Christ and His disciples at Supper, given by the late Right Reverend Father in God, Bryan Lord Bishop of Winchester, Prelate of the Order; the other, of Christ and the two disciples at Emmaus, wrought

THE ALTAR

after Titian's original, given by the Right Hon. the Lady Mordant, wife to the Lord Mordant, late Constable of Windsor. . . . It may be judged how other of the Sovereign's Chapels, wherein the solemn services at the Grand Feast were celebrated, besides this of St. George at Windsor, have been set forth and adorned by one or two examples. . . . At the feast of St. George, held at Whitehall, an. 5. Eliz. the Chapel was hung with cloth of gold, and the stalls both before and behind with cloth of tissue, set with scutcheons at their back. The Sovereign's royal stall was adorned with cloth of state, and furnished with cushions, as were the Emperor's, the French King's, and the Sovereign's Lieutenants. But an. 7 Eliz. all the stalls of the same Choir were hung with carpets, both before and behind. At the feast held there an. 19 Car. II. the Chapel was hung with rich hangings of silk and gold. . . . The altar was furnished with chased gilt plate, viz. one large bason in the middle, and two less on either side, two fair candlesticks with unlighted tapers, and two large water-pots: on the lower rank was set another bason, four flagons, and two service-books, covered with like gilt plate: and lastly, the Sovereign's stall had the rich furniture of cloth of gold and purple velvet, fetched from Windsor to adorn it.'—*Ashmole's Institution of the Order of the Garter*, pp. 497-500.

1643

PETERBOROUGH CATHEDRAL. 'The Table itself was thrown down, the table-cloth taken away, with two fair books in velvet covers, the one a Bible, the other a Common Prayer-book, with a silver basin gilt, and a pair of silver candlesticks.

'Now behind the Communion-table there stood a curious piece of stone-work, admired much by strangers and travellers; a stately screen it was, well wrought, painted and gilt, which rose up as high almost as the roof of the church in a row of three lofty spires, with

Ornaments and Furniture of the Altar. other lesser spires growing out of each of them, as it is represented in the annexed draft.[1] This now had no imagery-work upon it, or anything else that might justly give offence ; and yet, because it bore the name of the High Altar, was pulled all down with ropes, laid low and level with the ground.'—*Narrative of the Rifling and Defacing of the Cathedral Church of Peterborough. Gunton's History of the Church of Peterborough*, p. 334, fol. 1686.

1643

WINCHESTER CATHEDRAL. 'By virtue of an ordinance which had passed in 1643, all crosses, crucifixes, representations of saints and angels, copes, surplices, hangings, candlesticks, basins, organs, &c., were carried out of the cathedral and other churches.'—*Milner's History of Winchester*, i. 411, 412, 4to, 1809.

1643

'She keeps an altar on her brow,
  Her eyes two tapers on each side :
There superstitious lovers bow.'
  To a fair Lady weeping for her husband, committed to prison by the Parliament, 1643. *Rump Songs,* p. 131.

1643-1644

'The Lords and Commons in Parliament ordaining (Aug. 28, 1643) that, in order to remove all monuments of superstition and idolatry, all altars and tables of stone should be demolished, Communion-tables be removed from the east, rails taken away, chancels levelled, tapers, candlesticks, basins, etc., be removed from the Communion-tables ; and all crucifixes, crosses, images of the

---

[1] See the opposite illustration, which is copied from the above-mentioned 'draft.' It will be observed that the altar candles are burning.—EDD. 1848.

PLATE VII.] [*To face page* 100.

Hier. I.]

THE ALTAR

Trinity, or saints, etc., be taken away, and defaced.'—*Walker's Sufferings of the Clergy*, p. 25, fol. 1714.

<small>Ornaments and Furniture of the Altar.</small>

1644

ST. PAUL'S CATHEDRAL. 'April 17, 1644, The candlesticks, crucifixes, and other plate, that stood heretofore upon the altar, were ordered to be sold by the Committee at Grocers'-Hall, and the money to be employed for the publick safety.'—*Ibid.* p. 13.

1646

'Vestry plate (belonging to Charles I.), which was usually heretofore set upon the altar of his majesty's chapel at Whitehall; viz.

A pair of great candlesticks.
One gilt ship.
Two gilt vases.[1]
Two gilt layres.
A square basin and fountain.
A silver rod.'—*Peck's Desiderata Curiosa*, ii. 373. Lond. 1779.

c. 1650

'He [Bishop Cosin] also enriched that his new chapel at Aukland, and that in the castle at Durham, with divers pieces of fair gilt plate, books, and other costly ornaments, with purpose that they should remain to his successors in that bishoprick for ever. . . . He likewise gave to the cathedral at Durham a fair carved lectern and litany-desk, with a large scallop-patten silver and gilt, for the use of the communicants there, which cost £45.'—*Dugdale's Historical Account of the Cathedrals of York, Durham, and Carlisle*, p. 83, fol. 1715.

---

[1] It is to be observed that these were not vases for flowers.—ED. 1902.

c. 1650

Ornaments and Furniture of the Altar.

'First of all it is enjoined,[1] that the table or altar should be spread over with a clean linen cloth, or other decent covering, upon which the Holy Bible, the Common Prayer-Book, the paten and chalice are to be placed : two wax candles are to be set on.'—*Bishop Cosin's Notes on the Book of Common Prayer, Second Series. Works*, vol. v. p. 303. *Lib. Anglo-Cath. Theol.*

1661

'And here is to be noted, That such Ornaments of the Church, and of the Ministers thereof at all times of their Ministration, shall be retained, and be in use, as were in this Church of England by the authority of Parliament, in the second year of the reign of King Edw. VI.'—*First Rubric in the Book of Common Prayer.*

1662

* 'Two greate silver Flaggons double guilt,
Three silver Chalices guilt two of them with Covers,
Two small silver Plates,
Two small silver Basons,
Fowre Communion Table cloathes, two thereof dammaske one dyaper and one old wrought one
Two dammaske Napkins
Two small cloathes one dammaske thother dyaper,
One pecce of Hanging partely wrought with gold like Birds,
Item One Communion Table and an old Cloath,
Two kneeling purple cloath stooles to the same.
Item A faire Hanging with a gold fringe over the Communion Table,
alsoe another upon the Communion Table

---

[1] See Note, A, at the close of this volume.—ED. 1902.

THE ALTAR

Alsoe another round about the Communion Table, One large Carpett before the Communion table, Two Matts at each end of the Communion table. Two new common prayer books for the Communion table.'—*Inventories of Christchurch, Canterbury*, pp. 275 ff.

1662

* 'A carpett for the Communion table, a large cushion for the pulpitt and a litle one for the table.'—*Durham Parish Books*, p. 198. *Surtees Soc.*, 1888.

1666

* 'Then the bishop arising shall return to his chair, and sitting covered, some persons by the patron's appointment shall bring the Carpet, the Communion-cloth and Napkins, the Chalice, Paten, and the other Vessels, Books and Utensils for the Communion; and humbly presenting them on their knees to God, the bishop shall receive them severally, and deliver them to the deacon, to be laid orderly on the Communion-table; excepting only the Chalice, and the Paten, which two priests shall (when the Table is covered) humbly on their knees lay upon it. Then the bishop returning to the Altar, shall with reverence and solemnity (his face being Eastward) lay his hands upon the plate, and say this prayer standing. . . .'—*Irish Form of Consecration of Churches*, 1666, p. 19. *S. P. C. K.*, 1893.

1666

NORWICH CATHEDRAL.—'After the Restoration the city gave £100, with which the fine large offering dish and pair of silver candlesticks, all double gilt, were purchased.'—*Blomefield's Topographical History of Norfolk*, iv. 32, 8vo, 1806.

1667

<small>Ornaments and Furniture of the Altar.</small>

'ST. GEORGE'S CHAPEL, WINDSOR. 'A pair of plain gilt flagons bought with the money collected from the Knights' Companions, weighing 150 ounces.

A pair of wrought flagons with great bellies, having the figure of St. George on horseback on their covers, the rest all feather-work, bought with the Knights' money, weighing 414 ounces.

One plain small basin wrought and gilt only in the middle of it, weighing 25 ounces and one half.

A pair of plain gilt chalices and covers, bought also with the Knights' money, both weighing 163 ounces and one quarter.

A large embossed basin with the figure of Mary Magdalen washing our Saviour's feet, weighing 198 ounces.

A pair of large taper candlesticks embossed, with nozles to them, weighing 264 ounces.

These candlesticks and basin were obtained of her Highness Princess Mary, about November, 1660, by Dr. Brown; but she dying before the following Christmas, the charge (being £233 odd money) lay upon the College.

A pair of large basins gilt and embossed, with the history of Christ at his Last Supper upon one, and on the other, of Christ blessing the young children coming to him; being obtained by Dr. Brown of her Highness the Duchess of York, in 1661, both weighing 305 ounces.

A plain gilt corporas, the gift of Sir Richard Fanshaw, weighing 24 ounces.

A double-gilt chalice and cover, with a broad foot, having a cross on the cover, and another on the foot; the gift of the Lady Mary Heveningham, weighing 33 ounces.'—*Ashmole's Institution of the Order of the Garter*, p. 498.

THE ALTAR

1667

BP. WREN'S CHAPEL.   'Touching my chapel furniture. *Ornaments and Furniture of the Altar.* Now at this present the particulars of my chapel furniture are these : of silver plate richly gilt, there is a chalice with a cover of 37 ounces, a flagon above 46 ounces, a basin formed with a cross in it of 55 ounces, a pair of patens &c. above 34 ounces, a pair of candlesticks above 132 ounces,—in all about 305 ounces; there are also for the candlesticks two strong cases; then for the Holy Table there are two fronts (the upper and the nether), both of cloth-of-gold interpaned with like breadths of a brown velvet and well fringed ; a pall of cloth-of-gold fringed round, a long cushion of cloth-of-gold with four tassels backed with brown velvet: another such long cushion backed with satin, two shorter cushions of cloth-of-gold, the one backed with satin, the other with damask; a Bible in folio, the cover embossed with the arms of England ; the Book of Common Prayer suitable to that Bible ; another great Bible in folio, Cambridge edition ; another Bible in folio, and one Liturgy in folio ; another in 4to. bound in crimson satin, embroidered about with pictures ; two great folio Bibles in the English letter ; a great fair Liturgy for the Priest at the Table, in folio ; a fine linen corporal, embroidered with silk in colours ; a fine linen cloth over the pall at the Holy Communion ; sundry linen cloths to be spread before the communicants ; divers cloths of damask for the desks ; a canopy of damask and two long cushions thereunto ; a pulpit-cloth and a cushion of the like ; a blue velvet cushion, blue hangings, with suitable covers for the litany-desk and the forms ; three folding-chairs, an old carpet for the floor before the Holy Table ; a great standard to be set in the vestry of the new chapel.'[1]—*Bp. Wren's Will, proved* 10*th June,* 1667.

---

[1] Of Pembroke College, Cambridge, to which he bequeathed the said furniture.—EDD. 1848.

c. 1675

<small>Ornaments and Furniture of the Altar.</small>

* 'In the collection of W. Maskell, Esq., is a pair of small silver altar cruets of the latter half of the seventeenth century, on the lids of which are respectively the letters A. (*aqua*) and V. (*vinum*).'[1]—*Chronicle of St. Martin's, Leicester,* p. 27 *n.*

1689

* In the Inventory of Canterbury Cathedral taken in 1689, is mentioned *One Bible with plate covers double gilt with a case.* 'This bible which now lies upon the High Altar at the foot of the Cross, bound in precious metal, is placed in the inventory among the vestry stuff that would be set on the altar during a celebration of the Eucharist, much in the same way that the mediæval *textus* was set on the altar. This practice survived in many cathedral churches until lately, when the restorer, not taking the pains to understand its history, abolished the custom. Both candlesticks and bible are now (1902) always on the altar of Christchurch.'

In the same Inventory occurs, 'At the altar two Common Prayer Books bound in Turky leather with gilt leaves the one redd the other blew.' In the manuscript book of benefactors they are described as follows:—

<small>The Hon. Dr. Leopold Finch gave two large Common Prayer Books in folio of the Oxford print Curiously bound w[ch] lye on the top of the Altar.</small>

'One of these books may apparently be seen on the south side of the altar in Dart's plate of 1726.'

In the Inventory of 1735 we read, 'Two large Common Prayer Books (Dr. Finches Gift) with Ribbons and Gold Fringe over the Table.'—*Inventories of Christchurch, Canterbury,* pp. 278, 279, 294.

---

[1] Possibly these cruets were of foreign make.—ED. 1902.

1689-1752

* 1689. 'Three old starr cushions fower veluett purple cushions two whereof for the Communion Table.'   *Ornaments and Furniture of the Altar.*

1735. 'Two Cushions with Four Gold Tassels each.'[1]

1745. 'Two Velvet Cushions wth Tassels lying upon ye Table.'

1752. 'Two Velvet Cushions wth Tassels, lying on the Communion Table.'—*Inventories of Christchurch, Canterbury*, pp. 283, 294, 300, 306.

1703

'Grant that all these ornaments dedicated here to Thee, and given to the use of Thy service, may be by this my ministry thereunto consecrated, and for ever set apart from all common and profane uses whatsoever.

'Grant that these patens and chalice which I here offer up unto Thee, may be accepted by Thee. That they may ever continue hallowed vessels in Thy House. That no superstition may grow unto them in their service, nor no profanation unhallow them. And that all which come to be partakers of the Sacrament of Thy blessed Body and Blood may come worthily, and receive the earnest of their eternal salvation.'—*Form of Dedication and Consecration of a Church or Chapel*, 4to, 1703.

c. 1720

ALL SOULS' COLLEGE, OXFORD. 'The interior [of the Chapel] as we now behold it, was chiefly fitted up early in the last century, according to the taste which then prevailed. Dr. Clarke gave the massive altar-piece and panelling of marble, with two large gilt candlesticks, a purple velvet Communion-cloth, fringed with gold, &c.'—*Ingram's Memorials of Oxford*, i. 24.

---

[1] *Vide* p. 52, *sub* 1735.

1728

<small>Ornaments and Furniture of the Altar.</small> 'Several of the churches in that part of the country [near Oundle in Northamptonshire] are ornamented with altar-pieces of her performance, [Mrs. Elizabeth Creed]; she died in 1728.'—*Witfora's Memorials.*

1735

* 'It having been observed that 2 pair of the large Wax Tapers on the Communion Table were sufficient, viz. 1 Pair to Christmas, and 1 to Candlemas, instead of 3 pair which are usually bought, but not 2 thirds of them consumed; it was ordered by the prebendarys present that one of the 3 pair bought the last Winter should be kept entire for the use of this and not be just lighted and then go for a Perquisite to the vesterers, as it seems, has been the Practice, and by which the Church loses twenty shillings, that being the price of a pair of Tapers weighing 8L of white wax at 2*s.* 6*d.* pr pound.'—*Inventories of Christchurch, Canterbury,* p. 315.

1736

YORK CATHEDRAL. 'There is a particular account in our own records, of such plate, copes, vestments, and other things belonging to the choir, as they were given in charge to be kept by William Ambler, clerk of the vestry, anno 1633. By which it appears that our second reformers cleared off with what the first had left.

Lest the altar should again be robbed of its present ornaments, plate, &c., I think proper to give an account of what it is now enriched with; as likewise the donors of them.

King Charles I. bestowed upon the church a large quantity of Communion-plate, when there was scarce as much left out of their long inventory of riches, as to

THE ALTAR

perform the office with decency ; also a Common Prayer-book and Bible, large folio, bound in crimson velvet.

<small>Ornaments and Furniture of the Altar.</small>

Archbishop Stern gave plate to the weight of two hundred and eighteen ounces.

Archbishop Dolben gave one hundred and ninety-five ounces.

The Lord Beaumont gave two silver candlesticks weighing fifty-three ounces.

Archbishop Lamplugh gave the covering or *antependium* of the Table of crimson velvet, richly adorned with a deep embroidery of gold and fringe, with the velvet for the back of the altar. He gave also three pieces of fine tapestry for the same use. . . . And lastly he gave three large Common Prayer-books and a Bible, for the use of the altar.

In winter, from All Saints' to Candlemas, the choir is illuminated at every service by seven large branches, besides a wax candle fixed at every other stall. . . . These, with two large tapers for the altar, are all the lights commonly made use of. But on the vigils of particular holy days the four grand dignitaries of the church have each a branch of seven candles placed before them at their stalls.'—*Drake's Eboracum*, p. 524, fol. 1736.

1750

CAIUS COLLEGE, CAMBRIDGE. 'The altar is railed in, and paved with black and white marble ; the cloth of the Table is of velvet, on which stand two large silver-gilt candlesticks with wax tapers, a large silver dish, two books of Common-prayer, and two velvet cushions, all fringed with gold.'—*Blomefield's Collectanea Cantabrigiensia*, p. 101, 4to, 1750.

c. 1775

CANTERBURY CATHEDRAL. 'On Sunday, when this altar is dressed up for the Sacrament, and covered with its costly and splendid service of rich plate, it has an appearance of grandeur and magnificence that blots from the mind, as far as possible, a regret for its having been bereaved of its former ornaments. . . . All the plate (except the two great candlesticks) was new gilt, which altogether make a very handsome and splendid appearance.'—*Hasted's History of Kent*, iv. 526, 527, *and n*., fol. 1799.

Ornaments and Furniture of the Altar.

1780

* 'The allowance of Wax Candles for lighting the Church to be the same as usual, viz.: Two large Tapers for the Altar of Four pounds each.'—*Inventories of Christchurch, Canterbury*, p. 316.

1807

ST. PAUL'S CATHEDRAL. 'A silver-gilt chalice, with the paten, and another of the same material, are embossed with a saint bearing the Agnus Dei, and inscribed, "Bibite ex hoc omnes; est hic enim Calix Novi Testamenti sanguine meo." A pair of patens: "Benedixit, fregit, dedit; accipite, comedite; hoc est corpus meum."

'A most superb silver-gilt and embossed Prayer-book, adorned with angels, a glory, pillars, &c., inscribed "Oculi Domini super istos, et aures ejus in preces eorum," and "Fiant orationes pro omnibus hominibus, pro regibus."

'A Bible, edition 1640, with a silver-gilt cover, representing a temple, with Moses and Aaron in the intervals between the columns, and Jacob's dream on one side, with the inscription "Verbum Domini manet in æternum." On the other leaf, the prophet fed by a raven, and, "Habent Moysen et Prophetas; audiant illos."

'Two large silver-gilt plates, on which are engraven the following inscriptions: "The Rev. Mr. Charles Smith, fourth son of Sir Thomas Smith, of Hill Hall,

THE ALTAR

in the county of Essex, Bart., late Prebendary of St. Paul's, and Archdeacon of Colchester, gave this plate for the use of the church 1699." "Ex hoc non manducabo donec illud impleatur in regno Dei. Modicum et jam non videbitis me. Iterum, modicum et videbitis me quia vado ad Patrem." "Qui parcè seminat, parcè et metet. Si voluntas prompta est, secundùm id quod habet, accepta est; non secundùm id quod non habet."

'The bottoms of those plates are embossed with representations of the last Supper; and the widow bestowing her mite. The rims are adorned with his arms and crest, cherubim, and scrolls.

'A very large silver-gilt plate; plain, except that the centre contains an angel exhibiting a label, on which is engraved Τοιαύταις θυσίαις εὐαρεστεῖται ὁ Θεός. The arms of the Deanery on the back. Another very large silver-gilt plate has the Lord's Supper, extremely well done, on it; and a rich border of cornucopiæ and emblematical figures. There are large tankards of silver-gilt, very much but clumsily embossed.

'A large silver-gilt plate, with IHS in a glory.

'Two enormous tankards, finely embossed, given by the above Rev. Charles Smith, with the inscriptions "Verbum caro factum est, et habitavit in nobis." "Si mihi non vultis credere, operibus credite." "Qui biberit ex aquâ quam ego dabo ei, non sitiet in æternum." "Ecce Agnus Dei, Qui tollit peccata mundi; hic est qui baptizat in Spiritu Sancto." These words all refer to the embossings over them.

'A pair of silver-gilt candlesticks, two feet nine inches in height, exclusive of the spike, with triangular feet. "In lumine tuo videbimus lumen. De tenebris vos vocavit in admirabile lumen suum. Sic luceat lux vestra coram hominibus."

'Two other candlesticks of the same materials, about two feet in height.'—*Malcolm's Londinium Redivivum*, iii. 144, 145.

Ornaments and Furniture of the Altar.

1807

Ornaments and Furniture of the Altar.

ST. BENEDICT'S, GRACECHURCH. 'Two large and elegant candlesticks, supporting wax candles, stand on the altar.'—*Malcolm's Londinium Redivivum*, i. 323.

c. 1820

LINCOLN CATHEDRAL. 'A magnificent silver-gilt altar service, of the value of 1000 guineas, was presented some few years ago, for the service of his cathedral, by the present venerable Dean of Lincoln.'—*Anderson's Ancient Models*, p. 131 *n.*, 1842.

1828

ALL-HALLOWS BARKING. 'The rails of the altar are composed of a handsome balustrade entirely constructed of brass; on the altar, which is insulated, are two massive candlesticks.'—*Allen's History and Antiquities of London, etc.* III. ii. 172, 1828.

1838

* 'At Queen Victoria's coronation in 1838 the high altar of the Abbey was arranged much as it had been on such occasions since long before the Reformation, except that the candles in the two great golden candlesticks which stood upon it were not lighted. . . . The altar was vested in a frontal, in accordance with the universal custom of the Church. It was decorated with magnificent silver-gilt plate, some of it belonging to the Abbey, some to the Chapels Royal.'—*Eeles, The English Coronation Service*, p. 30, 1902.

1902

* 'The high altar (of Westminster Abbey), with its handsome new altar-cloth of the richest crimson, its two great golden candlesticks with tall lighted tapers, its

THE ALTAR

central cross of gold, and other ornaments of the like precious metal. . . . On a large credence-table to the south of the altar there was a noble display of additional gold plate from the Chapels Royal.'—*Coronation of Edward VII.* Vide *The Church Times*, Aug. 15, 1902, p. 182, col. 4.

<small>Ornaments and Furniture of the Altar.</small>

Summary of evidence from texts and engravings indicating usage as to Altar=lights.

* 'Before the Reformation lights on altars were common, not universal (a light before the Sacrament was universal).

In 1547-8, all lights in churches were ordered to be put out, except two to be retained upon the altar, by royal and episcopal Injunctions.

In 1549-51, certain Articles (wanting authorisation), and Bishops Ridley and Hooper order the putting out of those two lights; not known to be further ordered or done.

1558-1610, candlesticks remain in many places, and gradually disappear in most. Candles at first lighted, and then not, in the Queen's chapels.

1621-1641, candles apparently general, and lighted in many places, chapels, colleges, cathedrals.

1660-1678, candles apparently common, not universal, and no account of lighting.

1681-1737, independent evidences of lighting in 11 or 12 cases.

> De Laune, Hickeringill in 1681, Communicant's Guide, Addison, Loggan, William III. Coronation, Queen Anne at St. Paul's in 1706 [Christian's Manual, same as Addison; Brough, same as De Laune, above], Bishop Patrick 1717, Bishop Patrick 1731 (another picture), Orthodox Communicant, T. Burnett, ? York, Picart.

Ornaments and Furniture of the Altar.

1681-1737, none, or unlit, or lighted only for light, in 14 or 15 cases.

> Smythies, C. P. B. Plate 1684, Patrick 1684, ? Addison, James II. Coronation, Hickeringill in 1689, C. P. B. Plate 1693 [? Christian's Manual, same as Addison, above], Notes on Bishop Gilbert Burnet, Divine Banquet, Lawful Prejudices, C. P. B. Plate 1709, Wheatley (text and in 1714 picture), Whole Duty of Receiving, C. P. B. Plate 1717, ? York.

1750-1847, none are shown in 8 cases.

> Liturgia, Guide to Altar, C. P. B. Coronation George IV., Le Keux's St. John's Cambridge, Catherine Hall, Barnwell, Williams' Altar [13 illustrations].

,, ,, candles are shown in 11 cases.

> Caius, Canterbury, Dr. Parr, Builder's Mag. in 1788, Westminster, St. Paul's, St. Peter's Oxford, Magdalen Cambridge, and St. John's (1846).
> One picture of Communion at Shrewsbury with candles unlit, and [20 or 21 illustrations] in Williams' Altar.'

MORE BRIEFLY—

'Before the Reformation lighted candles on the altar common, not universal.

1547 and 8, two ordered.

1549-1551, were prohibited by some bishops, but not everywhere done away with.

1558-1610, the lighting ceased to a great extent, and the candles themselves in many places.

1621-1641, candles were general, and in many places lighted.

1660-1680, candles common ; no account of their being lighted.

1683-1737, almost as often lighted as not.

1737-1750, no evidence before us.

1750-1847, the lighting seems to have gone out.'

—*The Bishop of Lincoln's Case* (Roscoe ; Clowes and Sons, 1891), p. 189.

THE ALTAR

Consecration of Altar=Plate by Archbishop Sancroft
1685

'Now in the first year of the late king James, as Mr. Kettlewell was meditating in his heart how to heal, if possible, the growing animosities and dissensions among the people, and had frequently recommended the great duty of Christians, as such, to meet together at the holy Feast, where we are obliged to profess ourselves in perfect peace and charity with all men, and to perform the most solemn act of confederation with Christ, and with all that are Christ's, in commemoration of union with His sacrifice on the Cross; the good Lord Digby, as well to promote so desirable an end, as for the most decent celebration of the greatest of Christian offices, and in gratitude for the blessing and benefits by him received from the hand of God, made an offering of a set of new Communion-plate, for the use of the church of Coles-hill, the which, for the greater solemnity thereof, was by no less a person than the Archbishop of Canterbury himself then and there present, most reverently set apart and consecrated Deo Servatori, to God the Saviour. The manner whereof being somewhat rare and extraordinary, and having the approbation of two such excellent persons as were Archbishop Sancroft and Mr. Kettlewell, the one as Primate at that time of all England, and the other as priest or curate of that parish for whose use this solemn dedication was made, it will not be amiss in this place to relate; though some particulars thereof, which we could wish for, are not come to our hands.

'The plate then to be consecrated, having been presented by the aforesaid lord, the patron of the church, to Almighty God, that by the office and ministry of the first bishop in the kingdom it might be for ever dedicated to the holy service of God our Saviour,

Consecration of Altar-Plate.

Consecration of Altar-Plate. according to the usages and rites of the Church of England, was placed upon a table or buffet, below the steps of the altar, before the beginning of Divine service. And immediately after the Nicene Creed, and the first sentence of the Offertory, as being a command to let our light to shine before men, that they seeing our good works may thence glorify God; Mr. Kettlewell, the presenter of this plate in the name of the donor, officiating as parish priest under his Metropolitan, came forth and stood between the said table and the steps of the altar. When after his humble adoration made to Almighty God, and his obeisance to the archbishop, he humbly desired that the vessels there before him, prepared for the use of the church by his worthy lord and patron, (being a paten, two chalices, a flagon, and a basin,) might be by him presented to God and consecrated to His service, according to the donor's intentions. Whereupon the archbishop, after an answer of approbation, and a devout invocation of the holy Name of God, in terms very pathetical and appropriate to the occasion, standing before the midst of the altar, did receive, in the Name of God, from the hands of the presbyter kneeling, each piece of plate severally, and place it upon the altar decently spread; several sentences of Scripture, adapted to the offering of each of them, being alternately repeated, as he was thus placing them and praying over them, (viz. for the paten, Psalm lxxviii. 24, 25; for the chalices, Psalm civ. 15, Cant. i. 4; for the flagon, Psalm xxxvi. 8, Cant. v. 1; for the bason, Psalm liv. 6, Psalm cxix. 108). Which being ended, there followed the prayer of consecration, which was after this form, viz.:

"Unto Thee, O ever blessed Lord and Saviour, and to Thy most holy worship and service, do I here offer up and dedicate these oblations, [*here he laid his hands upon every piece of the plate*], which in humble acknowledgment of Thy sovereignty over all, and of Thy infinite mercy and goodness to him in particular, Thy pious and devout servant hath here presented before Thee. But who is he,

THE ALTAR

O Lord, that should be able to offer so willingly after this sort? Thine, O Lord, is the power, and the glory, and the majesty: for all that is in the heaven and the earth are Thine. Both riches and honour, and all things, come of Thee, and it is of Thine own that he hath given Thee. Accept, we beseech Thee, these his free-will offerings, and grant that they may be for ever holy vessels for the use of Thy sanctuary. Let no profane or sacrilegious hand ever withdraw them from Thine altar, or debase them to common use again; but let them continue always inviolable in that holy service to which they have by him been piously designed, and are now, by our office and ministry, solemnly set apart and consecrated. And sanctify, we beseech Thee, both the souls and bodies of all those who out of these holy vessels shall, now or at any time hereafter, partake of the holy Communion of Thy most blessed Body and Blood; that we may be all filled with Thy grace and heavenly benediction, and also pardoned and accepted, and everlastingly rewarded through Thy mercy, O ever blessed Lord and Saviour, who dost live and govern all things, world without end. Amen."

Consecration of Altar-Plate.

'After which the archbishop added this benediction following:

"And now blessed be Thou, O Lord, heavenly Father, almighty and everlasting God, for ever and ever; and blessed be Thy great and glorious Name, that it hath pleased Thee to put into the heart of Thy servant to give so freely for the more decent performance of Thy worship and service in the beauty of holiness. Accept, O Lord, this his bounden duty and service, not weighing his merits, but pardoning his offences; let these his oblations come up as a memorial before Thee, and let him find and feel that with such sacrifices Thou art well pleased. Bless him, O Lord, in his person and in his substance, and in all that belongs unto him, or that he puts his hand unto. Remember him, O my God, for good, and wipe not out the kindnesses that he hath done for the house of God, and the offices thereof; and give to all those that shall enjoy the benefit of this his piety and bounty, both a grateful sense, and a sanctified use of what is by him so well intended, that in all and by all, Thy praise and glory may now and for ever be set forth, O gracious and merciful Lord, who livest and reignest ever one God, world without end. Amen."

'Then the archbishop went on to read some other sentences in the Offertory: and bread and wine upon and in the vessels now consecrated were set upon the Communion-table or altar, and the alms of the communicants were gathered in the new basin; and the

Consecration of Altar-Plate.

order for the administration of the holy Communion was, according to the use of the Church of England, proceeded in, with which the solemnity ended. For the perpetual testification whereof there was an instrument drawn up in the Latin tongue, and signed by the consecrator, with the archiepiscopal seal thereto affixed. The copy of which instrument or act (dates and names omitted) was in the beginning of this century made public by Mr. Richard Tisdale, [see the form of dedication or consecration of a church or chapel, &c., printed for John Harley, in Holborn, 1703] chaplain to the late bishop of Norwich ; as was also the entire form of the consecration which then was used.'—*Kettlewell's Life and Works,* i. 56-58, fol. 1719.

The Form of Consecration of New Communion Plate

'¶ The plate to be consecrated is to be placed upon a table below the steps of the altar, before the beginning of Divine service.

'¶ Immediately after the *Nicene Creed,* and the reading of this sentence, *Let your light so shine before men, &c.,* the presenter of the plate (in his habit in which he is to officiate, if he be a priest) cometh forth, and standing between the said table and the steps of the altar, after his humble adoration made to God Almighty, and his obeisance to the bishop, saith as followeth :—

' " Right reverend father in God, in the name of [*the donor or donors, specifying the parish, county, and diocese*] I humbly desire that these vessels here before you, prepared for the use of that *church or chapel,* may be presented to God Almighty, and, by your office and ministry, consecrated to the holy service of God our Saviour."

¶ *The bishop answers :*—

'With a cheerful heart we are most ready to perform what you desire, in a matter so well becoming you and

THE ALTAR 119

them in whose name you come, and (as we are assured) so acceptable to God himself; and therefore let us begin with invocation of his holy Name :— Consecration of Altar-Plate.

'Bow down Thine ear, O Lord, and hear us; open, Lord, Thine eyes, and behold from the habitation of Thy holiness and of Thy glory Thy poor servants prostrate here before Thee, and have respect unto the supplications which, in confidence of Thy great mercies, and the all-sufficient merits of Thy blessed Son, we presume to make before Thee; begging Thy gracious assistance in what we are about, and Thy favourable acceptance of it. Let Thy Holy Spirit help our infirmities: give us hearts truly and deeply sensible of the greatness of Thy Divine Majesty. Increase our faith and inflame our love, and order our devotions. Make us always zealous for Thy glory; and give us ever to rejoice in Thy holy service, which is perfect freedom. And the glorious majesty of the Lord our God be upon us; prosper, Lord, the works of our hands upon us; O prosper Thou our handy-work, through Jesus Christ Thy Son, our Saviour. Amen.'

¶ The prayer being ended, the presenter taketh the *paten* into his hands, and (after adoration made) goeth to the bishop, (standing before the midst of the altar,) and kneeling upon the upper step saith :—

'I offer up this unto Thee, and to Thy holy service, O God, our Saviour.'

¶ While the bishop receiveth it, and reverently placeth it upon the altar, the chaplains, standing ready in their formalities at the north and south sides of the altar, say *alternatim* :—

'He rained down manna also upon them for to eat: and gave them food from heaven.
'So man did eat angels' food: for He sent them meat enough.'

¶ In the mean while the presenter is ready again with the *chalices*, and kneeling down, saith as before.

¶ While the bishop sets them on the altar, the chaplains pronounce :—

'That he may bring food out of the earth, and wine that maketh glad the heart of man.
'We will be glad and rejoice in Thee: we will remember Thy love more than wine.'

Consecration of Altar-Plate.

¶ The presenter, as before, offereth the *flagons*, which, while the bishop sets on, the chaplains say :—

'They shall be satisfied with the plenteousness of Thy house, and Thou shalt give them drink of Thy pleasures as of a river.

'Eat, O friends; drink, and be replenished, O beloved.'

¶ The *bason* is offered next by the presenter, which when the bishop hath taken, the chaplains say :—

'An offering of a free heart will I give Thee; and praise Thy Name because it is so comfortable.

'Let the free-will offerings of my heart please Thee, O Lord, and teach me Thy judgments.'

¶ Then shall the bishop say this prayer of consecration :—

'Unto Thee, O ever-blessed Lord and Saviour, and to Thy most holy worship and service, do I here offer up and dedicate these oblations, [*here the bishop lays his hands upon every piece of the plate,*] which, in humble acknowledgement of Thy sovereignty over all, and of Thine infinite mercy and goodness to *them* in particular, Thy pious and devout *servants have* here presented before Thee. But who *are they*, O Lord, that *they* should be able to offer so willingly after this sort? Thine, O Lord, is the power and the glory, and the majesty; for all that is in the heaven and in the earth is Thine. Both riches and honour, and all things come of Thee; and 'tis of Thine own that *they have* given Thee. Accept, we beseech Thee, these *their* free-will offerings, and grant that they may be for ever holy vessels for the use of Thy sanctuary. Let no profane or sacrilegious hand ever withdraw them from Thine altar, or debase them to common use again; but let them continue always inviolable in that holy service to which they have been by *them* so piously designed, and are now by our office and ministry solemnly set apart and consecrated. And sanctify, we beseech Thee, both the souls and bodies of all those who out of these vessels shall now or at any time hereafter partake of the Holy Communion of Thy most blessed Body and Blood; that we all may be filled with Thy grace and heavenly benediction, and also pardoned and accepted, and everlastingly rewarded through Thy mercy, O ever-blessed Lord and Saviour, who dost live and govern all things, world without end. Amen.'

¶ The bishop adds this benediction :—

'And now, blessed be Thou, O Lord, heavenly Father, Almighty and everlasting God, for ever and ever; and blessed be Thy glorious Name, that it hath pleased Thee to put into the heart of *thy servant* to give so freely for the more decent performance of Thy worship

THE ALTAR

and service in the beauty of holiness. Accept, O Lord, this *his* bounden duty and service, not weighing *his* merits, but pardoning *his* offences. Let these *his* oblations come up as a memorial before Thee, and let *him* find and feel, that with such sacrifices Thou art well pleased. Bless *him*, O Lord, in *his* person, and in *his* substance, and in all that belongs unto *him*, or that *he* puts *his* hand unto. Remember *him*, O my God, for good, and wipe not out the kindnesses that *he* hath done for the house of *his* God, and the offices thereof. And give to all those that shall enjoy the benefit of this his piety and bounty, both a grateful sense and sanctified use of what is by *him* so well intended; that in all and by all, Thy praise and glory may now and ever be set forth, O gracious and merciful Lord, who livest and reignest ever one God, world without end. Amen.'

Consecration of Altar-Plate.

¶ Then the bishop goes on to read the other sentences in the Offertory. And bread and wine, upon and in the vessels now consecrated, are set upon the altar, and the alms gathered in the new bason, and the rest of the Communion-service is proceeded in as is usual at other times.

[1] ¶ When there are *candlesticks* presented, while the bishop receiveth them and placeth them upon the altar, the chaplains say as before :—

'Thy word is a lantern unto my feet, and a light unto my paths.

'For in Thee is the fountain of life; and in Thy light shall we see light.'

¶ So likewise when a *censer* is presented and received, they say :—

'While the king sitteth at his table, my spikenard sendeth forth the smell thereof.

'Let my prayer be set forth before Thee as the incense; and let the lifting up of my hands be as the evening sacrifice.'

THE ACT.

'Notum sit omnibus quorum interest aut intererit, Quod die . . . die . . . scilicet mensis. . . . An. Dom . . . inter horas . . . et

---

[1] Archbishop Sancroft's Form of Consecration of New Communion Plate is printed at the end of *The Form of Dedication and Consecration of a Church or Chapel*, published by R. Tisdale in 1703. It was used by him at the church of Coleshill in 1685. After the paten, chalices, &c., have been provided for, there is an Appendix which deals with the candlesticks and the censer. It is very doubtful if this Appendix is Sancroft's, and it cannot be quoted as authoritative.—ED. 1902.

ejusdem diei antemeridianas in . . . in Com . . . notoriè situat. tempore Divinorum publice tunc et ibidem pro more solenniter celebratorum, Coram Reverendo in Christo Patre, ac Domino Domino . . . permissione divinâ . . . Episcopo, stante tunc temporis ad Altare in habitu Pontificali, comparuit personaliter . . . ad hæc infra-scripta specialiter requisitus et demandatus ; et adstitit mensulæ cuidam in medio positæ, et tapeto decenti coöpertæ, superquam stabant decenti ordine Vasa quædam (Patina nimirum, duo Calices, Lagena et Pelvis, etc. qualibus in sacris utimur) argentea omnia, et bis deaurata, ad usum Eccl. Paroch. de . . . in Agro . . . Diœceseos autem . . . sumptibus . . . præparata ; et post Deo debitam adorantiam, et Reverentiam Episcopo factam, nomine . . . humiliter petiit à Domino Episcopo antedicto, ut Vasa supradicta omnia, tam piè designata formata tam eleganter, et jam rite oblata Deo Servatori sisteret et præsentaret, suoque Pastorali Officio, et ministerio solenniter consecraret divino cultui in dicta . . . in perpetuum deservitura. Cui tam sancto desiderio toties dictus Episcopus lubenter annuens, et se promptum et paratum exhibens, Vasa illa omnia (Patinam et Calices, Lagenam et Pelvim, etc.) e manibus præfati . . . ante sacrum latare provoluti, sigillatim recipiens, et super altare, magnâ cum reverentiâ, reponens ; fusis ad Deum precibus, ab omni profano usu separavit, Deoque Servatori, et ejus Divino Cultui, juxta morem et ritus in Eccl. Angl. piè usitatos, solenniter in perpetuum consecravit; et eisdem Vasis ità Consecratis, eisque solis, mox usus est in Consecratione S. Eucharistiæ loco et tempore suprascriptis.'

—*Form of Dedication and Consecration of a Church or Chapel*, 4to, 1703.

Censers,[1] etc.

1550

* ST. DUNSTAN IN THE WEST, LONDON. 'Censer and chalice sold in the first year of Edw. VI. to pay for some repairs, but another Censer kept until the fourth year when sold.'—*Ex. Q. R. Miscell. Ch. Goods*, $\frac{4}{37}$. *Public Record Office.*

1552

* ST. MARY'S, COLECHURCH, LONDON. 'Two silver censers with chains, parcel gilt. A ship of silver, with a

---

[1] Extracts showing post-Reformation use of INCENSE will be found in the Second Volume of this work.—Ed. 1902.

THE ALTAR

spoon.'—*Milbourn's Hist. of the Church of St. Mildred,* Censers, etc. *Poultry, etc.,* p. 44, 1872.

1552

* YORK. 'A pair of censors of gold, 17 oz. A shell of silver for the same censors, 1 oz. . . . A pair of great censors of silver and guilt 100 oz. A pair of great censors, of silver 64 oz. [and four other "pair"].'— *York Fabric Rolls, Surtees Soc.,* vol. xxxv. p. 307.

1552

* WINCHESTER. 'ij silvar censors . . . j shippe of silvar with a little silvar spone.'—*Archæologia,* vol. xliii. p. 235.

1552

* CARLISLE. 'One pare of sencers.'—*Trans. of the Cumberland and Westmorland Antiquarian and Archæological Soc.,* viii. 194.

1552

* ST. PAUL'S, LONDON. 'ij faire Sensours of silver and gilte w^h high covers w^h vj wyndowes and batilments in the myddes of them wythe iiij chaynes of silver apeece. . . . cx unc.

on sensoure of silver and parcell gilte w^h iiij libardes heddes on the cover w^h vj wyndowes and pinacles and iiij chaynes of silver thereunto appertaynynge . . . xxxv^{ti} unc.

On little Sensour of Silver and gilte the cover is the forme of an old churche w^h wyndowes and pinacles w^h v shorte chaynes of Syllver wyer . . . xij unc. iij qu.

a greate large Sensoure all silver w^h mayne wyndowes and battilments usedd to sense w^h all in the penticoste weeke in bodie of the chirche of pawles at the procession tyme . . . clviij unc. iij qu.

Censers, etc.

on shyppe of silver all whight w^t a spone in it to take owte frankensence w^t all . . . xviij unc. di.'
—*The Ecclesiologist*, xvii. 198, 199.

1552

* EXETER. 'ij. silver censors. A silver shippe with a spone.'—*Ibid.* xxix. 42, 43.

1563

* CANTERBURY CATHEDRAL. '*Item* ij Sencers of Sylver.

'*Item* ij paire of Sensors of latten and one shippe of latten and another of copper.

Item ij payre of sensors of latten and j ship of latten. *Item* an other of copper.

Item one sensor wth a shipp and a spone of Syluer parcell guylt wayinge cvj ounz defased.'—*Inventories of Christchurch, Canterbury*, pp. 210 *n.*, 219, 229, 230.

1565

QUEEN ELIZABETH'S CHAPEL. 'A ship or ark, garnished with stone.'—*Ashmole's Order of the Garter*, p. 369.

1565

'The Communion-table was richly furnished with plate and jewels, viz., . . . a ship or ark garnished with stones . . . two ships of mother-of-pearl.'—*Christening of the child of Lady Cecile, at Westminster Palace, Sept.* 30, 1565. *Leland's Collectanea*, ii. 691, 692.

1565-1566

* 1565. '*Item*, . . . a paire of Sensors a crwett—Remainith in o^r pishe church of Gunbie.'

1566. '*Item*, one alb one sacring bell one paire of

THE ALTAR

sensors—Remaynith.'—*Peacock, English Church Furniture,* Censers, etc. pp. 92, 53.

1566

* 'A shype of tyn. A sencer of latten.'—*The Bodmin Indenture. Maclean's Hist. of the Deanery of Trigg Minor,* i. 341.

1570

* 'Whereas I am informed that certain monuments tending to idolatory . . . as Crosses, Censers . . . remaineth in your College as yet undefaced . . .'—*Letter of Horn, Bp. of Winchester, July 19, 1570, to Trinity College, Oxford,* qu. *Perry Lawful Ornaments,* 235 *n.*

1574

* ST. MARGARET'S, FENCHURCH STREET, LONDON. '*Item*, Payd for a parfuming pan.'—*The Case for Incense,* p. 162, 1899.

1630-1663

* 1630. 'A pann of coals well kindled with good perfumes.'

1663. 'One perfuming-pan of Iron.' — *Sheppard's Memorials of St. James's Palace,* ii. 29, 218.

1643

* 'In the chapel of Bishop Andrewes there stood on a table outside the sanctuary in front of the altar "a triquertrall censor wherein ye Clarke putteth frankincenes at ye reading of the first lesson," with "the Navicula like ye keele of a boat w^t a halfe cover and a foote, out of which the frankincense is poured."

'Prynne complained of this in the trial of Archbp. Laud, mentioning :—" A censor to burn Incense in at the reading of the First Lesson as in the Popish Masse and Churches. A little Boate out of which the Frankincense is poured etc., which Doctor Cosens had made use of in Peter house where he burned Incense."

Censers, etc.

'The inventory of the furniture, together with a plan, was found by Prynne among Laud's papers, and was quoted to incriminate him. It included "a triquertrall Censor" and "a Laton pan for it." Laud admitted that he had copied Andrewes.'—(W. Prynne, *Canterbury's Doom*, pp. 122-124. Lond. 1646.)

'In Peter House there was on the Altar a Pot which they usually called the incense pot.'—(*Ibid*. pp. 73, 74.)

'This was probably the Incense ship like those which stood on the Altar in Queen Elizabeth's Chapel in 1565 and Charles I.'s in 1646.[1]'—*The Case for Incense*, pp. 162, 163.

1641

* 'A Censer with fire and Incense: the book is crossed and perfumed.'—*A Parallel or Brief Comparison of the Liturgy with the Mass-book*, R. B. K., 1641.

1644

* Chillingworth 'being *Cancellarius* it was conceived that he should be buried *intra cancellos* and rot under the Altar near the pot of Incense, that the constant perfume of the Incense might excuse the thrift of his executrix.' —*Chillingworthi Novissima*, p. 31.

1646

Among the vestry plate belonging to Charles I., 'usually heretofore set upon the altar of his majesty's chapel at Whitehall, was One gilt ship.'—*Peck's Desiderata Curiosa*, ii. 373.

1674

* 'Robert Pye of Kendal was paid threepence for "glewing and varnishing ye censers in 1674."'—*The Parish Books of Kendal*, qu. Wilson's, *The Romance of our Ancient Churches*, p. 134, 1899.

---

[1] See page 124, and above *sub* 1646.

THE ALTAR

1685

* 'George Oldnar Grome of the Vestry in a scarlet <small>Censers, etc.</small> Robe with a perfuming pan in his hand burning perfumes all the way from Westminster Hall to the Quire-door in the Church.'—*Sandford's Hist. of the Coronation of James II.*, p. 70, 1687.

1703

* 'When a censer is presented and received, they shall say. . . .'—*Appendix to Archbp. Sancroft's Form of Consecration of New Communion Plate.*[1]

1761

* William Smith . . . 'in a scarlet dress holding a perfuming pan burning perfumes.'—*Thomson's Coronation of George III.*, p. 41, 1820.

The Houseling-Cloth[2]

1552

* ST. MARGARET'S, OCKLEY.   '*Item*, one housling <small>The Houseling-Cloth.</small> towell.'
   ST. MARY'S, SEND.   '*Item*, a long houseling towell.'
   ST. MARY'S, THORPE.   '*Item*, a howceling towell.'
'*Item*, j lyttill howceling towell of diaper.'
   ST. NICHOLAS', SUTTON.   '*Item* xij elles of lynen cloth for hosclyng towelles.'—*Daniel-Tyssen, Surrey Inventories*, pp. 13, 20, 34, 69.

1574

* '*Itm* two communion towels.' — *Inventory of the Church of St. Bartholomew, Smithfield.*

---

[1] See page 121 *n.* of this work.—ED. 1902.

[2] The houseling-cloth was a long towel or linen or silken sheet held before the communicants, as they knelt to receive the Eucharist. When altar-rails or kneeling-desks were introduced into our churches, the houseling-cloth was often spread over them: its purpose being to catch any particles of the Sacrament which, through accident, might be suffered to fall during the administration.—ED. 1902.

1586

The Houseling-Cloth.

* 'Suche churche goods and parishe goods as is this daye belonginge to this parishe and are as followeth. Imprimis 3 surplusses 8 ffonte clothes 3 towells vz^t 9 yards 1 tabell clothe of lynnen 1 silke clothe for the communyon table.'—*Church Goods of St. Columb Major, Cornwall,* qu. *Antiquary,* xxxiii. 344.

1593

* 'Her Majestie receaved the cuppe, havinge a moste princely lynned clothe layd on her cushion pillowe and borne at the four ends by the noble Erle of Herefford, the Erle of Essex, the Erle of Worcester, and the Erle of Oxford: the side of the sayd clothe her Majestie toke up in her hande, and therewith toke the ffoote of the golden and nowe sacred cuppe, and . . . did drinke of the same most devoutly (all this while knielinge on her knies).'—*Account of Q. Elizabeth's Communion on Easter Day,* 1593. Vide *The Old Cheque-Book of the Chapel Royal,* p. 150. *Camden Soc.* 1872.

1599

'*Item.* Paid for a long diaper cloth to make two towels for the communicants, 12s. 8d.'—*Churchwardens' Accounts of St. Margaret's, Westminster.* Vide *Nichols' Illustrations,* p. 26.

1623

* 'A fine Towel for the Prince, other Towels for the Houshold.'—*Arrangements for Prince Charles' Chapel at Madrid.* Vide *Collier's Eccles. Hist.,* II. viii. 726.

1651

* 'The King and the Duke received the Sacrament first by themselves, the Lords Byron and Wilmot

THE ALTAR

holding the long towel all along the altar.' (*Charles II.'s Chapel at Paris.*)—*Evelyn's Diary*, Dec. 25, 1651.

<small>The Houseling-Cloth.</small>

1661

'These four prelates having communicated, preparation was made for the King's receiving, who kneeled all this while before his faldstool. The towel was brought thither by Mr. Rumball on behalf of the Master of the Wardrobe, and presented to the Bishops of Hereford and Carlisle, who held it before the King while he received.'—*Coronation of Charles II.* Vide *Ashmole's Order of the Garter*, pp. 563-576.

1663

* '*Item*, Twenty ells of the like Holland Cloth for six Towells for the Communion.'—*Sheppard's Memorials of St. James's Palace*, ii. 218.

1667

'Sundry linen cloths to be spread before the communicants.'—*Bp. Wren's Will*, 1667.

1689

* ' When the ArchBp. and the Bps. assistant, have communicated in both kinds ; the ArchBp. administreth the Bread, and the Dean of Westm^r. the Cup to the King and Queen ; the Bps. that attend, holding a Towell of white Silk or fine linnen, 2. before the King and 2. before the Queen, while they receive.'—[*Coronation Order of William and Mary*] *MS. Heralds' Coll.* L. 19. qu. *Three Coronation Orders, H. Bradshaw Soc.* p. 34.

1714

* ' In Geo. I. the rubric is expanded as follows: "When the Archbishop the Dean of Westminster and the Bishops

The Houseling-Cloth. assist^ts. (vizt.) the Preacher and those two who read the Litanie, and those two that read the Epistle & Gospel) have communicated in both kinds, the Archbishop Administreth the Bread and the Dean of Westminster the Cup, to the King, the Bishops Assistants holding a Towel of white silk or fine linnen before the King while he receives."

'The first part of this rubric remains with a few verbal alterations until Victoria; but in Geo. II., III., and IV. the part about the towel is put off until after the words of administration, and in Geo. IV. it is only a bishop in the singular who holds a towel; while in Wm. IV. and Victoria the direction for the towel disappears altogether.'—*Three Coronation Orders*, pp. 156, 157.

1821

* 'Whilst the King receives, the bishop appointed for the service shall hold a towel of white silk or fine linen before him.'—*Order of Coronation of George IV*.[1]

c. 1845

* 'In Chesterfield parish church, large linen cloths covered the altar-rails and kneeling cushions during the celebration of Holy Communion, all through the vicariate of Archdeacon Hill; and when he resigned, though his successor abolished them, yet he brought them with him to his newly built church at Hasland and kept up the custom for some time. These were locally called "houselings" (pronounced *hoosling*), and the use of them was to prevent any of the crumbs from falling and being swept out with the dust of the church.'—

---

[1] This was the last occasion on which the houseling-cloth was used in the Coronation Service. It was not used at the coronation of William IV. in 1830, nor at that of Queen Victoria in 1838, nor yet at that of Edward VII. in 1902.—ED. 1902. 'Until the Order of K. William IV. it had been always directed, that "a towel of silk" or "houseling-cloth" should be held before the king, during the receiving of the Sacrament. It was then omitted, nor was it restored in the Order of Queen Victoria.'—Maskell, *Monumenta Ritualia*, vol. III. p. liii.

THE ALTAR

Letter from the Rev. R. K. Bolton, vide *The Guardian*, March 28, 1900. —The Houseling-Cloth.

1852

* 'An original custom is still continued in Wimborne Minster, namely, the use of the houseling or eucharistic-cloths of white linen, covering three plain oak benches, now kept to form the Communion-rail. Until about 1852 there were ten of these benches, and a rail stood on the top step at the entrance to the presbytery, covered with white linen.'—G. F. Score, *Guide to Wimborne Minster*, 1894, p. 30.

1879

* 'The communion or houseling-cloth is still spread in some churches in the diocese of Winchester; at St. Mary's, Oxford; at St. Mary's, Prestbury, near Cheltenham; and at All Saints', Leamington. It is placed over the rails before the communicants.'—*The Directorium Anglicanum*, p. 43 *n.*, fourth ed., 1879.

Ecclesiastical Vestments

Ecclesiastical Vestments

A.D. 1549

'Upon the day, and at the time appointed for the ministration of the Holy Communion, the priest that shall execute the holy ministry, shall put upon him the vesture appointed for that ministration, that is to say, a white albe plain, with a vestment or cope. And where there be many priests or deacons, there so many shall be ready to help the priest in the ministration, as shall be requisite; and shall have upon them likewise the vestures appointed for their ministry, that is to say, albes with tunicles.'

'Though there be none to communicate with the priest, yet these days [upon Wednesdays and Fridays], after the Litany ended, the priest shall put upon him a plain albe or surplice, with a cope, and say all things at the altar (appointed to be said at the celebration of the Lord's Supper,) until after the offertory.'

'And the same order shall be used all other days, whensoever the people be customably assembled to pray in the church, and none disposed to communicate with the priest.'

'In the saying or singing of Matins and Evensong, baptizing and burying, the minister, in parish churches and chapels annexed to the same, shall use a surplice. And in all cathedral churches and colleges, the archdeacons, deans, provosts, masters, prebendaries, and fellows, being graduates, may use in the quire, beside their surplices, such hoods as pertaineth to their several

Ecclesiastical Vestments.

degrees, which they have taken in any university within this realm: but in all other places, every minister shall be at liberty to use any surplice or no. It is also seemly, that graduates, when they preach, should use such hoods as pertaineth to their several degrees.'

'And whensoever the bishop shall celebrate the Holy Communion in the church, or execute any other public ministration, he shall have upon him, beside his rochet, a surplice or albe, and a cope or vestment; and also his pastoral staff in his hand, or else borne or holden by his chaplain.' [1]—*First Prayer-Book of Edward VI.*

1549

'After the exhortation ended, the archdeacon, or his deputy, shall present such as come to be admitted to the bishop, every one of them that are presented having upon him a plain alb, and the archdeacon or his deputy shall say. . . .

'Then one of them appointed by the bishop, putting on a tunicle, shall read the Gospel of that day.'—*The Form and manner of Ordering Deacons.*

'And when the archdeacon shall present unto the bishop all them that shall receive the order of priesthood that day, every of them having upon him a plain alb, the archdeacon saying. . . .'—*The Form of Ordering of Priests.*

'After the Gospel and Credo ended, first the elected bishop having upon him a surplice and a cope, shall be presented by two bishops (being also in surplices and copes, and having their pastoral staves in their hands) unto the archbishop of the province, &c.

---

[1] The best authorities maintain, that the meaning of this rubric of 1549, in which the expression 'a vestment or cope' occurs, is not that the cope was to be used indifferently with the chasuble; but that the use of the chasuble was to be reserved for actual and complete celebrations of the Holy Communion, whilst the cope was appointed for 'Table-prayers.' See Note B, at the close of the present volume.—ED. 1902.

'Then shall the archbishop put into his hand the pastoral staff, saying. . . .'—*The Form of Consecration of an Archbishop or Bishop.* ORDINATION OFFICES, *published by Grafton, in* 1549.

1550

'Archbishop Cranmer having on his mitre and cope, usual in such cases, went into his chapel, handsomely and decently adorned, to celebrate the Lord's Supper according to the custom, and by prescript of the book, intituled *The Book of Common Service.* Before the people there assembled, the holy suffrages first began, and were publickly recited, and the Epistle and Gospel read in the vulgar tongue, Nicholas [Ridley], Bishop of London, and Arthur [Bulkeley], Bishop of Bangor, assisting ; and, having their surplices and copes on, and their pastoral staves in their hands, led Dr. John Ponet, endued with the like habits, into the middle of them, unto the most reverend father, and presented him unto him, sitting in a decent chair ; and used these words, "Most reverend father in God, we present unto you this godly and well-learned man to be consecrated bishop" . . . These things being thus despatched, the Archbishop exhorted the people to prayer and supplication to the Most High, according to the order prescribed in the Book of Ordination, set forth in the month of March 1549. According to which order he was elected and consecrated, and endued with the episcopal ornaments, the Bishop of London first having read the third chapter of the first Epistle of Paul to Timothy, in manner of a sermon. . . . March 8, John Hooper was consecrated Bishop of Gloucester, just after the same manner, by the Archbishop, Nicholas Bishop of London, and John Bishop of Rochester, assisting, clothed (say the words of the *Register*) in linen surplices and copes, and John, elect of Glocester, in the like habit.'—*Strype's Memorials of Cranmer,* I. 363, 364, 8vo, Oxford, 1840.

1550

<small>Ecclesiastical Vestments.</small>

'BYNDON Chapel. A chalice of silver, a pair of vestments, an altar-cloth, a pair of crewets, one bell twenty inches broad and as much in depth.

'FARRINGDON, *alias* WINTERBOURNE GERMAGNE. Two bells, a chalice of silver, a cope of green satin, two pairs of vestments, two altar-cloths, a cross and censer, and two candlesticks.

'Chapel of FORSTEN in Charminster. One chalice, one cope of red satin, one cope of little value, one pair of vestments, two altar-cloths, and two little bells.

'BLANDFORD, St. Mary. Two chalices, one gilt, three vestments, three copes, three bells in the tower appointed to the parish, one cope with the table-cloths and surplices, delivered to Sir Thomas Eliston and others.'—*Return of Church Utensils in Dorsetshire in* 1550, *quoted by Hutchins from MS. in the Augmentation Office.*

1552

'John Scory (Ponet being translated to Winchester,) was consecrated Bishop of Rochester, at Croydon, by the Archbishop of Canterbury, assisted by Nicholas Bishop of London, and John Suffragan of Bedford. Miles Coverdale was, at the same time and place consecrated Bishop of Exon, all with surplices and copes, and Coverdale so habited also.'—*Strype's Memorials of Cranmer*, I. 389.

1552

* ST. PAUL'S CATHEDRAL, LONDON.

'The Inventarie of the Plate, Jewells, Coopes, Vestements, Tunacles, Albes, Bells, and other Ornaments

ECCLESIASTICAL VESTMENTS 139

appertayninge to the Cathedrall Churche of Sayncte Paule in London 1552.

(*Continued from p. 62.*)

Item, one faire large Coope of nedle worke full of ymages with perles in the orphers.
Item, two Coopes of Clothe of golde.
Item, five Coopis of Clothe of tisshewe blewe.
Item, one Coope of tisshewe greene with a goodlye orphery to the same.
Item, one fayre Coope of redd velvett tisshewe.
Item, Coopes of redde tisshewe in number three.
Item, two faire Coopis of redd tisshewe.
Item, a greate large Coope of nedell worke with divers ymages there uppon.
Item, two faier and goodlie Coopis of redd tisshewe.
Item, one fayer riche Coope of nedleworke.
Item, two goodlie Coopes of tisshewe blewe color.
Item, two verie faire Coopes of blewe tisshewe.
Item, one faire large Coope of blewe Clothe of tisshewe.
Item, two Coopes of black tisshewe for requiem.
Item, one Coope of redd velvett powdered with flowers of golde.
Item, a Coope of redde velvet powdered with egles and with books upon it.
Item, one Coope of redd velvett with crownis.
Item, two Coopes of redd velvett one with the Sonn and Moone thother with roses.
Item, a Coope of redd velvett powdered with flowers.
Item, one Coope of redd velvett with flowers of golde upon it.
Item, twelve Coopes of whight and greene velvett with branches and appuls of golde on them.
Item, one Coope of blewe velvett, goodlye with flowers of golde.
Item, a Coope of greene velvett with flowers of golde.
Item, two Coopis of blewe velvett with crownis of golde upon them.
Item, one Coope of blewe velvett with faire branches of golde uppon it.
Item, one Coope of blewe velvett with crownis.
Item, a Coope of redd velvett with a goodd orphery.
Item, foure greate and large Coopes with arms of golde and silver and ymages with a runnynge vyne.
Item, two Coopes of redd velvet havinge noe worke on them but playne.
Item, a Coope of redd velvett with egles and books upon it with an anngell and flowers and with redd stones in the orphris.

Ecclesiastical Vestments.

Item, one Coope of redd velvett with a runnyng vine and ymages thereon.
Item, a Coope of redd velvett.
Item, a Coope of blewe velvett fayre.
Item, one Coope of black velvett for requiem.
Item, foure goodlie newe Coopis of whight damaske with lillie potts and the splayde Egle of the Kyng's gifte.
Item, two faire newe Coopis of whight damask with anngells.
Item, two newe Coopes of whighte damaske with anngells and flowers there uppon.
Item, one Coope of whight damaske with the holye gost with a fayre ophres to it.
Item, a Cope of whight damaske with Egles and with this worde Russell.
Item, thre Coopes of whight damaske powdered with the holye goste.
Item, one Coope powdered, with the name of Jesus.
Item, one Coope of redd silke powdered with lyons and swannes in the orphres.
Item, thre Coopis of whight damaske with anngells and an M. crownedd.
Item, one Coope of whight silke powderedd with popinjayes.
Item, two Coopis of whight damaske one with the Sonn and thother with flowers.
Item, one Coope of grene silke.
Item, a Coope of redd silke with lyones.
Item, a Coope of redd silke with the name of Jesus.
Item, a large Coope fynelie made with ymages.
Item, a Coope of redd silke with lions of golde.
Item, Coopis of redd damaske with parrours of grene velvet and grene damaske to the number of seventene.
Item, a Coope of blewe damaske with a fayre orphery, the chalice and the hoste uppon it.
Item, twenty and foure Coopis of whight damaske with the orphreys of grene velvet and grene damaske powderedd with flowres de luce and flowres of golde.
Item, six Coopes of redd damaske with the orphres of grene velvett and grene damaske with flowers.
Item, whight Coopes of damaske and silk of divers sortis twentie and two.
Item, one large Cope of grene silke.
Item, thertie faire Coopis of grene silke with floures of gold wrought in them.
Item, a Coope of redd silke with lions and ooke treese.
Item, a Coope of crymesine damaske with greyhounds and birds.
Item, a Coope of redd damaske.
Item, two Coopis of blewe silke one with osteriche fethers, thother ooke trees.

ECCLESIASTICAL VESTMENTS 141

Item, nyne Coopis of faire blewe silke.
Item, a Coope of violett silke with wheate sheaves of golde.
Item, a faire Coope of whight damask with floures of golde.
Item, tenne fayre large Coopis of redd silke with ymagerie and other divers worke.
Item, twelve Coopis of blewe silke bawdekin with flowers of golde wrought in them.
Item, one whight Coope with perells in the orphres of the same.
Item, a large Coope of blewe silke with lions and oke tres.
Item, two Coopes of fayre redd bawdekin with the chalice and the hoste.
Item, twentie Coopis of redd bawdekin of divers sorts woven with golde.
Item, one Coope of goodlye bawdekin.
Item, eyghte Coopis of fyne bawdekin verye faire.
Item, foure Coppis of sadd coloredd bawdekin of blacke and redd silke.
Item, six Coopis of grene bawdkin.
Item, thre Coopes of sadd coloredd bawdekin.
Item, eleven Coopis of litell valor woven. Nott to be estemedd.
Item, a vestment and two tunicles of clothe of golde.
Item, two tunicles of redd velvett tisshew.
Item, two tunicles of blewe clothe of tisshewe.
Item, two tunicles of blacke clothe of tisshewe for requiem.
Item, two tunicles powderedd with the name of Jesus.
Item, two tunicles of redd velvett with Crownes.
Item, one vestment faire of redd velvett with the Vyne and ymagerie theruppon.
Item, two tunicles of blewe velvet with flowres of golde.
Item, a vestment and two tunicles of grene velvett with floures of golde.
Item, a vestment of blewe velvett with a fayre orphery with crowns of gold and two tunicles of the same.
Item, a goodlye fayre vestment of blue velvett powderedd with flowers of golde.
Item, a faire vestment of blacke velvett for requiem with two tunicles to the same.
Item, a vestment of redd velvett with crowns of golde uppon it.
Item, two tunicles of redd velvett with Egles and books uppon it with anngels and flours wythe redd stones in the orphres.
Item, two tunicles of redd velvett with a runnynge vyne and ymages theron.
Item, a vestment and two tunicles of redd velvett.
Item, two tunicles of blewe velvett.
Item, two tunicles of redd velvett with long stripes of golde.
Item, a vestmente of redd velvet with anngells and flowers of golde.

Ecclesiastical Vestments.

Ecclesiastical Vestments.

Item, a vestment and two tunicles of newe whight damaske with lillie potts and the splayde egle of the Kyng's gyfte.

Item, a vestment and two tunicles of whight damaske with anngells.

Item, two tunicles of whight damask powderedd with the holye goste.

Item, two tunicles of newe whight damaske with flowers of golde uppon them.

Item, two tunycles of whight damaske with lillie potts lyned wythe grene sarcenet.

Item, one vestment of redd silk with lions of golde.

Item, two tunicles of blewe silke with lions and ooke trees.

Item, a faire vestment of grene silke with anngells of gold and two tunicles.

Item, a vestment and two tunicles of blewe silke with crownes and osteriche fethers.

Item, a large vestment of redd silke with two tunicles with the crucifix on it.

Item, an other fayre vestment of redd silk full of crosses and two tunicles.

Item, a vestment and two tunicles of faire redd bawdkin with the chalice and the hoste.

Item, two tunycles of redd silke with lions and ooke trees.

Item, Two tunicles of crymesin damaske with greyhounds and birdes.

Item, a vestment of blewe silke with osteriche fethers.

Item, two vestments of redd silke one with lyons thother with greyhounds.

Item, two tunycles of whight damaske with flowers of golde.

Item, a vestment of redd silke for the lente with two tunycles to the same.

Item, tenn tunicles for the bisshopp, of bawdkin when he doth mynystre of divers sortis and colors.

Item, a vestment and two tunicles of fyne bawdkin, verie fayre.

Item, foure tunicles of faire blewe silke of one sorte.

Item, thre tunicles of sadd colouredd bawdkyn of blacke and redd.

Item, a vestment and two tunicles of grene bawdkin.

Item, two vestments of bawdkin.

Item, fourteen copes of bawdkin of diverse sorts.

Item, two vestments and two tunicles.

Item, two other vestments of litell valor and two tunicles to the same.

Item, a vestment and two tunycles of redd sylke.

Item, a vestment of whight fustian.

Item, a vestment of yelowe satin with two tunicles.

Item, a tunicle of redd silke onlye.

Item, a vestment of redd silke with two tunicles to the same with flours of golde.

Item, two tunicles with wheate sheaves.

ECCLESIASTICAL VESTMENTS 143

Item, one faire vestmente with wheate sheaves.
Item, six curtins of divers sortis.
Item, a riche fronte for the highe altar full of perels and goodlye wrought thereon.
Item, an other front wrought in golde and perell.
Item, a fronte richelie sett with perells with the Sonn and the Moone and thedds of the twelve Apostells.
Item, an hanginge of whight damaske powderedd, with the holye gost and richelie made with nedellworke in the myddes with curetines of whight Sarcenett.
Item, an hanginge of redd velvett with anngells a goodlye crucifix with Marie and John.
Item, an hanginge of blewe silke with fayre and goodlye ymages thereon.
Item, a hanginge of blewe silke with the Crucifix, Marie and John in the myddes, goodlye wroughte.
Item, a hanginge of redd silke with longe stripes of golde verie fayre.
Item, a hanginge of redd bawdkin for the lowere parte of the altar with a fronte.
Item, an hanginge of whight damask with flowers of silke.
Item, an hanginge of redd and pretie bawdkin with a Crucifix Marie and John with flowers.
Item, a fronte of blewe silke with ymagerye.
Item, an hanginge for the highe altar of black damask.
Item, fayre curtines of blacke sarcenett.
Item, an hanginge for a syde altar of whight damaske with floures of gold upon it.
Item, a greate and large canopie of tisshewe, redd color, fayre and newe fringedd abought, goodlie for the Kyng's Mai^{tie} to go under when he comethe to the chirche.
Item, one canopie of redd tisshewe for the Sacrament.
Item, an other Canopie of grene tisshew for the same purpose.
Item, two riche clothes for the garnishinge of the Sepulchre.
Item, two other smaller clothes for the Sepulchre of nedle worke one of them of the Sepulchre and thother of the resurrection.
Item, a pawle of blacke velvet to leye upon a corps with a large crosse of tisshewe.
Item, a greate pawle of whight silke with a large crosse of redd silke powderedd with lions of sylver.
Item, a greate clothe of redd silke miche like to a pawle with lions of golde upon it.
Item, a bordre of black sarcenet with a fringe of black silke myxte with golde well giltedd and of a greate lengthe.
Item, thertie and six bawdkins for to garnishe the quyer at enye trihumphe or at the Kyngs' Mai.$^{tis.}$ commynge of divers colors and sorts.

Ecclesiastical Vestments.

Item, a faire longe bawdkin for the quyer allsoe of the longeste.
Item, thirtie and one bawdekins for the quyer allsoe of divers sorts and colors.
Item, two faire longe bawdkins of the best sorte for the quyere.
Item, greate and weyghtie bawdkins for the bisshopps see for the garnishinge thereof when he mynystereth, in nombre therttene.
Item, five bawdekins to goe abroade.
Item, five Cusshyns to goe abroade.
Item, one greate cusshynne the one syde of Clothe of Tysshewe verie faire and thother syde of velvett longe to lene uppon.
Item, cusshins coveredd with blewe satin fayre and greate to lene uppon, in numbre three.
Item, other Cusshynes of fayre bawdekin to kneele uppon and to lene, greate and smale in nombre fourtene.
Item, eyghte fardells of Allbis with stoles fannels and parrours conteyninge the nombre of thertie and nyne.
Item, thertene Allbis with stoles fannels and parrours savinge two of them have none.
Item, thertie and one Allbis of divers sorts with their parrours.
Item, nyne Allbis goinge abroade for the Communyon.
Item, Altar Clothes of diaper and other playne Clothes for the table in nombre seven.
Item, fyve fyne towells for the Communyon.
Item, Corporax casis with the lynnyn therto belonginge, in nombre nyne.
Item, in the steeple of bells in nombre, fyve.
Item, doble hangings of tapestree for the quyere and one Turkeye carpett for the Communyon table.

    Ther was solde the xvij$^{th.}$ of Octobre in the same yeer one gylte crosse with a foote and a vice with Marie and John, etc. wayinge thre score and seven onces and an halfe bye the consente of the Deane and Chapiter unto Robert Raines goldsmith at Vs and six pence the once; sum, eyght tene poundes enleven shyllings and thre pence. Whiche moneye as yett remaynethe in the handes of the Keper of the vesturie towarde the greate charges of an alteracion and channge of a newe place for the ministracion of the Communion in our Churche.

WILLIAM MEY.
WILLIAM ERMYSTED.
GABRIEL DUNNE.
GILBERT BOURNE.

—*Exchequer Q. R. Church Goods*, $\frac{4}{7\frac{1}{1}}$ *Public Record Office.*

Plate VIII.] [*To face page* 145.

Hier, 1.]

1552

WYCOMBE, BUCKINGHAMSHIRE.

'An Inventorie of the Churche good$\mathfrak{f}$ that be lefte taken the xxiiij daye of Aprell in the vjth yere of the Reigne of ower soveraigne lorde Kinge Edwarde the sixte in the present$\mathfrak{f}$ of Mr George Parteferr then maier and his brethren Willm Corwyn Edwarde Carye Rowlande Wytnall and Gilys Scidmor churchewardens.[1]

> In primis a sute of blacke worsted w^t .R. of golde and the lynen y^t belongith therto w^t one cope of the same
> *Item* an olde sute of white bawdckyn w^t damaske flowrys w^{t}oute a coope havinge ij albys
> *Item* a sute of blewe and grene bawdekyn w^t hynd$\mathfrak{f}$ of golde and a coope w^t all the lynens therto belongynge
> *Item* a sute of Redde silke w^t sterris and the flowredeluce lackynge all the lynen w^t ij Coopis
> *Item* a sute of blacke w^t flowris of golde in y^e crosse wyth ij lynens therto belonginge
> *Item* a pawle of blewe velvet w^t flowris of golde
> *Item* an aulter Clothe of blewe worstede w^t flowris
> *Item* ij olde courteynez of sarcenet of purple colour
> *Item* ij Courteyns of Red sarcenet olde
> *Item* j Coope of Redde velvet
> *Item* j Redde Coope of Damaske w^t flowris
> *Item* iiij Albys for Chyldren w^t ij aulter clothis of Red damaske
> *Item* a vestment of Red satten w^t saint John baptist
> *Item* a vestment of blewe damaske w^t the albe therto belonginge
> *Item* vij towellez of lynen and iiij litle towels for the aulter
> *Item* vij Casis and xj corporas clothis
> *Item* a vestment of Redde dorneck$\mathfrak{f}$ wythous lynen
> *Item* a pilowe of Red velvet
> *Item* a pese of chaungeable sarcenet
> *Item* five aulter clothis of lynen one of them ys diaper
> *Item* twoo deske clothis

Ecclesiastical Vestments.

---

[1] Upon this inventory, Mr. St. John Hope comments thus:—'This inventory is of great interest and importance as showing what "Ornaments of the Church, and of the Ministers thereof at all times of their Ministration ... as were in this Church of *England*, by the authority of Parliament, in the second year of the reign of King *Edward* the Sixth," had continued to "be retained, and be in use" in the king's sixth regnal year.'

Ecclesiastical Vestments.

Item iij olde vestmentis with ij albys one of them Redde wythe the crosse of saint george and an other grene velvet and the thirde w^t flowris redde and grene
Item iiij silke stremers litle
Item an olde grene aultre clothe
Item a white Coope of Damaske wyth Imagis at the orphrasyies
Item v surplessez olde wyth a lynen courteyn
Item xj cofers ij candilstickꝭ of latten w^t one chayre
Item a vestment of white bustyan wyth the lynen.'

—*Inventories of the Parish Church of All Saints, and of the Chapel of the Blessed Virgin Mary, Wycombe, by W. H. St. John Hope, M.A.,* in *Records of Buckinghamshire,* 1899, p. 128, *being* vol. viii. no. 2., *of the Proceedings of the Architectural and Archæological Society for the County of Buckingham.*

1552

* In the sixth year of Edward VI., amongst other ornaments, there were remaining at the church of St. Mary, Colechurch, London—'iiij copes ij for hollye dayes and ij for worke dayes, and on other cope also.'—*Milbourn's Hist. of the Church of St. Mildred, Poultry, etc.,* p. 44.

1552

* [Wyken.] 'Reserved one vestment[1] of blue silk for the only maintenance of divine service in the said parish church.'

[Kenett.] 'Reserved one cope of green crewel for the only maintenance of divine service in the said parish church.'

[Knapwell.] 'Reserved the aforesaid vestment[1] for the only maintenance of divine service in the said parish church.'

[Graveley.] 'Reserved one cope of red damask and

---

[1] The context shows that these 'vestments' were not copes. The extracts given above refer to the 6th year of Edward VI.—ED. 1902.

ECCLESIASTICAL VESTMENTS 147

one cope of tawney silk for the only maintenance of divine service in the said parish church.'

[Over.] 'Reserved one cope of blue velvet and one cope of white damask for the only maintenance of divine service in the said parish church.'—*Cambridgeshire Church Goods*, ed. C. H. Evelyn White, pp. 29-32.

1552

* Mr. Edward Peacock, in his *English Church Furniture at the Period of the Reformation*,[1] Lond. 1866, mentions twenty parish churches in Lincolnshire in which, in the sixth year of Edward VI., the cope was retained at the time when other ornaments were sold or destroyed.—*Ed.* 1902.

1552

* 'Payde for makyng tow ratchetts for ye clarke, vj^d.'—*North's Chronicle of St. Martin's, Leicester*, p. 119.

1552

* '*Item*, ij gathered surplyses for the curat.
Item, x playne surplises for the quier.'—*Inventory of St. Peter's, Cornhill*, qu. *The Antiquary*, xxxiii. 279.

1552-1553

* 'The second year of Edward VI. was the year 1548-9. I have no more doubt as to what vestments were in use in the English Church in that year, than I have as to what king was then sitting on the English throne. But if I had any doubt, it is taken away by

---

[1] Pages 42, 47, 48, 49, 52, 75, 77, 81, 92, 106, 115, 117, 124, 130, 137, 148, 151, 154, 165, 167.

Ecclesiastical Vestments.

the inventory of those church-goods (still to be seen in the Public Record Office in London) which Edward's Commissioners found, and *left for use in the church of Newland*, as late as the sixth year of his reign—that is, in 1552-3.

'Let me give the list of vestments—

Capella de Newland

1 Cope of blue satin with branches.
1 Cope of green crewel.
1 Vestment of red satin with branches.
1 Vestment of green crewel.
1 Vestment of yellow crewel.
With albs, stoles, and fannels.'

—*Life of James Skinner*, pp. 277, 278, *Lond.* 1883.

1552-1553

* The inventory of Beckenham parish church, of the sixth year of Edward VI., contains the mention of 'two copes, nine vestments, two vestments for deacon and sub-deacon.'—*Exchequer Q. R. Church Goods*, $\frac{3}{43}$ *Public Record Office.*

1553

* 'An Inventory of the Plate, Jewels, &c., presented, at their request, to the Dean and Chapter of St. Paul's Cathedral in the year 1553 by the Commissioners for the Seizure of Church Goods.

'In the 7$^{o.}$ Edw. 6$^{ti.}$ upon the exhibiting of an Inventory of the Plate, Jewels, Ornaments, etc., belonging to the Cathedral Church of S. Paul, which was delivered into the Kings Commissioners at Guild-Hall; and request made to them by the Dean and Chapter, that certain things of necessary use might be permitted to

ECCLESIASTICAL VESTMENTS 149

remain, these following particulars were by them allowed of; viz.

Imp. Chalices ... III.
It. Two pair of Basyns for to bring the Communion bread, and to receive the offerings for the poor; whereof one pair sylver for every day: the other for Festivals, etc., gilt.
It. A Sylver Pot to put the wine in, for the Communion-Table, weighing xl. ounces.
It. The written Texts of the Gospels and Epistles.
It. A large Canopie of Tissew for the King's Majestie when he cometh thither.
It. A Pall of Black Velvet, to lay upon the Herse.
It. A Border of Black Sarcenet, with a Fringe of black silk mixt with gold for the burial of noble Persons.
It. Bawdkins of divers sorts and colours, for garnishing the Quire, at the Kings coming, and for the Bishop's seat; as also at other times when the Quire shall be apparailed for the honour of the Realm.
It. Eight Cusheons.
It. Thirty Albis, to make Surplices for the Ministers and choristers.
It. Twenty-four old cusheons to kneel on.
It. Seven Clothes of Lynnen, plain and diaper, for the Communion Table.
It. Five Towels.
It. Two Hangings of Tapestry, for the Quire.
It. A Turkey-Carpet for the Communion Table.
It. A Pastoral Staff for the Bishop.

'There was at that time also desired, by the said Dean and Chapter, allowance of xviii*l*. vi*s*. iii*d*. towards the Charges of taking down the steps and place of the High Altar; and for other furniture of convenient places and things for the administration of the Communion.'— *Exchequer Q. R. Church Goods,* $\frac{4}{71}$ *Public Record Office.*

1558

'Provided always and be it enacted, that such ornaments of the church, and of the ministers thereof, shall be retained and be in use as was in this Church of England, by authority of Parliament, in the second

<small>Ecclesiastical Vestments.</small>

year of the reign of King Edward VI., until other order [1] shall be therein taken by the authority of the Queen's majesty, with the advice of her Commissioners appointed and authorised under the great seal of England for causes ecclesiastical, or of the Metropolitan of this realm.'—*Act of Uniformity*, cap. 2.

1558

* '*Item* an albe which made a rochett for the Clarke anno primo Elizabeth.'—*Peacock's English Church Furniture*, p. 57.

1559

'And here is to be noted, that the minister at the time of the Communion, and at all other times in his ministration, shall use such ornaments in the church as were in use by authority of parliament in the second year of the reign of king Edward VI. according to the act of parliament set in the beginning of this book.' —*Book of Common Prayer*, 1559.

1559

'The chapel [of Lambeth palace] on the east part was adorned with tapestry, and the floor being spread with red cloth, and the Table used for the celebration of the Holy Sacrament, being adorned with a carpet and cushion, was placed at the east. Moreover, four chairs were set to the south of the east part of the chapel for

---

[1] 'Which *other order* (at least in the method prescribed by this Act) was never yet made; and therefore, legally, the ornaments of ministers in performing divine service are the same now as they were in 2 Edw. VI. Pursuant to the foregoing clause (though not by authority of Parliament) a rubrick was prefixed in the Book of Common Prayer in the first year of Queen Elizabeth, and continued till 1661 . . . which clause, somewhat altered, did, in 13 and 14 Car. II., become part of the Book of Common Prayer, by authority of Parliament.'—*Note by Bishop Gibson, Codex*, vol. i. p. 363, fol. 1713.—EDD. 1848.

Plate IX.] [*To face page* 151.

Hier. 1.]

ECCLESIASTICAL VESTMENTS 151

the Bishops, to whom the office of consecrating the Archbishop [Parker] was committed. There was also a bench placed before the chairs, spread with a carpet and cushions, on which the Bishops kneeled. And in like manner a chair, and a bench furnished with a carpet and a cushion, was set for the Archbishop on the north side of the east part of the same chapel. These things being thus in their order prepared, about five or six in the morning the Archbishop entereth the chapel by the west door, having on a long scarlet gown and a hood, with four torches carried before him, and accompanied with four Bishops, who were to consecrate him. . . . Sermon being done, the Archbishop, together with the four Bishops, go out of the chapel to prepare themselves for the Holy Communion; and, without any stay, they come in again at the north door thus clad: the Archbishop had on a linen surplice, the elect of Chichester used a silk cope, being to administer the Sacrament. On whom attended and yielded their service the Archbishop's two chaplains, Nicholas Bullingham and Edmund Gest, the one Archdeacon of Lincoln, and the other of Canterbury, having on likewise silk copes.'—*Strype's Life of Parker*, I. 113.

1559

* 'The archbishop of Canterbury, in his surplice and doctor's hood on his shoulders, who did execute, began the service, assisted by the bishops of Chichester and Hereford, appareled as the archbishop, and by two of the prebendaries in their grey amices [almuces].'— *Obsequy for Henry II. of France at St. Paul's, Sept. 8 and 9, 1559. Strype's Annals*, I. i. 189.

1559-1649

'In habits yet more glorious do the gentlemen of the sovereign's chapel at Whitehall, the petty canons and vicars of Windsor, appear, who at this time are also

Ecclesiastical Vestments.

joined in one body, to augment the solemnity, for they are all (or the most part of them) vested in rich copes of cloth of gold, cloth of bodkin, or most costly embroideries. . . . These kind of vestments have been at all times worn in the grand procession, whether the grand feast was kept at Windsor, or at Whitehall, or Hampton Court, or Greenwich, even to the beginning of the late wars, in which the covetous barbarism of the then reformers sent most of them to the fire : besides, they are sometimes taken notice of in the registers of the Order, to be used in the grand procession ; as, in particular, an. 15 Jac. Reg. it is noted, that the whole choir, being adorned in copes (for so we suppose the word *orarium* may signify, as well as *Dalmatica vestis*), descended from the altar, and sung the Litany; and to like purpose is that recorded, an. 21 of the same king.'—Ashmole's *Order of the Garter*, p. 574.

1560

' These Bishops [Parker, etc.] never appearing publickly but in their rochets, nor officiating otherwise than in copes at the holy altar.

' The liturgy was celebrated every day in the chapel [of Q. Elizabeth] with organs and other musical instruments, and the most excellent voices, both of men and children, that could be got in all the kingdom. The gentlemen and children in their surplices, and the priests in copes as oft as they attended the divine service at the holy altar.'—Heylyn's *History of the Reformation*, ii. 314, 315.

1560

' All such goods as doth appertain to St. Benet, Gracechurch, written out the 16th day of February, 1560 :—

One cope, of cloth of gold.
A cope of red silk with fringe of gold.
A cope of blue damask. A cope of satin with blue birds.
Another old green cope.
A vestment with lions of gold with all that appertaineth to it.

ECCLESIASTICAL VESTMENTS 153

A vestment of red velvet with the lily-pot.
A vestment of blue satin of Bruges.
A vestment of white fustian with roses and flowers.
A vestment of red saye with the lily-pot and all things to it.
A carpet, of cloth of gold, for the table, fringed.
A hearse-cloth of cloth of gold fringed.
A hearse-cloth for children, fringed, of blue damask, with five wounds.
A canopy of red velvet.
Three corporas cloths (with the linen cloths) of cloth of gold, in them.
Two canopies, one of cloth of gold, the other of red satin with birds of gold.
A canopy with white needlework, fringed.
Deacon and sub-deacon of blue satin.
A churching-cloth, fringed, white damask.
An altar-cloth, fringed, of yellow and red saye.
Two altar-cloths of yellow and red buckram, fringed.'
Malcolm's Londinium Redivivum, i. 315.

1560-1567

* ELIZABETHAN CHURCH ORNAMENTS. 'At the present juncture the following list of ornaments, made at a valuation by a "Commission to Survey the Duke of Lancaster's Almshouse, within the late College of Newarke [at Leicester], 26th June 1561," may be of interest to your readers.

'The Commission was issued by Elizabeth to five persons, including the mayor and the master of Wiggeston's Hospital, authorising them " to repair to Hospitall or Almeshouse called the Duke of Lancaster his Almeshous wthin the late College of Newarke nye Leicester," and to inquire " what implementes or housholde stuffe were ther at the time of thentre of John Clarke late mr. of the saide Hospitall, and what parcell or parcelles of the same were imbeseled, sold or given," etc.

'In accordance with their instructions, the Commissioners returned an account of their investigations with an inventory of the " Kytchin stuffe," and a list of " The churche stuffe that is remeninge withe use." The kitchen stuff does not now concern us, but the eccles-

Ecclesiastical Vestments.

iastical ornaments are of exceptional interest. I give the entire list, with the estimated values :—

> Fyrst iij Sherpless, vs.
> *Item* one vestment of red Satten, vjs. viijd.
> *Item* a nother of browne silke, xviijd.
> *Item* a nother of bustyon, viijd.
> *Item* a Cope of lynnen Pentid wythe Damaske worke, vs.
> *Item* iij albis vj ammis Kyrchieffes, viijd.
> *Item* ix aulter clothes, ixs.
> *Item* xj towelles, viijs.
> *Item* iiij Kyrcheffes, iiijs.
> *Item* ij Corporas cases one of linagere worke the other wt Fraunches wth over clothe, viijd.
> *Item* iij candlestickes, xijd.
> *Item* ij Pyllorves, vjd.
> *Item* a crorse wth a clothe Paynted, nihill.
> *Item* ij Paxes ye one of wood thother of everye, nihill.
> *Item* ij Coffers, ijs. viijd.
> *Item* ij cornetes, ijd.

'It will be seen that this list was not made for purposes of robbery, and the ornaments enumerated were "remeninge with use." Besides surplices there were three vestments, that is, chasubles with their appurtenances, also a cope, three albes and six amices, three candlesticks, and two paxes, one of wood, the other of ivory, with the usual altar-cloths, towels, etc. There is not a list of the plate.

'The document quoted is printed in the newly-issued part (vol. xxxiv., part i., page 270) of the *Associated Architectural Societies' Reports and Papers*, in a communication by the Rev. W. G. D. Fletcher, F.S.A.

'I may, perhaps, be permitted also to quote various items from another list of the same date, printed by Dr. Cox and myself in 1881, in *Chronicles of the Collegiate Church or Free Chapel of All Saints, Derby*, p. 173. The inventory of the church goods entered in the parish books for the 3rd year of Elizabeth's reign (1560-1561) contains *inter alia* the following :—

> ij. Chalecys and ij. pattens off sylver and gylte.
> A brasen Cross and a holy water Can of brasse.

ECCLESIASTICAL VESTMENTS 155

A fyne Cope of blak velvytt.
A fyne Vestment that Mr. Reyd gave.
Three blak Vestmentes of velvytte that be in the custody of Mr. Ward.

'That "vestment" here (as probably in the Leicester inventory) means a chasuble with its appurtenances is proved by the inventory for 1562-1563, which mentions the "vestment yt Mr. Reede gave except ye albe and ye amysse." Copes are enumerated in these Derby inventories until the 10th Elizabeth (1567-1568) and albes year by year until 1576-1577.

'In this year, 1576, the churchwardens of Chelmsford sold a lot of ornaments that, until then, had remained in their custody. In an inventory of these taken on 31st July 1560 (2 Elizabeth), there are enumerated twelve copes (of cloth of gold, red, blue, and black velvet, red satin, and red and blue baudekyn), twenty-four vestments, seven of which had also the tunicles for the deacon and sub-deacon, and a number of miscellaneous ornaments, such as albes, amices, a Lent cloth for the high altar, and the Lenten veil. The latten included twelve candlesticks, "an old shype for franckensence, ij hallowater pottes, a latten senser, ij hand bells, a latten crosse, and a latten pyx." Amongst the linen was "a lawne clothe to carry ye chrysmatory in."—(*Transactions of the Essex Archæological Society,* ii. 215-217.)

'To the same period belongs the indenture drawn up on Sunday after the Feast of St. Michael, 8 Eliz. (1566), between the Mayor of Bodmin on the one part, and the wardens of the church of St. Petherick in Bodmin on the other part, acknowledging the receipt by the latter of various goods and ornaments "to be used and occupyed to the honer of God ynn the same churche from the day and yere aforesayd fourthward."[1] To wit, five bells, four vestments of green, white, and blue, and "one hole sute of blew velvet, decon, sub-decon, and

---

[1] The indenture referred to above is printed in full later in this work.—ED. 1902.

Ecclesiastical Vestments.

pistolhere," a red cope and a white one, and "toe copes used on good fryday, and a obe [albe] of sylck." Among the other ornaments were sundry "frunts" of green, yellow, etc.; also a "cusshyn of velvet for the commūyon tabell," and "toe lent clothes for the commūyon tabell"; eight pair of surplices and four rochets; a ship of tin, a senser of latten, two pair of candlesticks, a bason of latten, "a lampe before the hye auter," a sacring bell, etc. (Maclean, *Parochial and Family History of the Deanery of Trigg Minor, co. Cornwall*, i. 341.)'— *Letter in 'The Church Times,' Decr. 3rd, 1898, from Mr. W. H. St. John Hope, M.A.*

1561

'The same 23rd of April, being St. George's day, the festival was kept solemnly at court in this manner. All her Majesty's chapel came through her hall in copes, to the number of thirty, singing, "O God, the Father of heaven, &c.," the outward court and the gate, round about being strewn with green rushes. After, came Mr. Garter and Mr. Norroy, and Master Dean of the chapel, in robes of crimson satin, with a red cross of St. George: and after, eleven knights of the garter in their robes. Then came the Queen, the sovereign of the order, in her robes; and all the guard following in rich coats. And so to the chapel.'—*Strype's Annals*, I. i. 400.

1561

* 'After matens done, they whent a prosessyon rond about the cherche, so done the mydes and so rond a-bowt . . . then the clarkes and prestes a xxiiij syngyng the Englys prossessyon in chopes xxxiiij, and sum of them in gray ames (*i.e.* almuce) and in calabur.'—*Diary of Henry Machyn, Camden Soc.*, 1848, p. 258. (*Procession at Windsor on St. George's Day, May 18, 1561.*)

ECCLESIASTICAL VESTMENTS 157

1562

* Archbishop Parker and his suffragans wore amess [almuce] and habit at Convocation, January 13, 1562.— *Cardwell, Synodalia,* ii. 497, 498.

1562

'Hereafter ensueth an inventory made by the said wardens' accountants, of all the goods, jewels, and ornaments to the said church of St. Margaret [Westminster] appertaining, anno Domini 1562 :—

First, one vestment of blue cloth of tissue with the tunicles for deacon and sub-deacon.
Item. One cope of crimson cloth of tissue, and two coarse copes of blue tissue.
Item. One cope of purple cloth of tissue, one other cope of crimson velvet with scallop shells of silver, and one other cope of crimson velvet with flowers of gold.
Item. One altar-cloth of crimson velvet and gold, and two other altar-cloths of blue and russet velvet with flowers of gold.
Item. Two cushions of cloth of gold and crimson velvet, two cushions of green velvet with escutcheons of needle-work, two cushions of cloth of bawdkin, and one little cushion with a tree of green silk.
Item. Six hearse-cloths, and a cloth for the pulpit, of black and red bawdkin with flowers of gold.
Item. Eight old altar-cloths of diaper, one great new altar-cloth of diaper fine, and five plain.
Item. Seventeen towels and two small towels.
Item. One chalice with the paten all gilt, and two great communion cups all gilt.
Item. A past for bird,[1] set with pearl and stone.
Item. A streamer of white sarcenet with a white cross.'
Malcolm's Londinium Redivivum, iv. 137, 138.

1562

'That the use of vestments, copes, and surplices, be from henceforth taken away.'—(*Notes of matters to be moved by the clergy*), *Strype's Annals,* I. i. 475.

---

[1] *i.e.* 'a paste for a bride.' The paste was a kind of crown, worn by brides at weddings. This one was the property of the parish, and was bought in 1540 for £3.—ED. 1902.

1563

Ecclesiastical Vestments.

* ELIZABETHAN CHURCH ORNAMENTS AT CANTERBURY.

'Mr. W. H. St. John Hope has given us some very interesting details from Elizabethan inventories in parish churches.[1] I should like to be allowed to follow in his footsteps with a short account of an Elizabethan inventory, not of a parish church, but of the mother church of all England—Christ Church, Canterbury.

'In 1563 Dr. Matthew Parker made a visitation of his cathedral church, and an inventory of its goods and ornaments was made at the time. Such an inventory has especial interest for the ecclesiastical historian, as it may be looked upon as representing Parker's view of what was fit and proper to be left in the way of ornaments for his cathedral church; it is his interpretation, acting at a visitation, of the Act of Parliament of 1559, which orders the ornaments of the second year of King Edward VI. to be retained and be in use. There are several copies of the inventory taken at this time, which show the several stages of the process of inventory making until a fair copy is reached.[2] The inventories themselves are too long to be given here in full. They were found at Canterbury not many years ago by Dr. Sheppard, to whom I owe my knowledge of them, and whose memory is cherished by scholars who frequented the chapter library for his invariable courtesy and kindness. The fair copy is quoted by Dr. Benson in the appendix to the Lincoln Judgment as showing the use of candlesticks in 1563 at Canterbury.

'The fair copy has this preamble :—

In this inventory indented is contained all such ornaments, stuff, and other implements remaining in the vestry of the said church in the charge and custody of Theodore Newton, treasurer there. The one part of which indenture is delivered to the most reverend Father in God, Matthew, by God's permission Archbishop of Canterbury, at

---

[1] See pages 153 ff.
[2] The fair copy alluded to above is printed in full on pages 160 ff., by kind permission of the transcribers and editors, and of the publishers of *Inventories of Christchurch, Canterbury*.—ED. 1902.

his visitation of the said church, holden and kept in the months of July and August, *Anno Domini* 1563.

'Next to no silver plate is found in the inventory; for a year after the accession of King Edward VI. the privy council send first for the silver table on the altar for themselves, and next they order all jewels of gold and silver to be delivered up to the officers of the mint. (January, 1548.) It was the reign of thieves. Thus the inventory opens with but one communion cup, recently made out of two chalices, three chalices with their patens, and two cruets, all silver gilt. Further, a cross of silver gilt with a staff; it could be used either to set on the altar, or be carried in procession. This meagre list nearly exhausts all the silver plate. Well may the Archbishop write to Cecil, in 1567, and say that not a tenth of the plate and ornaments then remained which were there when the first Dean took possession. But to leave the doings of the Edwardian robbers, let us note, of the ornaments, about which there has been dispute, what was left behind in 1563. There were ten corporases in cases (now called burses), many cushions (some for the altar), Lent cloths, and curtains of all sorts. With the vestments we find the copes conveniently arranged under the four liturgical colours. There were fifteen white copes, eight green copes, seventeen red copes, twenty blue copes. Besides a few single chasubles mentioned in other parts of the inventory there were twelve chasubles with tunicles to match, together with a number of albes and amices. There are a certain number of " albes for the choristers." Then we pass into metal ornaments. There are two crosses, copper and gilt, two candlesticks, copper and gilt, then eleven candlesticks of latten, and two small candlesticks with branches of latten. There were also two pair of censers of latten with ships, a lectern with a picture of an eagle, with hangings of arras, curtains, altar linen. We must not forget twenty-four stoles and twenty-two fannells, now commonly called maniples, two mitres and a pontifical ring, gloves, and buskins.

Ecclesiastical Vestments.

'Then at the end of the inventory, apart by themselves, are some few copes, tunicles, and chasubles, given by Mr. Parkhurst and Mr. Selinger; both these names occur in the list of the first holders of Prebends in Christ Church; and also a list of ornaments given by "the Late Lord Cardinall Poole." These are more plainly the results of the Marian reaction, and their treatment is noteworthy. All Cardinal Pole's silver ornaments, candlesticks, cross, censer, mitre, crosier, holy water pot, crismatory, are marked as "defaced," though like ornaments may be found in the body of the inventory above. Two pontifical rings of gold are not marked "defaced," nor are the vestments marked in this way. I have not yet satisfied myself of the cause of this different treatment, but it would seem to be likely that the destruction is due to some reason personal to Cardinal Pole, not that crosses, mitres, candlesticks, and censers are all superstitious rubbish; but that some must be destroyed, while others were to be retained for use in the church. Copes, we know, were used by the celebrant, epistoler, and gospeller in Parker's time at Christ Church.'—*Letter in 'The Church Times,' Decr.* 10*th*, 1898, *from Dr. J. Wickham Legg, F.S.A.*

1563

* ELIZABETHAN CHURCH ORNAMENTS AT CANTERBURY.

'In this Inuentorye Indented is contayned all suche Ornamentes Stuffe and other Implementes remayning in the Vestrie of the said Churche in the charge and costodye of Theodore Newton Treasorer there. The one parte of whiche Indenture ys delyuered to the moste reuerend ffather in god Mathewe by godes permyssion Archebusshop of Canterburye at his visitacion of the said churche holden and kepte in the montthes of July and Auguste Anno Domini 1563.

In primis one communyon cupp wth a cover of syluer an gilte made of twoo chalyces

ECCLESIASTICAL VESTMENTS 161

Item iij chalyces wth their pattentes whereof one princypall and the other Smaller of syluer and gilte
Item two crewettes of Syluer and gilte wth out covers
Item ix girdelles wth buckelles and pendauntes of syluer and gilte
Item a white crosse clothe olde an other grene olde
Item iiij banner clothes whereof ij blewe anto ij grene
Item ij banner clothes of lynnen Stayned
Item St Thomas Banner of my lorde cardenalles gifte
Item a Streamer
Item xiij^{en} banner clothes of Sarcenett stayned
Item xiiij pendauntes for the sepulture
Item a crose the staffe thereof wrethed wth syluer and gilte and the hedd syluer and gilte
Item a nother crosse covered wth white for goodfryday
Item a pynne to of syluer to mynister balme vppon maundey thursday
Item a redd boxe wth aglasse of balme
Item a pectorell of Iverye
Item one other pectorell sett wth pearle
Item iij beralle stones
Item a canopie of redd the . . . clothe of golde
Item a nother cannopie of white sylke wth a redd cros
Item four cannopie staues paynted
Item a heres clothe of blacke clothe of golde fringed wth Venis golde and silke
Item xij clothes of golde of the beast sorte vj red and vj grene
Item vj clothes of golde of the meane sorte
Item x corporaces in cases whereof v have clothes
Item v text cussheans
Item too other lesse cussheans
Item j other greate principall cusshen of red damaske and satten
Item j other princypall cusshen of blewe worsted
Item iiij rector cusshens of red sylke embrodered
Item iiij white rector cusshyns embrodered wth deringes
Item iiij rector cusshens of blewe arras
Item vij cusshyns of white arras of bockinge
Item iiij rector cusshens of golden lether
Item iiij other cusshens of lynnen white
Item a bigger cusshen of the same sorte
Item a cusshyn of tapstery woorke
Item a cusshen of grene Dornex
Item vj cusshens of Dornex
Item ij carpett cusshens of m and S
Item j other greate principall cusshen of red satten & ray silke
Item vj lent colothes of lynned stayned for the late highe Aulter and St Dunstones and Alphege aulters
Item the crosse clothe

L

Ecclesiastical Vestments.

Item a canopie for the founte
Item viij smalle tappettes for the Rectors whereof twoo redd twoo white two grene and ij blewe
Item iiij aulter clothes whereof iij dyaper for the late highe aulter
Item one cloth to drawe over the late highe alter for lent
Item a chisible of redd satten orpheras wth golde
Item iij aulter clothes of white lynnen embrodered wth whit threde
Item ij albes wth apparrelles of lynnen
Item a Tunycle of fustian
Item iij Stooles iij fannelles and a white girdell
Item vj gilte lether crownes
Item twoo syluer Bassons lately belonging to Canterburye Colledg and . . . in Oxford in Mr Deanes custodye

CURTAYNES

Firste a payre of red sarcenet of dyuers stories of master Goodnestones gifte
Item a payre of white sarcenet of dyvers stories wth deringes
Item a payre of blewe sarcenet wth Archaungelles
Item a payre of grene dyaper sylke wth Swannes
Item a payre of red sarcnet wth crownes and m S
Item a payre of blewe and red sarcenet wth the kinges armes
Item a payre of red sarcenet Stayned
Item a payre of blacke sarcenet rayed
Item a payre of olde blewe sarcnet wth archaungelles
Item a payre of olde blewe s . . . white sarcnet stayned wth m S

WHYTE COPES

Item of my lorde Mortons suyte tenne copes
Item a white cope called the Jesse wth orpheras embrodered
Item a cope of white velvet wth archaungelles and Orpheras embrodered
Item too copes of white velvet wth burres and orpheras embrodered
Item a cope of white Damaske wth colombynes and Orpheras embrodered

GRENE COPES

Item vj copes of grene silke wth Roo buckes Orpheras embrodered wth archaungelles
Item a cope of flower de lucis and orpheras of nedeleworke

ECCLESIASTICAL VESTMENTS 163

RED COPES

Item ij copes of clothe of golde wth pomegarnettes and roses wth orpheras embrodered wth pearle

Item a cope of Raye golde wth orpheras embrodered

Item ij copes of Tyssue

Item the cope called the Duke of Orlyans goune . . . wth Orpheras embrodered and sett wth pearle

Item ij copes of veluet wth vynes and orpheras embrodered

Item ij copes the one Crymsyn and the other purpule veluet wth Orpheras embrodered

Item a cope of Iesse wth orpheras embrodered

Item a cope of satten wth Images and braunches wth vyne trees and Orpheras embrodered wth nedeleworke

Item a cope of rede veluet wth sterres and birdes and Orpheras embroderede

Item a cope of satten wth lyons and orpheras nedeleworke

Item ij copes of satten wth Imagery in tabernacles and Orpheras nedeleworke

BLEWE COPES

Item a cope of clothe of Tyssue wth Orpheras embrodered

Item ij copes wth orpheras of white veluet embrodered wth archaungelles

Item j cope w^t Orpheras of Bawdekyn

Item a cope of the same clothe wth orpheras of red satten wth garters

Item a cope wth horses and trees embrodered

Item ij copes wth phesauntes and the orpheras embrodereds

Item a cope of velvet embrodered w^t gryffons and orpheras nedeleworke

Item a cope wth the Image of o^r ladey and flowers embrodered

Item ij copes of Satten wth scuchins of S^t george and the Orpheras whyte weluet wth archaungelles embrodered

Item ij copes of Damaske wth Images embrodered and Orpheras embrodered

Item ij copes of velvet wth Flower de lucys embrodered and Orpheras embrodered

Item ij copes of veluet wth flowers embrodered and the Orpheras embrodered called bredgers

Item j of blewe welvet wth orpheras of Images embrodered wth golde

CHESEBLES

Firste a chesible of cloth of golde wth pome granettes and rose and the orpheras embrodered and sett wth pearle

Item a chiseble of coper golde wth orpheras embrodered

Ecclesiastical Vestments.

Item a chisible of bawdekyn wth hindes and orpheras embrodered
Item j of grene velvet wth flower de lucis and orpheras embrodered
Item one of blewe Damaske of goldestones gifte
Item j of white velvet called the burres
Item j of blewe velvet embrodered wth gryffons
Item j of black velvet wth flower de lucis
Item ij chisibles of blewe satten wth and orpheras wth water flowers
Item a chisible of blewe velvet w^t cyrcles of golde and red roses

TUNYCLES

Firste first a payre of blewe velvet wth griffons
Item a payre of red clothe of golde wth pomegranettes and roses and orpheras embrodered
Item a payre of blewe Damaske of goldstons gifte wth orpheras of Tysshewe
Item a payre of red velvet wth vynes
Item a payre of whitt velvet w^t burres
Item a payre of blacke veluet wth flower delucis
Item a payre of red bawkekyn w^t hindes and runnynge orpheras
Item apayre of grene welvet w^t flower de lucys
Item a payre of grene called the birdes
Item a payre of blewe welvet wth circles and roses.

ALBES AND AMYSES
of blewe apparrelled

Inprimis j of Damaske wth pellycans of gold embrodered
Item an other of Damaske embrodered wth Ryses of golde
Item ij of blewe welvet embrodered w^t roundelles or circles of gold
Item ij of corser blewe velvet w^t flowers of gold sett out licke the sonne beames
Item ij of Satten embrodered w^t tonnes of gold and Waterflowers called coptons
Item iij of Satten red and blewe embrodered w^t waters flowers of gold

ALBES AND AMYSES
of red apparrelled

Item j albe of red rased velvet embrodered wth flowers of golde and spangled lackinge the sleves and amyses
Item j of Damaske embrodered wth lyllie pottes and fawkyns of golde lackinge apparrelles for the handes
Item j of crymsone velvet embrodered w^t flower de lyces of gold perfect

ECCLESIASTICAL VESTMENTS

Item j of red welvet w^t a pane in the myddes of ye apparrelles of lyons and chequier worke of golde
Item j of rased crynsone velvet embrodered wth white griffons of golde perfecte
Item j of rased crynsone velvet embrodered w^t flowers of golde
Item j of red welvet embrodered w^t the Image of S^t laurence and St Stphens ye amyse whereof is imbrodered w^t ye name of william hull in letters of golde
Item j of bawdekyn embrodered wth white hindes perfecte
Item j of olde red Damaske w^t flyinge Dragons of silke woven

ALBES AND AMYSES
apparrelled wth white

Item j whereof the grounde is white silke nedeleworke embrodered w^t dyuers Images of golde lackinge the amyse and apparell for the handes
Item ij of white Damaske embrodered wth waterflowers of golde per fratrem Thomam bredger
Item j apparelled w^t olde white Damaske embrodered w^t braunches of golde and red flowers
Item iij apparrelled wth white Damaske embrodered wth beastes of gold lycke lyons

ALBES AND AMYSES
apparrelled wth grene

Item j of grene Damaske embrodered wth beastes of gold their hornes licke a sawe
Item j of grene satten embrodered w^t flower De lucis of gold and silke

ALBES FOR THE
choristers

Item viij apparrelled perfectly for the same
Item ij crosses copper and gilte and stave parte coper and gilte
Item ij candelstickes coper and gilte
Item xj candelstickes of latten
Item ij smale candelstickes w^t braunches of latten
Item ij payre of sensors of latten and j ship of latten
Item an other of copper
Item an holly water stopp of latten
Item iij pewter pottes otherwise amples for oyle
Item v newe towelles and ij olde for the aulter
Item a lawne for the heres

166 HIERURGIA ANGLICANA

Ecclesiastical Vestments.

Item ij aulter clothes j of lawne and ye other licke anett for ye highe alter

Item a deske clothe wth letters of nedleworke and Thomas beckettes armes in it

Item iij payre of sandals compleate blewe red and white

Item a monstrant of latten to carrie the sacrement in vppon Festyvall Dayes

Item iiij shorte alter clothes for the side aulters

Item iij pewter basons wth brdges and spones in ye costody of the Sexton

Item an Ieron candelsticke for the rectors

Item a lectrone of latten wth a picture of an egle

Item a lectrone and foure stoles of Ieron for the rectors of ye quier.

Item iij hanginges for the quier wherof one of fayr clothe of arres and the other of olde arras and sylke

Item ij payre of pontyficall gloves

Item xxiiij^{ti} stoles of Dyuers facions

Item xxij^{ti} Fannelles

Item an olde vestment of blacke worsted

Item a crosse of leade

Item a myter and a pontyfycall of coper of the gifte of my lorde of Dover the myter besett w^t bruches of syluer and conterfett stones

Item an other olde myter embrodered

Item iiij pendauntes of arras wrought wth gold and ij frountes of the same of the gifte of S^r anthony Selenger knight

TAPETTES

Inprimis j great red Tapett
Item ij other red of a lesser sorte
Item ij greate blewe Tappettes
Item j greate white Tappett
Item ij pendauntes of red sylke

ORNAMENTS
geven by m^r Parhurst

Inprimis iij copes of white Damaske w^t orpheras embrodered and water flowers embrodered also

Item a vestment and too Tunycles of white Damaske lickewise embrodred

Item a vestm^t of white Damaske w^t orpheras embrodered w^t the picture of christ in gold and ij Tunycles licke embrodered

ECCLESIASTICAL VESTMENTS 167

Item j cope of white Damaske w^t orpheras embrodered wth the kinges armes in the backe and archaungelles of golde

Item ij other of white Damaske wth orpheras embrodered w^t lyllie pottes and the sprede egle of golde

ORNAMENTES

geven by m^r selenger

Item iij copes of grene silke w^t oken leves besides other iij geven by m^r Selenger and altered into v pendauntes

Item a vestment of white sattene wth agreat crosse

Item an olde vestmende of blewe silke

ORNAMENTS gyven by the Late L. Cardinall Poole.

Ffirste a payre of candelstickes of syluer and gillt wayinge ccxxvij ounz defased.

Item a greate crosse of syluer and gilte waying cxliij ounz j quarter Defased.

Item one sensor wth a shipp and a spone of Syluer parcell guylt wayinge cvj ounz defased.

Item a myter of syluer and gilte sett wth pearle and stone wayinge iiij^{xx} xvij ounz et di. defased.

Item a crosers Staffe of syluer and guylte wth a staffe in hit wayinge iiij^{xx}vij ounces Defased.

Item a crosse wth a staffe for a crosse bearer of syluer parcell guylte wayinge cxlvj ounces di. defased.

Item j payre of gloves of knyte crymson silke embrodered wth gold and Tasselles also.

Item a nother payre of gloves of white knitte silke embrodered wth golde and crymson silke.

Item ij pontyficall ringes of golde sett wth stones of Saphore the borders wherof are sett with Turkeyes Rubyes and pearles.

Item a payre of buskyns and a payre of Shoes of clothe of golde and a payre of shoes and a payre of buskyns of white Taffate.

Item a holy water pott wth a sprynckell of syluer parcell gilte waying lxj ounces defased.

Item a crismatorye of syluer gilte wayinge x ounces defased.

Item a vestment wth deacon and Subdeacon of cloth of golde braunched wth white syluer and the crosse of purple clothe of Tyssue wth ij albes for ye deacon and subdeacon and other furnyture for ye same.

Item j cope correspondent to the said vestmentes all whiche vestmentes and copes are lyned wth Crymson sarcenett.

Item a payre of Tunycles of crymsone Taffata wth a crosse and borders of purple Taffata and lyned wth crymsone sarcynett.

Ecclesiastical
Vestments.

Item an other payr of Tunycles of white Taffata layed wth lace and fringe and fringe of golde.

Item a fyne camerike clothe edged wth golde to take the myter of Tharchebusshopes hedd et cetera.'[1]

—*Inventories of Christchurch, Canterbury, with Historical and Topographical Introductions and Illustrative Documents, transcribed and edited by J. Wickham Legg, F.S.A., and W. H. St. John Hope, M.A.*, pp. 222 ff., *Westminster, Archibald Constable and Co.* 1902.

1564

'*Item.* In the ministration of the Holy Communion in the cathedral and collegiate churches, the principal minister shall use a cope with gospeller and epistler agreeably; and at all other prayers to be said at the communion-table, to use no copes, but surplices.

'*Item.* That the dean and prebendaries wear a surplice with a silk hood in the quire; and when they preach in the cathedral or collegiate church, to wear their hood.

'*Item.* That every minister saying any publick prayers, or ministering of the sacraments or other rites of the Church, shall wear a comely surplice with sleeves.'—*Advertisements of Queen Elizabeth. Cardwell, Doc. Ann.,* i. 326, 8vo, Oxford, 1844.

1564

'The Holy Communion is ministered ordinarily the first Sunday of every month through the year. At what time the table is set *east* and *west*. The Priest which ministereth, the Epistler and Gospeller, at that time wear copes.'—*The Certificate of the Vice-Dean of the cathedral and metropolitical church of Christ in Canterbury.* Vide *Strype's Life of Archbp. Parker,* i. 364, 365.

---

[1] The extract, 'Position of the Officiating Minister, *circa* 1563,' quoted in full later, pp. 245, 246, shows that most of the ornaments of the ministers named in the Canterbury Inventory of 1563, given above, were merely retained, and not used, about the time when it was taken.—ED. 1902.

PLATE X.] [*To face page* 168.

Hier. 1.]

1564

'The King's College church [Cambridge] was hanged with fine tapestry, or arras of the Queen's, from the north vestry door, round by the Communion-table, unto the south vestry door; and all that place strewed with rushes. The Communion-table and pulpit hanged richly. Upon the south side, between the vestry door and the Communion-table (which stood north and south), was hanged a rich travas of crimson velvet, for the Queen's majesty, with all other things appertaining. Also a fair closet glazed towards the quire was devised and made in the middle of the rood-loft; if the Queen's majesty perhaps would there repose herself, which was not occupied. The place between the north and south-west doors of the church was strewed with rushes, being not paved. And in the middle, between the north and south doors, a fair Turkey carpet laid, and upon that a little joined short form set, covered also with one other Turkey carpet, and one cushion to kneel upon, and one other to lean upon, of cloth of gold, and thereon was laid the Bible in Latin. All these were of the Queen's stuff. Also there was set a chair of red velvet for her Majesty to have sat in, whilst she heard the oration, if she had forsaken her horse. On the part of the College, Mr. Doctor Philip Baker, with all his company, was in copes, standing in a length from the quire-door unto the north and south doors, orderly, as in procession-wise. . . . When the Queen's majesty came to the west door of the church, Sir William Cecil kneeled down and welcomed her Grace. . . . Then she alighted from her horse, and four of the principal doctors bearing a canopy, she under the same, entered into the church, and kneeled down at the place appointed, between the two doors north and south, the lady Strange bearing the train; and all the other ladies followed in their degrees. Then the Provost, re-vested in a rich cope all of needlework, (standing about four yards from the Queen directly

Ecclesiastical Vestments.

towards the quire, in the middle of his company kneeling of both sides,) made his obeisance and courtesies three times, coming towards her Majesty. At the last, kneeling hard at her stool, he kissed her hand, and so pointed unto the psalm, *Deus misereatur*; inquiring, "Whether it would please her Majesty to answer and say with him?" And, understanding that she would pray privately, he likewise privately said the said psalm, and after that a collect for the Queen, which done, the whole quire began to sing, in English, a song of gladness; and so went orderly into the stalls of the quire. The Queen following, and going to her travas under the canopy; and marvellously revising at the beauty of the chapel, greatly praised it above all other within her realm. This song ended, the Provost began the *Te Deum*, in English, in his cope; which was solemnly sung in prick-song, and the organs playing. After that he began even-song, which also was solemnly sung, every man standing in his cope. . . . During all this time of prayer, the lords and other honourable persons, with the doctors, sat on the high stalls.'—*Grand Reception and Entertainment of Queen Elizabeth at Cambridge,* 1564. *Harl. MSS.* 7037, 109. *Nichols' Progresses of Queen Elizabeth,* i. 158-164, 4to, 1823.

1565

* 'On the last leaf of the accounts-book [of Christchurch, Bristol] made the first of June, Anno Domini, 1565, after some blank pages, appears the following list of ornaments :—

> Two copys of clothe of goulde
> A vestement & two chesebelle*s* of clothe of goulde
> A cope of crymsen velvet & one cope of greene damaske
> two vestement*es* the one of crymson velvet the other of grene sylke

ECCLESIASTICAL VESTMENTS

one other vestement of clothe of gowlde
A chalys with A cover of Sylver & gulte
fower clarkys surpeles for clarkes two surpeles for the curat
thre towelles
A pawlle of grene & Red satyn
A pawlle of Rede sylke, spangled with gowld
[an] Alter clothe wythe Rede & grene & damaske
A nother Alter clothe of grene & Rede sylke
Two cortens of sylk
fowere kussynge spangyde with goulde
two brasse pottes
two moldys of brasse fower salter bokys two in myter & of the salmys
two bokys of the omelys
the in-Junsyonys.'
—*Some Bristol Inventories, transcribed by Cuthbert Atchley, printed by G. du Boistel and Co., Bristol,* 1900.

1565-1566

* ROCHETS IN PARISH CHURCHES. 'Botheby Pañell.—*Item* an alb—w̃ch we made a Rochet of for or clerk, A° dñi 1565.'

'Market Deepinge.—*Item* fyve table clothes xv towelles a fonte clothe a surples a rocket or ij for the clark and a silver coppe—Remanith in oʳ pishe church a° dñi 1565 Wᵐ Harvie and Wᵐ affen churchwardens so that no popishe peltrie remaineth in oʳ said pishe church.'

'Lea.—*Item* a Rochet one crose clothe ij banner clothes and one old vestment—Remaynith in oʳ Church.'

'Tallington.—*Item* two albes—w̃ch were translated the one made a surplesse for the prieste the other made a rochet for the clarke.'—*Peacock's English Church Furniture*, pp. 53, 68, 113, 150.

1565-1566

* COPES IN PARISH CHURCHES. 'Basinghā, 18. March 1565.— . . . haue a cope in the churche the which

Ecclesiastical Vestments.

wee ar admitted [by the injunc]tions to kepe for oʳ mi'ster.'

'Billingborowe, 14. March 1565.—*Item* one cope—remayneth in or pishe churche w̃t a surplesse and 5 towelles wᶜʰ we occupie about the coion [communion] but all the tromperie and popishe Ornamentes is sold and defaced so that ther remaynethe no supersticious monumente w̃t in oʳ p̃ish churche of Billingborowe.'

'Lenton als Levington, 22. March 1565.—*Item* a cope w̃th all thother thinges according to thininctions [the injunctions]—remaineth in oʳ said pish church A° dñi 1565.'

'Lundonthorp, 11. April 1566.—*Item* one cope—remaynĩge in or said p̃ishe so that wee haue no monument of supersticon now remaynĩge.'—*Peacock's English Church Furniture*, pp. 42, 49, 114, 115.

1566

* 'Thys Indentuer made at bodmynn the Sunday next after the ffeast of Seynt mygell the archangell ynn the eyght yere of the Raygne of our Soueraygne Lady Elyzabeth by the grace of god of Englond ffrancie and Irelond quene defender of the ffaythe &c. Betwyne Nycolas Cory mayor of the towne of bodmyn on thone party and Rychard Water and Thomas Cole tanner Wardens of the Churche of Sᵗ Petherick ynn bodmyn aforesayd of thother party Wyttenesseth that the sayd Rychard Water and Thomas Cole Wardens and ther successors Wardens hath taken and receyved into ther handes and kepying of the sayd Nicholas Cory mayor and of all the hole paryshe aforesayd to be used and occupyed to the honer of god ynn the same churche from the daye and yere aforesayd fourthward all such goodes and ornamentes as folowth and hath taken uppon them for them and ther successors to yeld a true reckenyng of all the same goodes and ornamentes and delyvery therof to make withut deley to the sayd Nycholas Cory and his successors for the tyme beyng

ECCLESIASTICAL VESTMENTS 173

mayor and to all the hole paryshe of bodmynn aforesayd this tyme xij monethes that ys to wete.

> *Fyrst* fyve belles. . . .
> *Item*, one vestment of grene satyn of bryddes
> *Item*, one hole sute of blew velut decon subdecon & pistholere
>> a pere of vestmentes of whyte damaske
>> one cope of red satyn of bryddes
> *Item*, a vestment of blew velut
>> one whyte cope of satyn
> *Item*, one whyte vestment of satyn
>> and more toe copes used on good fryday and a obe [albe] of sylck
> *Item*, one crosse banner of grene sylck
> *Item*, one frunt of yelo . . . grene satyn of bryddes
>> toe cortens wherof one of sylck
>> a nother frunt of Arres, a nother frunt of sey and a curtens of the same
> *Item*, . . . cusshyn of velut for the communyon tabell and
>> a cusshyng of sylcke for Mr Mayor ys chere and a cloth of cheker work for Mr Mayor ys chere
>> a shype of tyn
>> viij pere of surpeles with one new for Mr Vycar
>> iiij^{or} rachetes [rochets]
>> a bybell & . . . of Erasmus
>> ij pere of candelstyckes, a bason of laten, a lampe before the hye auter
>> one corperal of red velut & a nother of green. . . .
>> a corpus cloth one dex cloth toe stoles for sett at the comunion tabell
>> a herse cloth of velut and a nother of black bocorum
> [*Item*, a] sencer of latten
>> toe lent clothes for ye commyon tabell
>> ij polys one of brasse & a nother of yron
>> ij new vant clothes¹ [and a nold *cancelled*]
>> a sacryng bell a cruat
>> iij Jesus cotes ij red wosterd & one of red bocrom
>> iij tormenttowers cotes of satyn of bryddes of yolo and blue . . .
>> ij cappes of sylck
>> ij develes cotes wherof one ys newe [toe sandyers cotes of whyte *cancelled*]
>> a croune of black
>> a nother for . . . a . . . ell of a cross . . . and a nold crosse

---

¹ *i.e.* font-cloths.—ED. 1902.

<small>Ecclesiastical Vestments.</small>

one comouyn cup of sylver and one other gylt wch hery Cock used at weddynges . . . andry & toe clottes of led

In [witnes]s herof the partes to thes present Indentuer interchayngabelly have putte [their] seles ye day & yere above w[ritten]

Endorsed. Betwene N. Cory Mayor Ric. Wat' & T. Cole tanner Wardens. Invent' ornament' eccl'ie.'—J. *Maclean, History of the Deanery of Trigg Minor,* i. 341. Lond. 1868, *cp. Journal Royal Inst. of Cornwall,* vii. 121.

1566

'You think that the small number can excuse them: as who they say were so few as you would have them seem to be. Cope, surplice, starch-bread, gospellers, pistlers, kneeling at Communion, crossing at baptism, baptism of [by] women, cap, tippet, and gown. Item, by authority of Parliament, albs, altars, vestments, &c. . . . These few things are more than may be well borne with. By the former Book of King Edward (whereto the Act of Parliament referreth us) an alb is appointed with a vestment, for a cope, for the administration of the Sacrament, and in some places the priest at this day weareth an alb.'—*An Answer for the Time,* pp. 54, 115. 1566.

c. 1566

* 'Grosse pointes of Poperie, evident unto all men. . . . Silken hoodes in their quiers, upon a surplesse. The gray amise [almuce] with cattes tayles.'—*The British Magazine,* xxi. 625. 1842.

1567

'And when one of them charged the government, that the Pope's canon law and the will of the Prince had the first place, and was preferred before the word

ECCLESIASTICAL VESTMENTS

and ordinance of Christ . . . the Bishop [Grindal] asked them, what was so preferred. To which another of them answered boldly, that which was upon his (the Bishop's) head and upon his back; their copes and surplices, their laws and ministers. . . . One of them presently said, tauntingly, that he went like one of the mass-priests still. To whom he gently said, that he wore a cope and surplice in Paul's.'—*Bishop Grindal's Concern with some Separatists. Strype's Life of Grindal*, pp. 172 ff., 8vo, Oxford, 1821.

1570

'He sold away the jewels, copes, vestments, and other ornaments of the said house.'—*Charge against Thurland, Master of the Hospital of the Savoy. Ibid.* p. 237.

1570

* 'Novr. 1570. *Itm* yt is agreid that the vestments and other vestrye stuffe remaynyng in the vestrye shall be viewed and solde, reseruyng some of the Coapes.'—*Inventories of Christchurch, Canterbury*, p. 235.

1570

'Do not the people, with the greater part of the inferior magistrates, everywhere think a more grievous fault is committed, if the minister do celebrate the Lord's Supper or Baptism without a surplice or cope, than if the same through his silence should suffer an hundred souls to perish, and many of his parishioners to die naked with cold for fault of garments?'—*Certain Questions, etc. Part of a Register*, p. 45.

1571

* 'No Deane, nor Archdeacon, nor Residentarie, nor Master, nor Warden, nor head of any college, or cathedrall

Ecclesiastical Vestments. churche, neither President, nor Rector, nor any of y^t order, by what name soeuer they be called, shall hereafter weare the Graye Amice [almuce].'—*Canons of* 1571. *Cardwell, Synodalia,* i. 115, 116.

1573

' In the second volume of the Homilies it is said thus : that the costly and manifold furniture of vestments late used in the Church is Jewish, and maketh us the more willingly (in such apparel of christians) to become Jewish. If I do subscribe to this, how can I subscribe to the ceremonies in cathedral churches, where they have the priest, deacon, and sub-deacon in copes and vestments, all as before?'—*An Answer unto Four Articles by Maister Edward Dering. A Part of a Register, etc.,* pp. 83, 84.

1574

'It is to be lamented that even amongst us who profess the gospel, there were some . . . who, being deceived with the fair and glittering show of the Babylonish garments, brought them, as Acan did, into the tents of Israel. For why do they command a cope and surplice to be used in divine service, or a tippet and a square cap to be worn daily, but because they think it is of some authority with the people, and bringeth some estimation to their office?'—*A Full and Plain Declaration, etc.,* p. 129.

1574

* ST. BARTHOLOMEW'S, SMITHFIELD. 'Certayne things appertaining to ye churche as followethe :—

> *Imprimis* a communion cloth of redd silke and goulde.
> *Itm* a communion coppe of silver withe a cover.
> *Itm* a beriall cloth of redd velvet and a pulpitte clothe of ye same.
> *Itm* two greene velvet quishins (cushions).
> *Itm* a blewe velvet cope.

ECCLESIASTICAL VESTMENTS

Itm a blewe silke cope.
Itm a white lynnen abe (albe) and a hedd cloth (amice) to the same.
    Itm a vestment of tawney velvet.
    Itm a vestment of redd rough velvet.
    Itm a vestment of greene silke with a crosse garde of redd velvet.
    Itm a crosse bannor of redd tafata gilded.
    Itm two stoles of redd velvet.
    Itm two white surplices.
    Itm two communion table clothers.
    Itm two communion towels.'

—*Inventory of the Church of St. Bartholomew, Smithfield*, A.D. 1574. Vide *Dearmer, Parson's Handbook*, 4th ed., p. 32.

1574

* 'Recd. of Mr. Trevor for a cope of blue vellvett, with a pere of vestments of the same, xxs.'—*Church and Parish Books of Dartington, Devonshire.* Vide *British Magazine*, vi. 376. 1834.

1588

'After the public had been hearers of several sermons upon the occasion [of the defeat of the Spanish Armada] from the Cross, the Queen went, on the 24th of November, in great splendour, to the church, seated in a kind of triumphal chariot, with four pillars, supporting a canopy and an imperial crown. Two others supported a lion and dragon on the front of the carriage, with the arms of England. This vehicle was drawn by two white horses. She was received at the church door by the bishop of London, the dean, and fifty other clergymen, habited in superb copes. At her entrance she kneeled, and pronounced a prayer; then proceeded to her seat, under a canopy, in the choir, when the Litany was chanted.'—*Malcolm's Londinium Redivivum*, iii. 166.[1]

---

[1] See also Nichols' *Progresses of Queen Elizabeth*, ii. 539.

1596

Ecclesiastical Vestments.

* ST. EWEN'S, BRISTOL. 'The Inventorie of all the ornament*es* app*er*teyninge to the p*ari*she church Sainte Audoens in Brystole as ffolloweth—

> *Inprimis* a silver comunion cup wth his cover.
> *Item* i ould bible i newe booke and ii ould booke*s* of comon praier.
> *Item* i ould booke of salter and salmis.
> *Item* the paraphrases of Erasmus.
> *Item* i booke of Homilies and the Abridgment of the act*es* and monument*es*.
> *Item* sixe smale booke*s*.
> *Item* A surples, i (*erased and* Tooe *written over*) diaper towells. and a holland table cloth fringed.
> *Item* i pawle for corses.
> *Item* iii banner staves. and iii banners.
> (*Item* xvii organ pipes. *crossed out*).
> *Item* iii bells.
> (*Item* A cope & a Vestemente,[1] and three stooles. *This is crossed out, and* sold at 50 S, 1598, to T. Wackley *added in another hand. In the margin also is added in the same hand* sold for 50 S by consent).
> *Item* a braunche wth xii sockts of tinn.
> *Item* ii smale candelsticke*s*.
> *Item* vi wale plate candelsticke*s*.
> *Item* i presse (wherein the copes doe lie. *Crossed out*).
> *Item* the organ case.

---

[1] This appears to be the latest notice, at present on record, of the vestment or chasuble, until recent times. The previous extracts, in which the chasuble is referred to, show a view of the ornaments of the minister, which, though comparatively rare, was at any rate a loyal view of the provisions of the Act of Uniformity and of the Book of Common Prayer. After the close of the sixteenth century, all mention of *the chasuble* practically ceases, whilst the evidence for the continuance of the use of *the cope* is abundant, as the following extracts in the text testify. On the question of the disuse of the chasuble in the face of its authorisation by the Ornaments Rubric, and the survival for a considerable period of the cope, see Note B at the end of this volume.

It has been stated that Mr. Hawker of Morwenstow and Mr. Darwall revived the use of a special vesture for the Holy Communion about the year 1840: but this vesture appears to have been a cope. Dr. Neale began to wear the chasuble in the year 1850, and he was followed almost immediately by Mr. Chamberlain. There is, however, on record the case of Dr. Theophilus Leigh, Master of Balliol, 1726-85, who used to wear a peculiar dress when celebrating the Holy Communion at his living of Huntspill, near Bridgewater. This was later than 1780. *Vide* letter in *The Church Times* of Febry. 5, 1897, from Mr. C. F. S. Warren, Longford, Coventry.—ED. 1902.

In a different hand.

    Item iiijor canvas bolsters to knele to the comunion.
    Item a comunion frame.
    Item a old cheast wth manie lock*es* to kepe the churches record*es* and writing*es*.
    Item one faier bible of the largest volume imbossed & was bought in the yere that mr miles Hobson was churchwarden.
    Item a grene carpett of Carsey frenged

In a different hand.

    Item added to this Inventory in anno d*omi*ni 1605. one nue comunion booke, one booke of cannons appointed & set forth by the King*es* ma*jes*tie, & a present quarte pott geven to the vse of the church by myles hobson pewterer

In another hand.

    Itm a green cossen for the pollpit
    Itm a cran wth an owre glasse (*in the margin is added in a different hand* waity)

In another hand.

    Item a booke of Channons
    Item a Joyned forme for the Comunion table

In a different hand.

    A new table cloth & a presen pott given by Thos: Hobsons wife and m ffillingham and A newe surplise.'

—*Inventories of the Church-Goods at St. Ewen's, Bristol, from the Vestry Book,* 1596-1746, in *Some Bristol Inventories, transcribed by Cuthbert Atchley, printed by G. du Boistel and Co., Bristol,* 1900.

1597

'*Imprimis.* The Queen's majesty to be received at the north door of the said church. But before her entry into the porch of the said door, a form with carpets and cushions to be laid, where her Majesty is to kneel and to receive a sceptre of gold, having the image of a dove in the top, and to pronounce a prayer. The dean of the said church is to deliver the said sceptre, and to shew the said prayer.

At her Majesty's entry into the church, the dean of

Ecclesiastical Vestments.

her Majesty's chapel, with all the company of the chapel, and the dean of Westminster, with his brethren and company, in copes, to meet her Majesty at the north door of the church.

The whole quire then to sing a solemn psalm, going before her Majesty.

The Queen's majesty to come to the body of the church, and so to enter in at the west door of the quire, and so up to her travise by the Communion-table.

Upon her entrance into her travise *Te Deum* to be sung, after that the Litany.

Then the sermon.

After the sermon, a solemn song with a collect for the Queen. That being ended, the whole quire to go before her Majesty, singing, to the south-east door, where the dean kneeling, with two of his brethren, is to receive of her Majesty the golden staff with the dove in the top.'—*The Order of receiving Queen Elizabeth in the College Church of Westminster, the first day of the Parliament, October* 13, 1597. *From the British Museum Donation, MSS.* 4712. *Nichols' Progresses of Queen Elizabeth*, iii. 115.

1604

'In all cathedral and collegiate churches, the Holy Communion shall be administered upon principal feast-days, sometimes by the bishop, if he be present, and sometimes by the dean, and sometimes by a canon or prebendary, the principal minister wearing a decent cope, and being assisted with the Gospeller and Epistler agreeably, according to the Advertisements published ann. 7 Elizabethæ.'

'In the time of divine service and prayers, in all cathedral and collegiate churches, when there is no Communion, it shall be sufficient to wear surplices: saving that all deans, masters, and heads of collegiate churches, canons, and prebendaries, being graduates, shall daily, at

ECCLESIASTICAL VESTMENTS 181

the times both of prayer and preaching, wear with their surplices such hoods as are agreeable to their degrees.'— *Canons* xxiv., xxv.

1605

'At the chapel . . . the Lord Archbishop of Canterbury, assisted with the deans of Canterbury and of the chapel, in rich copes, received the child; and bringing the child into the traverse, the quire sung certain anthems, and the lords took one side of the stalls, and the ladies the other.'—*Christening of the Princess Mary. Nichols' Progresses of James I.*, i. 512.

1605

'The lords embassadors and their great train took up all the stalls, where they continued about half-an-hour, while the quire-men, vested in their rich copes, with their choristers, sang three several anthems with most exquisite voices before them.'—*Westminster Abbey; Visit of the French Ambassadors.* Vide *Hacket's Life of Williams*, i. 210.

1605

'As for copes, surplices, crosses, candles at noondays, and such like superstitious ornaments, rites, and ceremonies . . . we affirm that they ought to be cast away.' —*Certain Demands with their Grounds, etc.*, p. 29, 1605.

1607

'As for the cope appointed by the 24th Canon, by the principal Minister to be worn, when he ministers the Communion in collegiate and cathedral churches, we need not here trouble ourselves at all, for there is none that I know or hear of in such places that refuse therein to conform themselves.'—*A Brotherly Persuasion to Unity, etc.*, by Thomas Sparke, D.D., p. 18, 4to, 1607.

1612-1613

Ecclesiastical Vestments.

'The chapel [at Whitehall] was in royal sort adorned: the upper end of it was hung with very rich hangings, containing part of the history of the Acts of the Apostles, and the Communion-table was furnished with rich plate. . . . The royal assembly being . . . settled in the chapel, the organ ceased, and the gentlemen of the chapel sung a full anthem; and then the Bishop of Bath and Wells, dean of his Majesty's chapel [Dr. Montague], went into the pulpit, which stood at the foot of the step before the Communion-table, and preached upon the second of S. John, the marriage of Cana in Galilee: and the sermon being ended, (which continued not much above an half-hour,) the choir began another anthem. . . . While the choir was singing the anthem, the Archbishop of Canterbury and dean of the chapel went into the vestry, and put on their rich copes, and came to the Communion-table, where they stood till the anthem was ended. They then ascended the hautpas, where these two great princes were married by the Archbishop of Canterbury, in all points according to the Book of Common Prayer.'—*Marriage of Princess Elizabeth. Nichols' Progresses of James I.*, ii. 546, 547.

1617

'When he [King James I.] received the Communion in this cathedral church upon Easter-day, 1617 . . . two copes indeed were worn, but decent, as the canons prescribe.'—*Canterbury's Cruelty, by Peter Smart*, p. 19.

1617

* 'The Book of Benefactors records the gift of a rich cope in 1617 by Jo. Marsten, the Vicar.'—*Walcott's Hist. of Christchurch, Hants*, 2nd ed. p. 81.

ECCLESIASTICAL VESTMENTS 183

c. 1619

'*As were in use.* And then were in use, not a surplice and hood, as we now use, but a plain white alb, with a vestment or cope over it; and therefore, according to this rubrick, we are all still bound to wear albs and vestments, as have been so long time worn in the Church of God, howsoever it is neglected. For the disuse of these ornaments, we may thank them that came from Geneva, and in the beginning of Queen Elizabeth's reign, who, being set in places of government, suffered every negligent priest to do what him listed, so he would but profess indifference and opposition in all things (though never so lawful otherwise) against the Church of Rome, and the ceremonies therein used. If any man shall answer, that now the 58th canon hath appointed it otherwise, and that these things are alterable by the discretion of the Church wherein we live; I answer, that such matters are to be altered by the same authority wherewith they were established; and that if that authority be the Convocation of the clergy, as I think it is (only that) that the 14th canon commands us, to observe all the ceremonies prescribed in this book, I would fain know how we should observe both canons?'—*Bp. Overall's Notes in Nicholls' Commentary on the Prayer Book*, p. 18.

1620

'Upon Midlent Sunday, anno 1620, accompanied by the prince [Charles I.], attended by the Marquis of Buckingham, the bishops, lords, and most of the principal gentlemen about the court, he [James I.] intended to visit St. Paul's. From Temple-bar he was conducted in most solemn manner by the Lord Mayor and Aldermen of London; and at his entrance into church, received under a canopy by the dean and canons, attired in rich copes and other eccleciastical habits. Being by them brought into the quire, he heard with very great rever-

Ecclesiastical Vestments.

ence and devotion the divine service of the day, most solemnly performed with organs, cornets, and sagbuts, accompanied and intermingled with such excellent voices that seemed rather to enchant than chant.'—*Cyprianus Anglicus*, 1. i. 52.

'The king [James I.] entered at the great west door of Paul's, where he kneeled, and having ended his orisons, he was received by the dean and chapter of that church, being all in rich copes. The canopy was supported by the archdeacons of the diocese, and other doctors of divinity, being likewise all in rich copes. The gentlemen of the king's chapel and the quire of Paul's were likewise all in rich copes, and so with solemn singing brought the king into the quire, through which he went unto his traverse, which was set up on the south side of the high altar: and it being then three of the clock, they began to celebrate divine service, which was solemnly performed with organs, cornets, and sagbuts.'—*Howes' Chronicle, cited in Nichols' Progresses of James I.*, iv. 601.

1625

* 'Have you a comely large Surplice, with wide and long sleeves?'—*Visitation Article of Bp. Andrewes.*

1625-1649

'The third sort of innovations in my chapel charged against me, is the setting up of a *Credentia*, or side-table, my own and my chaplains' bowing towards the table or altar at our approaches to it, our going in and out from the chapel; my chaplains' with my own using of copes therein, at the celebration of the Lord's Supper, and solemn consecration of Bishops, attested by Dr. Heywood my own chaplain, who confessed that he celebrated the Sacrament at Lambeth Chapel in a cope; that my other chaplains did the like, and that he thought I was sometimes present when they did it; that the bread, when the Sacrament was administered, was first laid upon the *Credentia*, from whence he took it in his hand, and then carried it to, and kneeling down upon his knee presented it, laid it on the Lord's Table, on which there were candlesticks with tapers, but not burning, as he had seen them at Whitehall; which Mr. Cordwell, once my servant, likewise deposed, adding that I was present sometimes when this was done, and that my chaplains bowed down thrice towards the altar at their approaches to it.

'To which I answer—*First*, that I took my pattern of the *Credentia*, from Bishop Andrewes' chapel. *Secondly*, that this bowing towards the altar was used in the king's chapel and in many cathedrals, both in Queen Elizabeth and King James their reigns. *Thirdly*, that the use of copes is prescribed by the 24th Canon of our Church, anno 1603. . . . This therefore is no innovation.'—*Abp. Laud's Defence, in Rushworth's Collections, Second Part*, pp. 279-280, fol. 1680.

1625-1649

'He [Archbp. Williams] also repaired one side of Lincoln College in Oxford, and built a chapel there, where the Mysteries of our Saviour Christ, while he was upon earth, being neatly coloured in the glass windows, make a great and solemn appearance. The screen and lining of the walls is of cedar-wood. The copes, the plate, and all sorts of furniture for the Holy Table, being rich and suitable.'—*Hacket's Life of Williams*, p. 146, 8vo, 1715.

1625-1649

'There was not that care and moderation used in reforming the cathedral church [Norwich] bordering upon my palace. It is no other than tragical to relate the carnage of that furious sacrilege whereof our eyes and ears were the sad witnesses under the authority and presence of Linsey, Toftes the Sheriff, and Greenwood. Lord, what

Ecclesiastical Vestments.

work was here! what clattering of glasses! what beating down of walls! what tearing up of monuments! what pulling down of seats! what wresting out of iron and brass from the windows and graves! what defacing of arms! what demolishing of curious stone-work that had not any representation in the world, but only the cost of the founder and skill of the mason! what tooting and piping upon the destroyed organ-pipes! and what a hideous triumph on the market-day before all the country! when, in a kind of sacrilegious and profane procession, all the organ-pipes, vestments, both copes and surplices, together with the leaden cross, which had been newly sawn down from over the Green-yard pulpit, and the service-books and singing-books that could be had, were carried to the fire in the public market-place; a lewd wretch walking before the train, in his cope trailing in the dirt, with a service-book in his hand, imitating in an impious scorn the tune, and usurping the words of the Litany used formerly in the Church.'—*Bishop Hall's Hard Measure. Select Works by Pratt*, vol. i. pp. lv-lvi.

1626

CONSECRATION OF WHITE, BISHOP OF CARLISLE, IN DURHAM CATHEDRAL. 'The service executed by John Cosin, Archdeacon of the East Riding in York, the sermon by him preached.

'The hymns and psalms sung solemnly by the choice of the king's quire, with those of St. Paul and Westminster.

'The Communion-service, and the consecration, executed by the Bishop of Durham.

'The Epistle read ⎫ in the king's ⎰ by John Cosin,
'The Gospel read ⎭   copes   ⎱ by H. Wickham,
                                    Archdeacons of York.

'The offertory solemnly made by more than twenty persons, bishops, doctors, and other divines of note.'—*Cosin's Works*, i. 85, *Lib. Anglo-Cath. Theol.*

1627

* 'Have you a comely and a large surplice, with wide and long sleeves?'—*Visitation Articles of Archdn. Cosin.*

1628

DURHAM CATHEDRAL. 'But what a trick is this which our new-fangled ceremony-mongers have taken up of late, to go in a cope to the altar, to say two or three prayers after the sermon? Why use they this ceremony, not mentioned in the Communion Book or Canons? Why suffer they not the preacher to dismiss the congregation with the blessing of God's peace, as was wont to be done, and our last bishop esteemed to be best? How dare they put off and put on a cope so often in one service, not only to pray, but to read the Epistle and Gospel and Ten Commandments at the altar only? . . . Is it because they are enamoured of copes? do they dote upon copes? or are the psalms and chapters, read in the body of the church, not such good gospel, nor so worthy to be coped? or is there so near affinity between copes and altars, are they so married together, that they cannot be parted? . . . Again, why sing they the Nicene Creed in a cope at the altar, the book appointing it to be said as the Apostles' Creed is said, not sung. . . . A decent cope is commanded by our canons to be used sometimes, only at the Communion. Whether a stately cope, a sumptuous cope, a cope embroidered with idols of silver, gold, and pearl; a mock cope, a scornful cope, used a long time at mass and May games, as some of ours were; whether, I say, such a cope be a decent cope, fit for the Lord's Table, judge ye, beloved.'—*Sermon by Peter Smart*, pp. 18-25.

1633

'That the copes which are consecrated for the use of our chapel be delivered to the dean to be kept upon

Ecclesiastical Vestments.

inventory by him, and in a standard provided for that purpose, and to be used at the celebration of the Sacrament in our chapel-royal.'—*Instructions of Charles I. to be observed in the Chapel Royal of Holyrood. Cyprianus Anglicus*, II. iv. 11.

1634

YORK CATHEDRAL. 'The sumptuous ornaments and vestments belonging to this cathedral are carefully kept in the vestry aforesaid, viz. the gorgeous canopy, the rich Communion Table-cloths, the copes of embroidered velvet, cloth-of-gold, and silver and tissue, of great worth and value. There the verger shewed us St. Peter's chair (which we made bold to rest in), wherein all the archbishops are installed; two double-gilt coronets, the tops with globes and crosses to set on either side of his grace, upon his said instalment, when he takes his oath: these are called his dignities. In this consecrated place is a dainty, sweet, clear well, of which we tasted for the saint's sake.'

DURHAM CATHEDRAL. 'The vestry, and therein we saw divers fair copes of several rich works of crimson satin embroidered with embossed work of silver, beset all over with cherubims curiously wrought to life. A black cope wrought with gold, with divers images in colours. A high altar-cloth of crimson velvet to cover the Table; another of purple velvet to hang above; and a third of crimson and purple to lay beneath, and four other rich copes and vestments. And although they cannot shew the like royal gift of plate as we viewed at York, yet they glory in that rich gift they presented to his majesty in his progress, the richest of all their ancient copes, which his majesty graciously accepted, and esteemed at an high value.'

LICHFIELD CATHEDRAL. 'Rich copes of cloth-of-tissue, a fair Communion-cloth of cloth-of-gold for the high altar.'—*A Topographical Excursion in the year* 1634. *Graphick and Historical Illustrator*, pp. 94, 127, 208, 4to, 1834.

c. 1634

* CANTERBURY CATHEDRAL. 'A scarlett Cope lyned with miniuer left unto the Church by Dr. Clarck.'—*Inventories of Christchurch, Canterbury*, p. 256.

1635

'At Winton . . . he [Archbishop Laud] required them, by Brent his vicar-general, to provide four copes, to rail in the Communion-table, and place it altarwise, to bow towards it, and daily to read the Epistles and Gospels at it. . . . The like injunctions [were] given by Brent to the church of Chichester, to provide copes by one a-year for God's publick service, till they were sufficiently furnished with them: with the like adorations toward the Communion-table, as before at Winchester. The statutes of Hereford being imperfect, he caused to be cast in a new mould, and sent them thither under the broad seal for their future reglement, to be there sworn to and observed. In which it was required, First, that every residentiary should officiate twice every year, under the pain of paying forty shillings, to be laid out on ornaments of the church. Secondly, that they should officiate on Sundays and holydays in their copes. Thirdly, that they should stand up at the Creeds and Gospel, and Doxologies, and to bow so often as the name of Jesus was mentioned, and that no man should be covered in church. Fourthly, that every one should bow toward the altar. Fifthly, that the prayer afore their sermons should be made according to the 55th canon. . . . From Lincoln it was certified, that the Communion-table was not very decent, and the rail before it worse; that the organs were old and naught, and that the copes and vestments were imbezzled, and none remained. From Norwich, that the hangings of the choir were old, and the copes fair, but wanted mending. From Gloucester, that there wanted copes, and that many things were grown amiss since he

Ecclesiastical Vestments.

left the deanery. From Lichfield, that the furniture of the altar was very mean, care therefore to be taken in it for more costly ornaments. The like account from other places, which drew on by degrees such reformation in cathedral churches, that they recovered once again their ancient splendour, and served for an example to the parish churches which related to them.'—*Cyprianus Anglicus*, II. iv. 29, 30.

1635

DURHAM CATHEDRAL. 'Herein a stately pair of double organs which look both into the church and chancel ; a stately altar-stone, all of fine marble, standing upon a frame of marble pillars of the same marble as the font. When the Communion is here administered, which is by the Bishop himself, there is laid upon this altar, or rather Communion-table, a stately cloth of gold : the Bishop useth the new red embroidered cope, which is wrought full of stars like one I have seen worn in St. Denis, in France : there are here two other rich copes, all which are shaped like unto long cloaks reaching down to the ground, and which have round capes.'—*Brereton's Travels. Chetham Soc.*, p. 83.

1636

* 'Have you a comely large surplesse, with wide and long sleeves?'—*Visitation Articles of Curle, Bp. of Winchester.*

1636

'He [Bishop Wren] in the said year 1636, commanded and enjoined all ministers to preach constantly in their hood and surplice. . . . And the parishioners of Knatshall wanting a surplice, he did by his officers, in the year 1637, enjoin the churchwardens there, that no prayers should be read in that church till they had got a surplice, which they not getting for the space of two

ECCLESIASTICAL VESTMENTS

Lord's days after, had no prayers during that time there.'—*Articles of Impeachment, etc.*, p. 4.

1636

WINCHESTER CATHEDRAL. 'In this cathedral these injunctions were not only obeyed, copes provided, an altar with all popish furniture erected, bowed to, and second service read thereat, but likewise a large naked crucifix set over it, to the great scandal of many.'—*Canterbury's Doom*, p. 80.

1639

'Some zealous protestants beheld his [Laud's] actings with no small fear, as biassing too strongly toward Rome; that the puritans exclaimed against him for a papist, and the papists cried him up for theirs, and gave themselves some flattering hopes of our coming towards them: but the most knowing and understanding men amongst them found plainly, that nothing could tend more to their destruction, than the introducing of some ceremonies which by late negligence and practice had been discontinued. For I have heard from a person of known nobility, that at his being at Rome with a father of the English College, one of the novices came in and told him with a great deal of joy, that the English were upon returning to the Church of Rome; that they had began to set up altars, to officiate in their copes, to adorn their churches, and to paint the pictures of the saints in the church windows: to which the old father made reply with some indignation, that he talked like an ignorant novice; that these proceedings rather tended to the ruin than the advancement of the Catholick cause; that by this means the Church of England coming nearer to the ancient usages, the Catholicks would sooner be drawn off from them, than any more of that nation would fall off to Rome.'—*Cyprianus Anglicus*, II. iv. 107.

c. 1640

<small>Ecclesiastical Vestments.</small>

'*Such ornaments, &c.* The particulars of these ornaments (both of the church and of the ministers thereof, as in the end of the Act of Uniformity,) are referred not to the fifth of Edward VI. . . . but to the second year of that king, when his Service-book and Injunctions were in force by authority of parliament. And in those books many other ornaments are appointed; as, two lights to be set upon the altar or communion-table, a cope or vestment for the priest and for the bishop, besides their albs, surplices, and rochets, the bishop's crosier-staff, to be holden by him at his ministration and ordinations; and those ornaments of the church, which by former laws, not then abrogated, were in use, by virtue of the statute 25 Henry VIII.; and for them the provincial constitutions are to be consulted, such as have not been repealed, standing then in the second year of King Edward VI., and being still in force by virtue of this rubrick and act of parliament.

'That which is said for the vestures and ornaments, in solemnizing the service of God, is, that they were appointed for inward reverence to that work, which they make outwardly solemn. All the actions of esteem in the world are so set forth, and the world hath had trial enough, that those who have made it a part of their religion to fasten scorn upon such circumstances, have made no less to deface and disgrace the substance of God's public service.

'These ornaments and vestures of the ministers were so displeasing to Calvin and Bucer, that the one in his letters to the Protector, and the other in his censure of the liturgy, sent to Archbishop Cranmer, urged very vehemently to have them taken away, not thinking it tolerable, that we should have any thing common with the papists, but shew forth our Christian liberty, in the simplicity of the gospel.

'Hereupon, when a parliament was called, in the fifth

year of King Edward, they altered the former book, and made another order, for vestments, copes, and albs not to be worn at all; allowing an archbishop, and a bishop, a rochet only, and a priest or deacon to wear nothing but a surplice.

'But by the Act of Uniformity [1 Eliz. c. 2.] the parliament thought fit, not to continue this last order, but to restore the first again; which since that time was never altered by any other law, and therefore it is still in force at this day.

'And both bishops, priests and deacons, that knowingly and willingly break this order, are as hardly censured in the preface to this book concerning ceremonies, as ever Calvin and Bucer censured the ceremonies themselves.'—*Bp. Cosin's Notes on the Book of Common Prayer, Third Series, Works*, vol. v. pp. 438, 439, 440. Lib. Anglo-Cath. Theol.

1640

'The like [persecution by the House of Commons] happened also unto Heywood, Vicar of St. Giles's-in-the-Fields; Squire, of St. Leonard's, in Shoreditch; and Finch, of Christchurch. The articles against which, and some others more, being for the most part of the same nature and effect, as, namely, railing in the Communion-table, adoration toward it, calling up the parishioners to the rail to receive the Sacrament, reading the second service at the table so placed, preaching in surplices and hoods, administering the Sacrament in copes, beautifying and adorning churches with painted glass, and others of the like condition; which either were to be held for crimes in the clergy generally, or else accounted none in them.'—*Cyprianus Anglicus*, II. v. 14.

1640

'One and the same [with the Church of Rome] in your episcopal robes and vestments, both rare and rich,

Ecclesiastical Vestments.

as purple and scarlet, and fine linen ; . . . so also in your mitres, your rochets, palls, semiters [chimeres?], square caps, tippets, and so *cap-à-pied*. One and the same in your Liturgy, Service or Mattins, or Service-book, which even your Jesuit confessed to be catholick ; and so one and the same in all your service, dressing and garb, as rich copes, palls, and other altar-ornaments, goodly gilt plate, fair crucifixes over them, and devout adoration unto them, and praying toward the East, where your altar and crucifix standeth, goodly gay images, and loud sounding organs, and sweet chanting choristers and chanters, deans and subdeans, and prebends, epistlers and gospellers, singing-men and vergers, and a huge stately pomp and equipage, more than I can tell.

'I suppose you would be loath to have your rich cloth-of-gold copes, and the like, to be turned into coarse frieze.

'How would too few [ceremonies] leave your service naked? Surely many ways, now when I better consider it. Without the surplice and hood, the minister naked ; without rich ornaments and a crucifix, the altar naked ; without a sign of the cross, baptism is naked ; without kneeling before the altar at the Communion, the sacrament naked ; . . . without looking towards the East when you pray, prayer naked ; without goodly images, the walls naked ; without the rich copes, the Epistle and Gospel naked ; without a fair pair of organs and chanting to it, the whole service naked.

'As to that inscription which the Apostle found upon that altar at Athens, "To the Unknown God," may it not be written as well upon your whole service, which you dedicate to the unknown God ; which being patched up like a fool's gay coat of so many divers coloured shreds, wherein your service being dressed up, you think it is wondrous pleasing to God : doth not all this bewray that you do all this service to a God whom you know not, as whom your fancy frameth to be some carnal man, whose senses are delighted with such service ; as his ears

ECCLESIASTICAL VESTMENTS 195

with organs, his eyes with goodly images, curious wrought copes, rich palls, fair gilded plate; his smell with sweet incense, his Majesty with sitting upon your stately high altar as upon his throne, and to keep his residence in your goodly cathedral as in his Royal Court?

'The main, the all, and sum of all your religion is your altar. On this your goddess, all your other devotions and ceremonies, as so many handmaids, give their devout attendance. Your face prayeth towards your altar; your body boweth towards your altar; your second solemn service, (as the *Secundæ Mensæ*) for your daintier cates, must be served upon your altar, which the main body of the Church must not taste of; your third service (which is instead of the preacher's concluding prayer and blessing after his half-hour's sermon) must be served by your priest at your altar, when with his blessing he dismisses the people with an *Ite Missa est*; and all the while of your second and third service, your serving men in their liveries, or rich copes, stand and give their attendance about your altar; your crucifixes and images, like the cherubims, have their aspect and respect upon your altar; all must come and offer at your altar, while for joy your organs merrily play.'—*Reply to a Relation of the Conference*, etc., pp. 66, 100, 102, 104, 343, 344.

1640

* 'May 2, 1640. Paid for mending the Copes, 19s. 9d. —*Fowler's Hist. of Corpus Christi College*, p. 359.

1641

'And these faults [sundry "corruptions" before enumerated] there are in that Book of Ordination which is of the last edition and most reformed. In the former edition (which seems by the words of the 36th Article to be, that we are required to subscribe unto, and which it may be some of the bishops do still use,) there are other

Ecclesiastical Vestments.

corruptions, as that the cope, alb, surplice, tunicle, and pastoral staff are appointed to be used in ordination and consecration.'—*The Abolishing of the Book of Common Prayer by reason of above Fifty gross Corruptions in it, etc.,* p. 13, 4to, 1641.

1641

'The Bishop of Ely [Dr. Wren], Dean of the Chapel, and the Clerk of the Closet, Dr. Steward, being in rich copes, and having the Liturgy in their hands, stept forward, and stood by the hautpas, where the Dean began the service appointed for Matrimony.'—*Marriage of the Prince of Orange and the Princess Mary. Leland's Collectanea*, vol. v. p. 346.

1641

'In which diocese [Gloucester], proceeding in his former courses, he [Godfry Goodman] turned Communion Tables, railed them altar-wise, set up an altar or two in his own private chapel, with tapers on them (one of which altars, many say, he dedicated to the Virgin Mary); besides he set up divers crucifixes and images in the cathedral at Gloucester and elsewhere; and after the popish manner consecrated divers altar-cloths, pulpit-cloths, with other vestments for the cathedral, whereon crucifixes were embroidered to the great scandal of the people. And as if this were not sufficient to proclaim his popery to the world, he hath bestowed much cost in repairing the high cross at Windsor, where he was a prebend: on one side whereof there was a large statue of Christ in colours (after the popish garbs in foreign parts) hanging on the cross, with this Latin inscription over it, *Jesus Nazarenus Rex Judæorum*, in great gilded letters; on the other side, the picture of Christ rising out of the sepulchre, with his body half in and half out of it. And to manifest that he is not ashamed of this scandalous work, it is thereupon engraven, *that this was*

ECCLESIASTICAL VESTMENTS

done at the cost of Godfry, Bishop of Gloucester, one of the prebends there.'—The Second Part of the Antipathy . . . by W. Prynne, pp. 316, 317, 4to, 1641.

1643

'Ordered [by the House of Commons], that the Committee for pulling down and abolishing all monuments of superstition and idolatry, do take into their custody the copes in the Cathedrals of Westminster, Paul's, and those at Lambeth; and give order that they be burnt, and converted to the relief of the poor in Ireland.'—*Malcolm's Londinium Redivivum*, iii. 143.

1643-1644

'About the latter end of the same year, I find also mentioned in the Journals of the House, an order for selling the copes, surplices, &c. in all cathedral, collegiate, and parish churches. And by another ordinance of May 9, 1644, "to accomplish the blessed reformation, so happily begun," they enlarged the clause about removing of images and pictures, which before was confined to churches, chapels, or places belonging to them, to all open places whatsoever; and then proceeded to forbid the use of surplices, superstitious vestments, &c.; provided that no cross, crucifix, picture, &c. as before should "continue upon any plate, or other thing used about the worship of God": ordered the taking away of all organs; and in the close, commanded that all those copes, surplices, superstitious vestments, roods, fonts, and organs, be not only taken away, but utterly defaced.' —*Walker's Sufferings of the Clergy*, p. 25, fol. *Lond.* 1714.

1644

YORK CATHEDRAL. 'Furthermore, they [the Royalists] demanded [in their Treaty with the Parliamentary Generals] that all within the town [York] should have

Ecclesiastical Vestments.

liberty of their conscience to use their religion, the prebends to enjoy their places, and to have the Common Prayer, organs, copes, surplices, hoods, crosses, &c. Whatsoever is used by popish idolaters, they would have to be continued in use there, to beautify the Protestant religion, which they profess to fight for. These things were denied by the three generals [Leslie, Fairfax, and the Earl of Manchester].'—*The Scottish Dove*, p. 185, 4to.

c. 1650

'By authority of parliament, in the first year of Queen Elizabeth . . . for the ornaments of the church, and of the ministers thereof, the order appointed in the second year of his [Edward VI.] reign was retained, and the same we are bound still to observe. Which is a note wherewith those men are not so well acquainted as they should be, who inveigh against our present ornaments in the church, and think them to be innovations introduced lately by an arbitrary power, against law ; whereas, indeed they are appointed by the law itself. And this Judge Yelverton acknowledged and confessed to me (when I had declared the matter to him, as I here set it forth) in his circuit at Durham, not long before his death, having been of another mind before.'—*Bp. Cosin's Notes on the Book of Common Prayer, Second Series, Works*, vol. v. p. 233. *Lib. Anglo-Cath. Theol.*

c. 1660

'He does not say the mass indeed in Latin : but his hood, his cope, his surplice, his rochet, his altar railed in, his candles, and cushions and book thereon, his bowing to it, his bowing at the name of Jesus, his organs, his violins, his singing-men, his singing-boys, with their alternate jabbering and mouthings (as unintelligible as Latin service), so very like popery, that I profess, when I came from beyond sea, about the year 1660 to Paul's

ECCLESIASTICAL VESTMENTS 199

and Whitehall, I almost thought at first blush that I was still in Spain or Portugal; only the candles on our altars, most nonsensically, stand unlighted, to signify, what? The darkness of our noddles, or to tempt the chandlers to turn down-right papists, as the more suitable religion for their trade; for ours mocks them with hopes only. He gapes, and stares to see the lucky minute when the candles should be lighted; but he is cheated, for they do not burn out in an age.'—*The Ceremony Monger, Hickeringill's Works,* ii. 405.

c. 1660

'The present organ was set up by Dean Crofts and the Chapter, . . . the old organ . . . being altogether demolished by the rebels, as were the five or six copes belonging to the church, which, though they looked somewhat old, were richly embroidered. The present cope was given at the Restoration, by Philip Harbord, Esq., then High Sheriff of Norfolk.'—*Blomefield's Topographical History of Norfolk,* iv. 6.

1660

'The Bishops elect in their albs.'—*Consecration of Bishops in Dublin. View of the Prelatical Church of England,* p. 33.

1661

'And here is to be noted, That such Ornaments of the Church, and of the Ministers thereof at all times of their Ministration, shall be retained, and be in use, as were in this Church of England by the authority of Parliament, in the second year of the reign of King Edward VI.'—*First Rubric in the Book of Common Prayer.*[1]

---

[1] See Note C., at the close of this volume.—ED. 1902.

1661

Ecclesiastical Vestments.

'Forasmuch as this rubrick [*And here is to be noted, &c.*] seemeth to bring back the cope, albe, &c., and other vestments forbidden by the Common Prayer Book, 5 and 6 Edw. VI., and so our reasons alledged against ceremonies under our eighteenth general exception, we desire it to be wholly left out.'—*The Exceptions of the Presbyterians against the Book of Common Prayer. Cardwell's History of Conferences*, p. 314. 8vo, Oxford, 1840.

1661

'As soon as he [Bishop Wilson] had put on his episcopal robes, he hasted the performance of his devotions in the quire. When he entered the body of the church, the Dean (Dr. Henry Bridgman, brother to the Lord Chief-Justice Bridgman) and all the members of the cathedral, habited in their albs, received a blessing from his Lordship, sung the *Te Deum*, and so compassing the quire in the manner of a procession, conveyed him to his chair.'—*Bp. Kennet's Register, etc.*, vol. i. p. 537, fol. 1728.

1661

* 'July 2. For the President's surplice, £4, 0s. 0d.'—*Fowler's Hist. of Corpus Christi College*, p. 359.

1662

* 'For 11 yeardes of Holland att 3s. 2d. a yeard for a new surplice for our minister, £1, 14s. 10d. For making the surplice, 8s.'—*Vestry Book of St. Oswald's, Durham. Durham Parish Books*, p. 198. Surtees Soc., 1888.

1671

'Bishop Creyghton's effigy at Wells represents him as vested in a cope.'—*Ecclesiologist*, vol. iii. p. 50.

1680

'Went to see the Abbey : viewed the exceedingly rich copes and robes: was troubled to see so much superstition remaining in Protestant churches: tapers, basins, and a richly embroidered IHS upon the high altar; the picture of God the Father, like an old man, the Son as a young man, richly embroidered upon their copes. Lord, open their eyes, that the substance of religion be not at length turned into shadows and ceremonies.'—*Ralph Thoresby's Diary*, i. 60, 61.

1681

'January 1. Afternoon returned to Durham, 2 die Dom. In the forenoon went to the Minster; was somewhat amazed at their ornaments, tapers, rich embroidered copes, vestments, &c. Dr. Brevin, a native of France, discoursed on the birth of Christ.'—*Ibid.* i. 75.

1684

* 'In Wats' glossary, published in 1684, he says, with reference to the word *Capa*,—"*Coaps* nos Angli dicimus et in liturgia adhuc iis utimur." '—*British Magazine*, xv. 669. 1839.

1709

* 'Rich copes preserved and made use of by the Episteler and Gospeler in the Cathedral Church of Durham so late as the year 1709.'—*Ibid.* xv. 423. 1839.

1713

* '*Until other Order.*—Which other order, at least in the method prescribed by this Act [1 Eliz. c. 2, s. 25] was never yet made : and therefore, *legally*, the Ornaments of Ministers in performing Divine Service, are the

Ecclesiastical Vestments.

same now as they were in 2 Ed. VI.'—*Bp. Gibson's Codex*, i. 13, 2, f. 297.

1738

'Bishops, Deans, Canons, in Cathedral churches, wear a cope besides the surplice, and are to put it on at the Communion service, administration of Sacraments, or any other religious function, which is to be performed with solemnity.'—*Picart's Religious Ceremonies*, vi. 55, fol. 1738.

1746

* 'Upon the fifty-eighth canon (1604), which enjoins "ministers reading divine service, and administering the sacraments, to wear surplices, and graduates therewithal hoods," I need say the less, because it is superseded by the rubric before the Common Prayer, in 1661, which is statute-law, and determines, that "all the ornaments of the ministers, at all times of their ministration, shall be the same as they were by authority of parliament in the second year of king Edward VI."'—*Archdn. Sharp, The Rubric*, p. 203. Oxford, 1834.

1759

'I believe some of the ancient vestments formerly belonging to the Cathedral of Durham are still preserved there. If we may credit an anecdote, the cause of their ceasing to be worn was this. Bishop Warburton, who was a hot-tempered man, could never be pleased by the verger in putting on his robe; the stiff high collar used to ruffle his great full-bottomed wig, till one day he threw the robe off in a great passion, and said he would never wear it again; and he never did, and the other dignitaries soon afterwards left off theirs.'—*Quarterly Review*, vol. xxxii. p. 273, *quoted in Hartshorne's Funeral Monuments*, p. 51 *n.*, 8vo, 1840. Vide *Notes on the Purchas Judgment*, by *T. W. Perry*, p. 49 *n.*

ECCLESIASTICAL VESTMENTS

1771

* 'Paid the clerk for washing the table-cloth, napkins, the surplice, and the alb, 7s. 0d.'—*Churchwarden's Accts. of Bledlow, Bucks.*, qu. *Notes on the Purchas Judgment*, by T. W. Perry, p. 105 n.

1783

* 'An alb, a short surplice for funerels and another for the clark without sleeves, 15.0.'—*Visitation of Archdn. Heslop, Bledlow, Bucks*, 1783. *Ibid.* p. 105 n.

1784

* 'The use of copes at Durham does not seem to have been totally discontinued until 1784.'—*Abbey and Overton, The English Church in the eighteenth century*, ii. 467.

1804

'In the vestry of Durham Cathedral are five ancient copes, which were, until these twenty years, worn at the altar on festivals and other principal days of the year.'—*Gentleman's Magazine*, vol. lxxiv. part 1. p. 232.

1842

'I apprehend, that for some time after the Reformation, when sermons were preached only in the morning as part of the Communion service, the preacher always wore a surplice, (or possibly an alb or close-sleeved surplice); a custom which has been retained in cathedral churches and college chapels. . . . When there is only one officiating clergyman, and the prayer for the Church militant is read, which must be read in a surplice, it seems better that he should preach in the surplice, than quit the church after the sermon for the purpose of changing his habit. It would perhaps be most consonant with the intention of the Church, if the preacher wore a

Ecclesiastical Vestments. surplice when preaching after the morning service, and a gown when the sermon is in the evening.'—*Charge by Bishop Blomfield of London*, pp. 53, 54.

1842

'The case [submitted to me] is the difficulty experienced in resuming the service after the sermon, by reason of the requisite change of the dresses appropriated in practice respectively to the pulpit and the Communion-table. My solution of the difficulty is comprised in the following suggestions. First, what is the obligation on a clergyman to use a dress in the pulpit different from that which he wears during his other ministrations? Secondly, does not the order for his dress, during his ministrations in general, *include his ministration in the pulpit*? and thus would not the surplice be properly worn at any time for the sermon by the parochial clergy, as it is by those in cathedral churches and college chapels? But thirdly, at all events, where the circumstances of the case make the dress desirable, does there appear any impropriety in its use?

'If, indeed, it were *at all times* worn by the preacher, it might tend to correct an impropriety, not to say an indecency, which is too apt to prevail in our churches, by reason of the change which takes place before the sermon: when the preacher, attended perhaps by the other clergy, if others be present, quits the church for the vestry-room, after the Nicene Creed; thus leaves his congregation to carry on a part of the service, admitting psalmody to be such, without their minister; an absolute anomaly, as I apprehend it, in Christian worship, that the people should act without their minister; deprives them of his superintendence during that exercise, and of his example in setting before them the becoming posture and a solemn deportment in celebrating God's praises; and at length, after an absence of several minutes, during which he has been employing himself in any way but that of common worship with his people in God's house, he returns at the close of the psalm to the congregation, and ascends the pulpit in the character of the preacher. Now all this is, in my judgment, open to much animadversion. And the best mode of correcting it appears to be, for the minister to proceed immediately after the Nicene Creed to the pulpit, attired as he is—for the Church certainly gives no order or sanction for the change of his attire—and so be prepared to take part with his people in the singing, *if* singing be at that time desirable, or if not, to proceed at once with his sermon.'—*Charge by the Lord Bishop of Down and Connor and Dromore*, pp. 26, 27.

1844

'I have no difficulty in saying, that Mr. Blunt has been right, since he has preached in his surplice. The sermon is part of the Communion service; and whatever be the proper garb of the minister in the one part of that service, the same ought to be worn by him throughout. The rubrick and canons recognise no difference whatever. The rubrick, at the commencement of "The Order for Morning and Evening Prayer," says, "That such ornaments of the church, and of the ministers thereof at all times of their ministration, shall be retained, and be in use, as were in this Church of England by the authority of Parliament, in the second year of the reign of king Edward VI."—in other words, "a white alb plain, with a vestment or cope." These were forbidden in king Edward VI.'s second book, which ordered that "The minister at the time of the Communion, and at all other times of his ministration, shall use neither alb, vestment, nor cope: but being an archbishop or bishop, he shall have and wear a rochet; and being a priest or deacon, he shall have and wear a surplice only." This was a triumph of the party most opposed

Ecclesiastical Vestments.

to the Church of Rome and most anxious to carry reformation to the very furthest point. But their triumph was brief—within a few months queen Mary restored popery; and when the accession of queen Elizabeth brought back the Reformation, she, and the convocation, and the parliament, deliberately rejected the simpler direction of Edward's second book, and revived the ornaments of the first. This decision was followed again by the crown, convocation, and parliament, at the restoration of Charles II., when the existing Act of Uniformity established the Book of Common Prayer, with its rubrics, in the form in which they now stand.

'From this statement it will be seen, that the surplice may be objected to with some reason; but then it must be because the law requires "the alb and the vestment, or the cope."

'Why have these been disused? Because the parishioners—that is, the churchwardens, who represent the parishioners—have neglected their duty to provide them; for such is the duty of the parishioners by the plain and express canon law of England (Gibson, 200). True, it would be a very costly duty, and for that reason, most probably, churchwardens have neglected it, and archdeacons have connived at the neglect. I have no wish that it should be otherwise. But, be this as it may, if the churchwardens of Helston shall perform this duty, at the charge of the parish, providing an alb, a vestment, and a cope, as they might in strictness be required to do (Gibson 201), I shall enjoin the minister, be he who he may, to use them. But until these ornaments are provided by the parishioners, it is the duty of the minister to use the garment actually provided by them for him, which is the surplice. The parishioners never provide a gown, nor, if they did, would he have a right to wear it in any part of his ministrations. For the gown is nowhere mentioned nor alluded to in any of the rubrics. Neither is it included, as the alb, the cope, and three surplices expressly are, among "the furniture and ornaments proper for divine service," to be provided by the parishioners of every parish.

'The 58th canon of 1604 (which however cannot control the Act of Uniformity of 1662) enjoins that " every minister, saying the publick prayers, or ministering the sacraments or other rites of the church, shall wear a decent and comely surplice with sleeves, &c., to be provided at the charge of the parish." For the things required for the common prayer of the parish were and are to be provided by the parish. If a gown were required, it would be to be provided by the parish.

'But the commissioners say, that Mr. Hill told them at the time of the inquiry, that " he should not object to the use of the surplice, if it were not the badge of a party." This, I am aware, is a very common cry. But I cannot forbear from saying, that if any of the clergy deserve to be called a party, in an invidious sense of the phrase, they who agree in violating the law of the Church ought to be so designated, not they who observe it. But in the present case I do not think that any such reproachful name would properly be applied to either the one or the other. Those who observe the law ought to be protected from all reproach by their faithfulness; they who do not observe it, by the long and general, however irregular, prevalence of such non-observance on the part of the clergy, and of connivance on the part of the bishops.

'There is one, and one way only, in which all appearance of party and division among the clergy, in this respect, may be avoided. I mean by all of them complying with the easy requisition of the Church, that they wear one and the same garb during the whole of the Communion service, including the sermon, which, I repeat, is only a part of that service. And the experience which I have had, not only at Helston, but at several other places, of the great practical evils and scandals which have arisen, and are daily arising, from suffering the law of the Church in this instance to be set

<small>Ecclesiastical Vestments.</small> at nought, will make me earnestly call upon my clergy throughout the diocese to return to obedience to the law, by wearing throughout their ministration that dress which is provided for them, the surplice, if the use of the other more costly garments be not (as it is not desired by any that it should be) revived among us.'—*Judgment of Henry Philpotts (Bishop of Exeter) re William Blunt, Oct. 23, 1844;* cited in *Stephen's Eccles. Stat.,* ii. 2049, and *Bk. of C.P.,* i. 377; also in *The English Churchman,* No. xcviii.

Copes worn at Coronations.

1546

<small>Copes at Coronations.</small> CORONATION OF EDWARD VI. 'First. There was a goodly stage richly hanged with cloth of gold and cloth of arras, and the steps from the choir contained two-and-twenty steps of height, and down to the high altar but fifteen steps, goodly carpeted, where the King's grace should tread with his nobles. Secondly. The high altar richly garnished with divers and costly jewels and ornaments of much estimation and value. And also the tombs on each side the high altar, richly hanged with fine gold and arras. Thirdly. In the midst of the stage was a goodly thing made of seven steps in height, where the King's majesty's chair-royal stood; and he sat therein, after he was crowned, all the mass-while. Fourthly. At nine of the clock all Westminster choir was in their copes, and three goodly crosses borne before them: and after them other three goodly rich crosses, and the King's chapel, with his children, following all in scarlet, with surplices and copes on their backs. And after them ten bishops in scarlet, with their rochets, and rich copes on their backs, and their mitres on their heads, did set forth at the west door of Westminster towards the King's palace, there to receive his Grace; and my Lord of Canterbury

PLATE XI.] [*To face page* 208.

Hier. 1.

ECCLESIASTICAL VESTMENTS

[Cranmer], with his cross before him alone, and his mitre on his head. And so past forth in order as before is said.'—*Strype's Memorials of Cranmer*, I. 203, 8vo, Oxford, 1840.

Copes at Coronations.

1558

CORONATION OF QUEEN ELIZABETH. 'On the 15th day [of January] she was crowned with the usual ceremonies at Westminster Abbey. She first came to Westminster-hall. . . . There her Grace's apparel was changed. In the hall they met the bishop that was to perform the ceremony, and all the chapel, with three crosses borne before them, in their copes, the bishop mitred; and singing as they passed, *Salve festa dies*.'—*Strype's Annals*, I. i. 44.

1603

CORONATION OF JAMES I. 'The king's chaplains in copes.'—*The Proceeding to the Coronation, etc. Nichols' Progresses of James I.*, i. 229.

1626

* CORONATION OF CHARLES I. 'Fuller tells us (*Ch. Hist.* bk. xi. p. 123) that, after the Sermon, the Lord Archbishop "invested in a rich Coape tendered to the King (*kneeling down on cushions at the Communion-Table*) a large Oath."'—*The Manner of the Coronation of King Charles the First* . . . 1626, ed. Chr. Wordsworth, H. Bradshaw Soc., Lond., 1892, p. 24, note 5.

1633

CORONATION OF CHARLES I. AT EDINBURGH. 'The archibishop of Sanctandroiss, the bischopis of Morray, Dunkell, Ross, Dumblane, and Brechyn, servit about the coronatioun . . . with white rochetis, and white sleives, and koopis [copes] of gold, haueing blew silk to thair

Copes at Coronations. foot.'—*Spalding, Memorials of the Troubles in Scotland and England, 1624-1645, I. 36. Spalding Club, 1850.*

1661

CORONATION OF CHARLES II. 'A great pleasure it was to see the Abbey raised in the middle, all covered with red, and a throne (that is a chair) and footstool on the top of it; and all the officers of all kinds, so much as the very fiddlers, in red vests. At last come in the Deans and Prebends of Westminster, with the Bishops (many of them in cloth of gold copes),[1] and after them the nobility all in their parliament robes, which was a most magnificent sight.'—*Memoirs of Samuel Pepys, Esq., F.R.S.,* i. 120, 4to, 1825.

1685

* CORONATION OF JAMES II. 'The Dean and Prebendaries of Westminster . . . brought the regalia in solemn procession into the hall, being habited in white surplices and rich copes, and preceded by the Gentlemen of the King's Chapel and Choir of Westminster.'—*Sandford's Historical Account of the Coronation of James II. Gentleman's Magazine,* xxxi. 349.[2]

* 'While the Anthem is singing, ye Archbishop goeth down, and before ye Altar revesteth himself with a Cope.'

'Then followeth ye Litanie; to be sung by two Bishops, vested in Copes.'—*Coronation Order of James II., St. John's Coll., Cambridge,* MS. L. 14; *L. G. Wickham Legg, English Coronation Records,* pp. 293, 295.

1689

* CORONATION OF WILLIAM III. AND MARY II. 'While

---

[1] The Archbishop of Canterbury was 'vested in a rich ancient cope.' *Kennet's Register,* p. 416.—EDD. 1848.

[2] The Dean and Prebendaries of Westminster wore rich copes at the Coronation of Queen Anne in 1702.—EDD. 1848.

ECCLESIASTICAL VESTMENTS

the Anthem is Singing, the ArchBishop goeth down, and before the Altar puts on his Cope . . .'[1] *Copes at Coronations.*

'Then followeth the Litanie; to be sung by two Bishops, vested in Copes.'—[*Coronation Order of William and Mary*] *Heralds' Coll.* MS. L. 19; *Three Coronation Orders, H. Bradshaw Soc.*, pp. 16, 17.

1714

CORONATION OF GEORGE I. 'The twelve Prebendaries of Westminster in their surplices and rich copes, according to their seniority, four abreast, the youngest first. The Lord Bishop of Rochester, as Dean of Westminster, in a surplice, and a rich cope of purple velvet, embroidered with gold and silver.'—*The manner of the grand Proceeding, &c. Account of the Ceremonies used at the Coronation of the Kings and Queens of England*, p. 33, 4to, 1761.

1761

CORONATION OF GEORGE III. 'Children of the chapel-royal in surplices, with scarlet mantles over them.

Choir of Westminster in surplices.

Gentlemen of the chapel-royal, in scarlet mantles.

The Subdean of the chapel-royal, in a scarlet gown.

Prebendaries of Westminster, in surplices and rich copes.

The Dean of Westminster, in a surplice and rich cope.'
—*Procession of the Coronation of George II. Gentleman's Magazine*, xxxi. 418.

1821

* CORONATION OF GEORGE IV. 'Prebendaries of Westminster, in surplices and rich copes, three abreast. . . .

'The Dean of Westminster, in a surplice and rich

---

[1] 'This rubric throws into definite shape the customs practised in earlier coronations. It has continued, with some unimportant variations, to the last coronation.'—*Three Coronation Orders*, p. 136.

cope....'—*Sir George Nayler, The Coronation of His Most Sacred Majesty King George the Fourth,* p. 113, Lond., 1839.

1831

CORONATION OF WILLIAM IV. 'His Majesty took his seat: and the Bible, the chalice, and the patina were carried to and placed on the altar by the Bishops who had borne them. The Archbishop of Canterbury put on his cope, and the Bishops who were to read the Litany, were also vested in copes.'—*Gentleman's Magazine,* ci. 226.

1838

CORONATION OF QUEEN VICTORIA. 'The Archbishop of Canterbury then proceeded to the altar, put on his cope, and stood on the north side. The Bishops who read the Litany also vested themselves in their copes.'— *Ibid.* x. (new series), 195.

Copes worn at Funerals.

1559

OBSEQUIES OF HENRY II. OF FRANCE IN ST. PAUL'S CATHEDRAL. 'A royal obsequy on the king deceased was performed ... in most solemn manner, with a rich hearse made like an imperial crown, sustained with eight pillars, and covered with black velvet, with a vallance fringed with gold, and richly hanged with scutcheons, pennons, and banners of the French king's arms. The principal mourner for the first day was the Lord Treasurer Paulet, Marquis of Winchester, assisted with ten other Lords, mourners, with all the heralds in black, and their coat-armours uppermost. The divine offices performed by Doctor Matthew Parker, Lord elect of Canterbury, Doctor William Barlow, Lord elect of Chichester, and Doctor John Scory, Lord elect of Hereford, all sitting

PLATE XII.] [*To face page* 212.

Hier. 1.]

ECCLESIASTICAL VESTMENTS   213

in the throne of the Bishop of London, no otherwise Copes at
at that time than in hoods and surplices : by whom the Funerals.
Dirge was executed at that time in the English tongue ;
the funeral sermon preached the next morning by the
Lord of Hereford, and a Communion celebrated by the
bishops then attired in copes upon their surplices.'—
Heylyn's History of the Reformation, ii. 304.

'Saturday, the 9th of September, about the hour
assigned, they met together at the said bishop's palace.
And about nine of the clock they proceeded up to the
hearse, as the day before; the three bishops elect in copes,
and the two prebendaries in grey amices [almuces], came
forth from the vestry unto the table of administration.'—
Strype's Annals, i. i. 189.

1603

'Gentlemen of the chapel in copes; having the
children of the chapel in the middle of their company, in
surplices, all of them singing.'—*The True Order and
Formal Proceeding of the Funeral of Queen Elizabeth.
Nichols' Progresses of Queen Elizabeth*, iii. 622.

1612

'Gentlemen of the chapel in rich copes.'—*Funeral
of Henry, Prince of Wales. Nichols' Progresses of James I.*,
ii. 495.

1625

'The whole chapel and vestry in their copes.'—
Order of Procession of the King's [James I.] Funeral. Ibid.
iv. 1043.

1670

' At the entrance into the Abbey [Westminster], the
Dean and Prebends in their copes, and the quire in their
surplices attended, and proceeded between the great
banner, and the officers-of-arms that carried the trophies.'
—*Sanford's Account of the Solemn Interment of George, Duke
of Albemarle*, fol. 1760.

1721

<small>Copes at Funerals.</small>

'The late Duke of Buckingham . . . was on Saturday night interred in Westminster Abbey . . . In the abbey they [of the funeral procession] were received by the Dean and Chapter in their copes, the whole choir in their surplices singing before the corpse, which was carried up to a vault in King Henry VII.'s chapel, the ensigns of honor being all borne by the proper officers.'—*The Weekly Journal or Saturday's Post, March* 18, 1721.

1722

'Having all entered into the church, a velvet canopy being laid over the body, and the pall-bearers having taken up the corners of the pall, the Prebends in their rich copes, and the choir in their surplices, placed themselves after the great banner, and before the heralds, who carried the trophies, and sung the sentence in the office for Burial, "I am the resurrection and the life," with the two following sentences, and continued singing till the body was placed in King Henry the VII.'s chapel. . . . An altar, by the Dean's order, was erected at the head of King Henry VII.'s tomb. After the body was set down in the chapel, an anthem was performed with vocal and instrumental music. . . . The anthem being ended the body was carried to a vault at the foot of King Henry VII.'s tomb, the choir singing "Man that is born of a woman," and the three following sentences, and continued singing them till the body was deposited in the vault. Then the Lord Bishop of Rochester, the Dean of Westminster, in his cope, read, "Forasmuch as it hath pleased Almighty God," &c. Then the choir sung, "I heard a voice from heaven," &c.'—*Funeral of the Duke of Marlborough. The Daily Journal, Aug.* 13, 1722.

1737

'As soon as the procession came to the north door of

Westminster Abbey, the Lord Bishop of Rochester, as Dean, and the Prebendaries, with the masters, scholars, and choir belonging to the same, and the choir of the chapel-royal, attending there in their proper habits, with wax tapers in their hands, and the Dean and Prebendaries in their copes; they all joined the procession.'—*Funeral of the Queen of George II. Gentleman's Magazine*, vii. 765.

<small>Copes at Funerals.</small>

1760

'At the entrance within the church [Westminster Abbey] the Dean and Prebendaries in their copes, attended by the choir, all having wax tapers in their hands, received the royal body, and fell into the procession just before Clarencieux king-of-arms, and so proceeded singing into Henry VII.'s chapel.'—*The Ceremonial of the Interment of King George II. Gentleman's Magazine*, xxx. 540.

Clerical Outdoor Apparel.

1564

'First, That all Archbishops and Bishops do use and continue their accustomed apparel.

'*Item*, That all Deans of Cathedral churches, Masters of Colleges, all Archdeacons, and other dignities in Cathedral churches, Doctors, Bachelors of Divinity and Law, having any ecclesiastical living, shall wear in their common apparel abroad, a side gown with sleeves straight at the hand, without any cuts in the same; and that also without any falling cape; and to wear tippets[1]

<small>Clerical Outdoor Apparel.</small>

---

[1] From the previous words, it is evident that the tippet is not a cape: see also p. 217. That the tippet is not a hood, obs. *Culmer's Cathedral News from Canterbury*, p. 18,—'All this time the priest stood dumb at the altar, with his service-book, in his surplice, hood, and tippet.' This extract refers to a date about the year 1641. In 1566, Grindal, referring to the advertisement of 1564, quoted above, speaks of the requirement of 'a tippet, coming over their necks, and hanging down almost to their heels,' see Strype's *Grindal*, p. 158.—ED. 1902.

Clerical Outdoor Apparel.

of sarcenet, as is lawful for them by the act of Parliament, *anno* 24 *Henrici octavi.*

'*Item*, That all Doctors of Physick, or of any other faculty, having any living ecclesiastical, or any other that may dispend by the Church one hundred marks, so to be esteemed by the fruits or tenths of their promotions; and all Prebendaries, whose promotions be valued at twenty pounds or upward, wear the like apparel.

'*Item*, That they and all ecclesiastical persons, or other having any ecclesiastical living, do wear the cap appointed by the Injunctions. And they to wear no hats but in their journeying.

'*Item*, That they in their journeying do wear their cloaks with sleeves put on, and like in fashion to their gowns, without guards, welts, or cuts.

'*Item*, That in their private houses and studies they use their own liberty of comely apparel.

'*Item*, That all inferior ecclesiastical persons shall wear long gowns of the fashion aforesaid, and caps as before is prescribed.

'*Item*, That all poor parsons, vicars, and curates do endeavour themselves to conform their apparel in like sort, so soon and as conveniently as their ability will serve to the same; provided that their ability be judged by the Bishop of the diocese. And if their ability will not suffer to buy them long gowns of the form afore prescribed, that then they shall wear their short gowns, agreeable to the form before expressed.

'*Item*, That all such persons as have been or be ecclesiastical, and serve not the ministry, or have not accepted, or shall refuse to accept, the oath of obedience to the Queen's Majesty, do from henceforth abroad wear none of the said apparel of the form and fashion aforesaid, but go as mere laymen, till they be reconciled to obedience; and who shall obstinately refuse to do the same, that they be presented by the Ordinary to the Commissioners in causes ecclesiastical, and by them to be reformed accordingly.'—*Advertisements of* 1564. *Cardwell Doc. Ann.* I. 329.

Clerical Outdoor Apparel.

1564

'In the month of January, Archdeacon Mullins, by the Bishop's commission, visited at St. Sepulchre's church. Whither the ministers being cited and appearing, he signified to them the Queen's pleasure, which was, that all in orders should wear the square cap, surplice, and gown. . . . They were therefore prayed in a gentle manner to take on them the cap, with the tippet to wear about their necks, and the gown; (which Earl, one of these ministers, incumbent of St. Mildred's, Bread Street, in a journal of his, yet extant, describes to be a Turky gown with a falling cape;) and to wear in the ministry of the Church the surplice only. And lastly, they were also required to subscribe their hands, that they would observe it. Accordingly an hundred and one, all ministers of London, subscribed; and eight only refused. . . . On the 24th of March following, this reformation in ministers' habits began: when the use of the scholar's gown and cap was enjoined from that day forward; the surplice to be worn at all divine administrations. . . . and subscription required to all this; or else a sequestration immediately to follow; and after three months' standing out, deprivation *ipso facto*; which was afterwards executed upon some. This was done at Lambeth, the Archbishop, the Bishop of London, and others of the ecclesiastical commission sitting there; when the Bishop's Chancellor spake thus: "My masters, and the ministers of London, the Council's pleasure is, that strictly ye keep the unity of apparel like to this man," pointing to Mr. Robert Cole, (a minister likewise of the city who had refused the habits awhile, and now complied, and stood before them canonically habited), "as you see him; that is, a square cap, a scholar's gown priestlike, a tippet, and in the church a linen surplice."'— *Strype's Life of Grindal,* pp. 143, 144.

1604

Clerical Outdoor Apparel.

'The true, ancient, and flourishing Churches of Christ, being ever desirous that their prelacy and clergy might be had as well in outward reverence, as otherwise regarded for the worthiness of their ministry, did think it fit, by a prescript form of decent and comely apparel, to have them known to the people, and thereby to receive the honour and estimation due to the special messengers and ministers of Almighty God : we therefore following their grave judgment, and the ancient custom of the Church of England, and hoping that in time newfangleness of apparel in some factious persons will die of itself, do constitute and appoint, That the Archbishops and Bishops shall not intermit to use the accustomed apparel of their degrees. Likewise all Deans, Masters of Colleges, Archdeacons, and Prebendaries, in Cathedral and Collegiate churches, (being priests or deacons,) Doctors in divinity, law, and physic, Bachelors in divinity, Masters of arts, and Bachelors of law, having any ecclesiastical living, shall usually wear gowns with standing collars, and sleeves strait at the hands, or wide sleeves, as is used in the universities, with hoods or tippets of silk or sarcenet, and square caps. And that all other ministers admitted or to be admitted into that function shall also usually wear the like apparel as is aforesaid, except tippets only. We do further in like manner ordain, That all the said ecclesiastical persons above mentioned shall usually wear in their journeys cloaks with sleeves, commonly called priests' cloaks, without guards, welts, long buttons, or cuts. And no ecclesiastical person shall wear any coif or wrought nightcap, but only plain nightcaps of black silk, satin, or velvet. In all which particulars concerning the apparel here prescribed, our meaning is not to attribute any holiness or special worthiness to the said garments, but for decency, gravity, and order, as is before specified. In private houses, and in their studies, the said persons ecclesiastical may use any comely and scholar-like apparel,

PLATE XIII.] [*To face page* 218.

Hier. 1.]

ECCLESIASTICAL VESTMENTS 219

provided that it be not cut or pinkt ; and that in publick they go not in their doublet and hose, without coats or cassocks ; and that they wear not any light-coloured stockings. Likewise poor beneficed men and curates (not being able to provide themselves long gowns) may go in short gowns of the fashion aforesaid.'—*Canon* LXXIV.

<small>Clerical Outdoor Apparel.</small>

The Churching-Veil.

A.D. 1552

* ALL SAINTS', WANDSWORTH. '*Item*, a clothe serving for the purificacion of silke.'—*Surrey Inventories*, p. 46.

<small>The Churching-Veil.</small>

1573

* 'The woman must come covered with a veil.'

'The coming of women in veils to be churched is not commanded by law, but yet the abuse to be great, by reason that superstition is grown thereby in the hearts of many, and others are judged that use it not.'—*The Defence of the Answer to the Admonition. Whitgift's Works*, ii. 563 ; iii. 490, *Parker Soc.*

1603

* 'In the reign of King James I. an order was made by the chancellor of Norwich, that every woman who came to be churched, should come covered with a *white vail* : A woman, refusing to conform, was excommunicated for contempt, and pray'd a prohibition ; alledging, that such order was not warranted by any custom or canon of the Church of England. The judges desired the opinion of the Archbishop of Canterbury, who convened divers bishops to consult thereupon ; and they certifying, that it was the ancient usage of the Church of England, for women who came to be churched, to come veiled, a prohibition was denied.'[1]—*Gibson's Codex Juris,* XVIII. xii. 373, *Oxford,* 1761.

1620

* '*Item,* whether doth he give thanks for women after their child-birth : And doth he admit any to the performance of that holy action, that do not come having a decent vail upon their heads Matronlike as hath been accustomed heretofore?'—*Visitation Articles of Harsnet, Bp. of Norwich.*

c. 1630

* 'Whether have you any women which have not decently and orderly come to the Church with a vail or other grave attire, thereby discerned from the rest of the company to give God thanks after child-birth?'—*Visitation Articles of Williams, Bp. of Lincoln.*

1635

* 'Is it not more seemly, that women, when they goe to be churched, bee so covered on their heads according as in former times, rather than be so attired, like as those be which goe to a market, or a faire, or to a wedding, or the like?'—*Reeve's Christian Divinitie,* p. 174, 4to, 1635.

1636

* 'That women to be Churched come and kneele at a side neare the Communion-table without the Raile, vailed according to the Custome, and not covered with a hatt, or otherwise not to be churched.'—*Visitation Articles of Wren, Bp. of Norwich.*

1637

* 'Whether, when they come to church to give

---

[1] At this time, the direction that the woman should come into the church 'decently apparelled,' was not inserted in the rubric.

thanks to God for their safe delivery, they are apparelled with a fair white vail of linen cloth?'—*Visitation Articles of Archbp. Laud.* The Churching-Veil.

1637

* '*Item*, for 2 yeardes of Kersey for a churching cloth, 7s.'—*Vestry Book of St. Oswald's, Durham. Durham Parish Books,* p. 190. Surtees Soc., 1888.

1638

* 'Doth any woman refuse to give God thanks openly in the Church in a decent vayle or (as we terme it) to be churched?'—*Visitation Articles of Thornburgh, Archdn. of Worcester.*

1638

* 'Doth she come to church in her ordinary habit and wearing apparel, or with a fair veil dependent from her head, that she may be distinguished from her accompanying neighbours?'—*Visitation Articles of Montague, Bp. of Norwich.*

1640

* 'Doth any woman in your parish after her delivery from the paines and perill of Childbirth refuse to come into the Church to render thanks to God for so great a mercy: Doth she go thither covered with a decent veil according to the laudable and ancient custome?'—*Visitation Articles of Juxon, Bp. of London.*

1640

* '*Item*, Whether doth married Woman within your Parish after Childbirth, neglect to come to the Church to give Thankes, Vailed in a decent manner, as hath been anciently accustomed?'—*Visitation Articles of Bostock, Archdn. of Suffolk.*

1657

The Churching-Veil.

* 'The woman that is to be churched is to have a veil.'—*Bp. Sparrow, Rationale upon the Book of Common Prayer*, p. 286. Oxford, 1843.

1661

* 'The woman shall come into the Church decently apparelled.'—*The Churching of Women. Book of Common Prayer.*

1662

* 'When the women come to make their public thanksgiving to God, do they come decently veiled?'—*Visitation Articles of Cosin, Bp. of Durham.*

1662

* 'Doth any woman in your parish after her delivery from the pains and peril of Childbirth refuse to come into the Church to render thanks to God for so great a mercy: Doth she go thither covered with a decent veil according to the laudable and ancient custome?'—*Visitation Articles of Pory, Archdn. of Middlesex.*

1735

* 'A Churching Cloth of Course diaper.'—*Inventories of Christchurch, Canterbury*, p. 293.

1745

* 'A smaller Huckaback Cloth formerly us'd at the Churching of Women *struck through and over it between lines written*, cut in pieces for dusting Cloths.'—*Ibid.* p. 299.

PLATE XIV.] [*To face page* 223.

Mitres, Pastoral Staffs, and Processional Crosses.

A.D. 1546

CORONATION OF EDWARD VI. '. . . ten bishops *Mitres, etc.* in scarlet with their rochets, and rich copes on their backs, and their mitres on their heads, did set forth at the west door of Westminster towards the King's palace, there to receive his Grace; and my Lord of Canterbury (Cranmer), with his cross before him alone, and his mitre on his head.'—*Strype's Memorials of Cranmer*, 1. 203.

1548

'No mention is here [in the rubrick] made of that very ancient and beautiful part of the episcopal dress, the Mitre: but in the original frontispiece to Cranmer's Catechismus, "set forth" about the same time as Edward's first Prayer-book, the Bishops are represented wearing their copes and mitres, and with their pastoral staffs in their hands.'[1]—*The Rubrick, its strict Observance recommended*, p. 14 *n.*, 1839.

1550

CONSECRATION OF BISHOPS PONET AND HOOPER. 'Archbishop Cranmer, having on his mitre and cope, usual in such cases, went into his capel, handsomely and decently adorned, to celebrate the Lord's Supper according to the custom.'—*Strype's Memorials of Cranmer*, 1. 363.

---

[1] See the accompanying illustration, which represents King Edward and his Court, and is a copy of the 'frontispiece' referred to in the text. Mitres were worn, and crosses, &c. carried, at the coronations of Edward VI. and Elizabeth. We also find mention made of pastoral staffs in King Edward's first Prayer-book and Ordinal, and in the accounts of the consecrations of several bishops during his reign. There is an engraving of a pastoral staff preserved at Oxford, and said to have been Latimer's, in Wade's *Walks in Oxford*, vol. ii. p. 241.—EDD. 1848.

1552

Mitres, etc.

*ST. PAUL'S CATHEDRAL.

'*Item*, a principall myter all the ground worke whereof is sett with saphires and other stones in the middes.

Item, a new myter the groundwork whereof is clothe of silver sett full with perles with iiij. broches silver and gylte lynedd with crymosin velvett and ij. labells with v. bells at eche lable silver andd gylte.

. . . .

Item, iiij. myters with perles and stones sett and wroughte with goldsmith worke.

Item, a myter the grounde whereof is sett with perles and stones and wrought with goldsmyth worke, havinge manye silver plates about it gylte and manye thinges befallen from it.

Item, a staffe silver and all gylte with ij. bosses : in thover bosse are vi. apostels and divers pinnacles are lacking thereof. This staffe hath iiij. partes. } lxxxxvij. unc.

Item, a staffe all silver and parcell gylte with muche fyne worke ; in the hedd whereof ar th ymages of ower Ladie and Pawle. This staff hath iiij. partes to be joynedd together with vices. } lxxxix. unc.

Item, a staffe of timber with a picke and iij. bosses with a hedd silver and all gylte having in the hedd ij. ymages and a dragon under them. } xxxviij. unc. di.

Item, a staffe of yverie for the chaunter of the queere with a hedd and a crosse of birall wrought with goldsmith worke with vij. joyntes silver and gylte beside the picke and the bosse.

Item, iij. longe staves usedd to carie the crosses upon in processions all throughlye platedd with silver except one which is not throughoughtlye platedd with silver but to the myddes onlye.'

—*Exchequer Q. R. Church Goods*, $\frac{4}{71}$ *Public Record Office.*

1552

'The Protestant Bishops had their crosses borne before them, and wore copes, till the 1st of November, 1552, 6 Edward VI.'—*Nichols' Illustrations of the Manners and Expenses of Ancient Times in England*, p. 318.

1553

'*Item* a pastoral staff for the Bishop.'—*Inventory of plate, etc., permitted to remain at St. Paul's Cathedral*, 7. Ed. VI. *Dugdale's Hist. of St. Paul's*, p. 274, 1658.

ECCLESIASTICAL VESTMENTS 225

1554

'The effigy [of Thomas Goodrich, Keeper of the Mitres, etc. Great Seal to Edward VI. and Bishop of Ely, in Ely Cathedral] which, with the exception of one small piece in the upper part, is quite perfect, represents the full episcopal robes. The alb, which is handsomely ornamented in the orfray, reaches to the feet, which are sandaled; above these is the tunic; between the latter and the dalmatic the fringed ends of the stole are visible; the maniple and chasible are both richly embellished. [A mitre adorns the head.] In the left hand is the pastoral staff adorned with the vexillum : in the right, the Bible and great seal.'[1]—*Illustrations of Monumental Brasses*, No. i. p. 14, *Cambridge Camden Soc.*, 4to, 1840.

1555

* 'Robert Ferrar, Bishop of St. David's, who was burnt in Queen Mary's reign, left no male descendants, and Elizabeth, his daughter and heiress, married the Rev. Lewis Williams, rector of Marberth, temp. Ed. VI. Their descendants inherited certain relics of the bishop, including his seal and pastoral staff: the latter, which he had with him at his martyrdom, shewed traces of the fire, and was in the possession of the Williams family certainly as late as the early part of the nineteenth century.'—*From the Genealogical Magazine*, May, 1898, p. 39.

1558

'In the hall [Westminster Hall] they met the bishop that was to perform the ceremony, and all the chapel, ... the bishop mitred.' [*Coronation of Queen Elizabeth.*] —*Strype's Annals*, I. i. 44.

---

[1] Boutell (1st ed. pp. 18, 19), in noting this brass, says, 'The effigy itself is almost perfect; it represents the prelate in his full episcopal vestments, as he wore them after the Reformation.'—ED. 1902.

1560

Mitres, etc.

* '1560. It'm payd for beryng ye crosse and banner and stremers uppon St. Marke's day and saynt gorge's day, viij^d.

'1560. It' payd for beryng ye Crosse and banner, in Crosse wyke, iiij^d.'—*Trinity Church Accounts, Coventry,* qu. *Brit. Mag.* vi. 615, 1834.

1563

* '*Item* ij payre of pontyficall gloves.

Item a myter and a pontyfycall of coper of the gifte of my lorde of Dover the myter besett w^t bruches of syluer and conterfett stones.

Item an other olde myter embrodered.'—*Inventories of Christchurch, Canterbury,* p. 229.

1604

* 'What bishop is there that in celebrating the Communion, and exercising every other publike ministration, doth weare, besides his rochet, a surplice, or albe, and a cope or vestment, and doth hold his pastoral staff in his hand, or els hath it borne by his chaplain? To all which, notwithstanding hee is bound by the first Book of Common Prayer made in King Edward the 6 his time, and consequently by authority of the same statute whereby we are compelled to use those ceremonies in question.'—*The Abridgement,* qu. *Lathbury, Hist. of the Book of Common Prayer,* 2nd ed. p. 134.

1621

'Archbp. Magrath died at Cashel in December 1622, in the hundredth year of his age. . . . In his lifetime he erected a monument for himself in the Cathedral of Cashel. It is placed on a high basis on the south side

ECCLESIASTICAL VESTMENTS

of the choir, between the episcopal throne and the altar, on which is his effigies cut in stone in high relief; his mitre on his head, and his pastoral staff in his hand.'— *Ware's History of Ireland*, i. 485, fol. 1764.

1631

'The effigy of Harsnett, Archbp. of York, deserves particular notice, as being, perhaps, the latest instance in which a reformed bishop is exhibited in the vestments, the use of which is still enjoined by our Church in the rubrick which refers to the first book of Common Prayer of King Edward VI., and in the twenty-fourth canon. The exterior vestment gathered up over the right arm is the cope, beautifully embroidered with flowers, and having a rich flowing border. . . . Beneath the cope may be observed the alb, its upper part being fringed with lace. His right hand bears a Bible; his left the pastoral staff.'—*Illustrations of Monumental Brasses*, No. i. p. 32.

1636

* At Pembroke College, Cambridge, are 'Wren's Episcopal mitre and staff—these are rarely shown.'— *Jarold's Guide to Cambridge*, p. 66.

1645

'The crosier, or pastoral crook, of Archbishop Laud, with the staff or walking-stick, which supported his steps in his ascent to the scaffold . . . have been lately deposited here.'—*Ingram's Memorials of Oxford. Account of St. John's College*, p. 13.

1661

'Novr. 20. The Bishop of Gloucester [Dr. W. Nicholson] preached at the Abbey at the funeral of the Bishop

228 HIERURGIA ANGLICANA

<small>Mitres, etc.</small> of Hereford, brother to the Duke of Albemarle. It was a decent solemnity. There was a silver mitre with episcopal robes, borne by the herald before the hearse, which was followed by the Duke his brother, and all the Bishops with divers noblemen.'—*Evelyn's Diary. Memoirs*, i. 331, 4to, 1818.

1661

'On Tuesday the 25th day of March, the corpse of Henry Ferne, Bp. of Chester, being privately brought out of Paul's Churchyard (where he died) to the Deanery at Westminster, and there placed in the chamber called the Jerusalem : there first proceeded two conductors with black staves ; then the clerks of Convocation, procurators of Cathedral churches, Archdeacons, Deans, with their prolocutor ; then Blue-mantle Pursuivant-at-arms in his coat ; then divers Bishops in their rochets ; then York Herald carrying the mitre ; then the body covered with a fair pall of velvet, whereon his arms, impaled with those of the Bishoprick of Chester mitred, were fixed ; the Bishops of London, Durham, Chichester, and Carlisle supporting the pall.'—*Ibid.* i. 30. 5, 6.

c. 1662

* 'There is kept at the palace (Norwich) a silver mace for carrying before the bishop. It is 3 ft. 6 in. in length. The head is not cup-shaped like Corporation maces, but has an oval shield, with the arms of the see surmounted by a tall mitre. Its date is, probably, shortly after the Restoration of 1662.'—*The Antiquary*, ix. 278.

1662

'Upon Thursday the 24th of April, in the afternoon, the body of Brian Duppa, Bp. of Winchester, was (with all solemnity due unto his dignity, whereat were present

ECCLESIASTICAL VESTMENTS

and assisting most of the Bishops, the Convocation of Divines, Doctors of Law, and many other persons of quality,) carried thence to the Abbey church of Westminster, and there interred. The Bishop of Llandaff was chief mourner, and the Bishop of Chichester preached the funeral sermon. The officers of arms that directed and attended at this funeral were, Sir Edward Walker, Knight, Garter Principal King of Arms; George Owen, York Herald (who carried the mitre), and William Ryley, Lancaster Herald, who carried the pastoral staff.'
—*Certificate in the College of Arms*, i. 8, 85.

1663

'The body of William Juxon, Bp. of London, was carried to St. John's College [Oxford], and there interred. William Ryley, Esq., Lancaster Herald, carried the mitre on a cushion; Elias Ashmole, Esq., Windsor Herald, carried the pastoral staff or crosier staff.'—*Ibid.*

1664

'The officers-of-arms that directed the funeral of Dr. Frewen, Archbp. of York, were Henry Saint George Richmond, who carried the mitre. . . . Robert Challoner, Blue-mantle, who carried the crosier and pastoral staff.'[1]
—*Ibid.* i. 31, 6, 7.

1667

'The Right Rev. Father in God, Matthew [Wren], Lord Bishop of Ely, departing this mortal life at his palace called Ely House, in Holborn (in the suburbs of London), upon Wednesday the 24th of April, anno 1667 . . . his corpse was wrapped in cere-cloth, and carried thence to Bishop Stortford in Essex [Herts.] on

---

[1] It does not appear by the funeral certificates in the College of Arms prior to the Restoration of Charles II., whether any episcopal insignia were carried at the funerals of bishops before that period.—EDD. 1848.

Mitres, etc. Wednesday the 8th of May ensuing, accompanied by his children, alliance, and family, and so to Cambridge, on Thursday the 9th of the same month, where it was solemnly conveyed under a pall of black velvet into the schools, into a room there, called the Registry, (the Vice-Chancellor, with the whole University, there met together, attending it from the end of the Regent Walk, Rougedragon, Pursuivant-at-arms, carrying before it the crosier [of silver with the head gilt, which was provided by the said Bishop about a twelvemonth before], and Norroy, King-of-arms, as deputy to Clarenceux, the mitre [of silver and gilt, provided as aforesaid]), which room was hung and floored with black cloth, and adorned with escutcheons of his arms. The said pall of velvet having also the like escutcheons upon it; and being there placed with the mitre and the croiser thereon betwixt six silver candlesticks, supporting as many large tapers of wax, burning night and day about it, twenty-eight poor scholars (viz. four at a time) waiting also thereon by turns, continued till Saturday following, being the 11th of May. And about three of the clock, afternoon, the Vice-Chancellor and whole University being again there met, the funeral proceeding past thence unto the beautiful chapel of Pembroke Hall . . . and evening prayer thereupon solemnly read by the President (the mitre and crosier also offered in due form), and an elegant oration there made in Latin by Dr. Pearson, Master of Trinity College . . . [the corpse] was carried into the vault under the east end of the chapel, by him made and ordained for his sepulchre, and there laid in a fair coffin of one whole stone, on which his name and day of his death is legibly engraven.'—*Certificate in the College of Arms*, i. 30, 28-30.

1671

'The Right Rev. Father in God, John [Cosin] Lord Bishop of Durham, departing this life at his lodging in the street called Pall Mall, within the suburbs of West-

minster, upon the fifteenth day of January, anno 1671, Mitres, etc.
being then 77 years of age, had, in order to his funeral
at Aukland, in the bishopric of Durham, (as by his last
will and testament was appointed) his corpse wrapt in
cere-cloth, and coffined with lead, and upon Friday 19
April next ensuing, thence conveyed in an hearse drawn
by six horses, with banner-rolls on each side, borne by
gentlemen of quality through the Strand and Chancery-
lane, to the end of Gray's Inn-lane; a solemn proceeding
made by seventy-seven poor men in mourning gowns,
led by two conductors, with black staves, and after them
his servants, with divers gentlemen, &c. Then his
chaplains, next the great banner, borne by Miles Staple-
ton, Esq. After him, Rougedragon, Pursuivant-at-arms.
Then York Herald bearing the crosier, and Norroy,
King-of-arms, the mitre; the chief-mourner and his
assistants, all in their gowns and hoods, following in
coaches. Whence it was carried the same night to
Welling in Hertfordshire; and so, by several stations,
to North Allerton in Yorkshire; and upon Saturday
27 April, to Durham; the greatest part of the gentry,
with many of the clergy of that county-palatine, meeting
it at the river of Tese, and attending thereon to that
city; into which a solemn proceeding on horseback was
made from Farwell Hall (a mile distant), the mayor and
aldermen standing within the west gate, in their liveries,
and following it to the castle; whence, after a short stay,
a new proceeding being formed on foot, it was borne to
the Cathedral a little before evening prayer-time, in this
manner: first, two conductors with black gowns and
staves, then the poor of those his two hospitals of
Durham and Aukland, by him founded. Next, servants
to gentlemen; then his own servants. After them,
Gentlemen Esqrs. and Knights (all in mourning), with
many clergymen in that diocese in their canonical habits.
Then Sir Gilbert Gerrard, Bart. Sheriff of the same
county-palatine. Next to him the Bishop of Bristol.
Then the great banner, crosier, and mitre (carried as

before is expressed), and the corpse by eight men in gowns, under a large pall of velvet, supported by four of the Prebends of that Cathedral; on each side thereof the banner-rolls were likewise borne as above. After which followed the chief-mourner and his assistants in close mourning; and after them the mayor and aldermen of Durham, with a multitude of the chief gentry thereabouts; the whole quire in their surplices, falling in next to the chaplains at the entrance of the churchyard. And thus coming to the upper end of the middle aisle of that Cathedral, the poor people, conductors, and servants dividing themselves, the rest entered the quire and placed the corpse in the midst thereof, where it continued till Monday ensuing, and then was carried to Bishop's Aukland (about seven miles distant) in like manner as into Durham. At which place the poor of the hospitals before mentioned, attending, were added to the proceeding, made again on foot from the market-cross there, to that sumptuous chapel adjoining to the castle, by him totally built; where, after evening service regularly completed, and a sermon preached by the learned Dr. Bazier, one of the Prebends of Durham, it was solemnly interred in a fair vault prepared under a large stone of black marble, the Bishop of Bristol performing the office of burial.'—*Certificate in the College of Arms*, i. 30, 61, 62.

1670-1713

The effigy of Bishop Hackett, in Lichfield Cathedral, represents him with his mitre on his head and his pastoral staff in his left hand. His monument is figured in the folio edition of his Sermons, 1675. He died in 1670.

The effigy of Bishop Creyghton, in Wells Cathedral, subsequent to the Restoration, has mitre and pastoral staff.

In Drake's *Eboracum*, folio, 1736, are figured the monuments of Archbishop Sterne, who died 1683; Archbishop Dolben, who died 1686; Archbishop Lamp-

ECCLESIASTICAL VESTMENTS 233

lugh, who died 1691; and Archbishop Sharp, who died 1713: all these Prelates are represented with mitres on their heads, and one of them [Archbishop Lamplugh] with a pastoral staff in his hand.—*Editors of the Hierurgia Anglicana*, 1848.

Mitres, etc.

'The monumental effigy in Croydon church, Surrey, of Archbishop Sheldon, who died in 1677, appears with long hair, a mitre on his head, bands below the chin, the rochet fitting close to the body, and the chimere, with large lawn sleeves attached, worn above it. In his hand he holds the pastoral staff.'—*Mon. Arch.* p. 271. *Book of Fragments*, p. 195.

1684, 1706

'I have only to add that both the mitre and the crosier appear upon the monuments of many modern Bishops of the Established Church since the Reformation; and, among others, upon that of Bishop Hoadley, in Winchester Cathedral; and that real mitres and crosiers of gilt metal are suspended over the remains of Bishop Morley, who died in 1684, and of Bishop Mews, who died in 1706.'—*A description of the Limerick Mitre and Crosier, by Dr. Milner. Archæologia*, vol. xviii. p. 38, 4to, 1814.

1721

'On Thursday, the corpse of Sir Jonathan Trelawny, Bart., late Bishop of Winchester, was carried with great funeral pomp and state, in order to be interred at his lordship's seat at Trelawny in Cornwall; the procession was made through Chelsea, Kensington, &c. The trophies of honour belonging to his quality and office were carried before the hearse, viz. crown and cushion, mitre and crosier, great banners and bannerolls.'—*The Weekly Journal or Saturday's Post*, Aug. 5, 1721.

1724

Mitres, etc.

'The solemnity observed at the funeral of Dr. Lindesay, Arbp. of Armagh, was as follows: first, the beadle of St. Ann's; second, two conductors; third, seventy old men in black gowns and caps, the number of his age; fourth, his porter with a truncheon, sable, fourteen servants in cloaks, and steward with a white rod; fifth, two conductors; sixth, the crosier and pastoral staff, both gilt, forty-two clergy, two and two; the mitre carried on a cushion by Will Hawkins; the hearse with the body in it, with escoucheons on both; four mourning coaches with six horses, and eleven coaches with pairs, &c.'—*Mason's History, &c. of St. Patrick's Cathedral*, p. 215 *n*., 4to, 1820.

1781

* At the funeral of Mrs. Mathew (first wife of Francis Mathew, afterwards Earl of Landaff) the Anglican Archbishop of Cashel wore a mitre and conducted the obsequies.—*Genealogy of the Earls of Landaff*. Vide *Gentleman's Magazine*, 1781.

1785

* 'Learning that the mitre worn by Bishop Seabury in his episcopal ministrations, was yet in existence, I had the curiosity to obtain it through the Rev. Dr. Seabury of New York, and placed it in the Library of Trinity College with an appropriate Latin inscription. An aged presbyter, the Rev. Isaac Jones of Lichfield, came into the Library on Commencement-day, 1847, and betraying some emotion at the sight, I said to him: "You probably have seen that mitre on Seabury's head." He answered: "Yes; in 1785, at the first ordination in this country, I saw him, wearing his scarlet hood and that mitre; and though I was then a Dissenter, his stately figure and solemn manner impressed me very much." *Mitres, etc.*

'The mitre is of black satin, adorned with gold-thread needlework. The cross is embroidered on the front; and on the reverse, a truly significant emblem, the crown of thorns.'—*Coxes Christian Ballads and Poems*, pp. 210, 211, *nn. Oxford,* 1858. *In explanation of a poem, Seabury's Mitre in Trinity College, Hartford.*

Fabrics, Ornaments, &c., temp. Elizabeth

Fabrics, Ornaments, &c., temp. Elizabeth

Ecclesiastical Fabrics, Ornaments, and Observances in the Reign of Elizabeth

Cathedral and Parochial Churches

'I WILL now address myself to speak a little of their holy synagogues or places of assembly, commonly called their parish church, whereunto all this rabble of worshippers resort at their appointed seasons to hear this divine book [of Common Prayer], together with their learned priests' sermons. . . . These synagogues are built altogether to the form of the old temple of the Jews, in a long square east and west, with their holy court walled round about, commonly called the churchyard which is holy ground, and serveth for Christian burial, being altogether exempt for [from] civil use: yet is it lawful for the young men and maids to play there together upon their sundays and holy-days. But whoso smiteth any in that holy ground, by statute is to have his hand cut off therefore. These synagogues have also their battlements, and their porch adjoining to their church, not here to speak of the solemn laying of the foundation where the first stone must be laid by the hands of the Bishop or his suffragan with certain magical prayers and holy water, and many other idolatrous rites. They have unto it their folding-doors and an

_{Churches temp. Eliz.}

Churches temp. Eliz.

especial levite, their parish clerk, to keep the key. They have at the west end their hallowed bells, which are also baptized, sprinkled, &c. They have their aisles and their body of the church. They have also their cells in the sides of the walls, their vestry to keep the priests' ministerial garments, where they are to attire and dress themselves before they go to their service. They have their treasury. All the Cathedral or mother-churches also have their cloisters for their dean, prebendaries, canons, petty canons, singing men and singing boys, &c., within their precincts and walls to abide and dwell, that they may keep the watch of the temple, and their hours of orisons. Again, they have in the body of the church their hallowed font to keep the holy water wherewith they baptize, all other vessels and waters to the use of baptism being, by express law, forbidden. They have also their holiest of all, or chancel, which peculiarly belongeth to the priest, and the quire which help the priest to say and sing his service. They have their rood-loft, as a partition between their holy and holiest of all. The priest also hath a peculiar door into his chancel, through which none might pass but himself. Now this church thus reared up is also thoroughly hallowed with their sprinkling water, and dedicated and baptized into the name of some especial saint or angel, as to the patron and defender thereof, against all enemies, spirits, storms, tempests, &c. Yet hath it within also all the holy army of saints and angels in their windows and walls, to keep it. Thus I think can be no doubt made, but that the very erections of these synagogues (whether they were by the heathens or papists) were idolatrous.

'But here I look to have objected against me for the defence of the present state of them, that now (thanks be to God) they are quite purged of all these idols in the walls and windows, and used to the pure worship of God; therefore it do not well so to write of them in this estate. . . . How then (I answer) do they still stand in their old idolatrous shapes, with their ancient appurten-

FABRICS, ORNAMENTS, ETC. 241

ances, with their courts, cells, aisles, chancel, bells, &c. Can these remain, and all idolatrous shapes and relicks be purged from them? which are so inseparably inherent unto the whole building, as it can never be cleansed of this fretting leprosy until it be desolate, laid on heaps, as their younger sisters the abbeys and monasteries are. We see how suddenly, even in few days, they may be replenished and garnished with all their idols again. We had a late proof thereof in Queen Mary's time, which is not yet taken out of the common people's minds; who, in doubt of the like hereafter, partly upon superstition, but generally because they would not be at the like charge to buy new, have reserved the old relicks still: some of them standing up in their church windows, others kept in their chests and vestries; yea, sundry of them are still in use, as their bells, font, organs, copes, surplices, the covering cloth of the altar, &c., which way can these be purged so long as they remain in this shape? Their whole church also, is it not still a fit shrine to receive all the rest? What letteth but they might not be set up again (if the idols were in readiness) in one hour? seeing their very roomths still remain as they left them, and want but a little sweeping so that every saint may know and take his old place again. And as it standeth with the whole frame of their church walls, windows, and implements, so standeth it in like manner with the whole ministry of the church, from the highest bishop to the lowest priest, curate, preacher, or half-priest. They may altogether within the space of one hour, with a little changing of their copy, serve again in their old roomths which they held in the Church of Rome, to which this ministry of theirs a great deal better fitteth than unto the Church of Christ, which can bear no such adulterate and antichristian ministry. Well then you see what good reformation they have made, and how thoroughly they have purged their churches both within and without, from the very foundation to the covering stone thereof. So that now they must be driven either absolutely to justify these their

Churches temp. Eliz.

cathedral and parish churches in this form, with these appurtenances, furniture, and use, by the word of God, or else we may resolutely by the same word detest them as abominable idols.'[1]—*A brief Discourse of the False Church*, pp. 129, 132.

Celebration of Divine Service

'In all their order of service there is no edification according to the rule of the Apostle, but confusion. They toss the psalms in most places like tennis-balls. . . . The people, some standing, some walking, some talking, some reading, some praying by themselves, attend not to the minister. He again posteth it over as fast as he can gallop; for either he hath two places to serve, or else there are some games to be played in the afternoon, as lying for the whetstone, heathenish dancing for the ring, a bear or a bull to be baited, or else Jackanapes to ride on horseback, or an interlude to be played, and if no place else can be gotten, this interlude must be played in the church, &c. Now the people sit, and now they stand up. When the Old Testament is read, or the lessons, they make no reverence; but when the Gospel cometh, then they all stand up. . . . When Jesus is named, then off goeth the cap, and down goeth

---

[1] This extract, and many others in the *Hierurgia*, may be cited to prove that 'the changes effected by the Reformers of the Anglican Church, in the sixteenth century, neither extended nor were intended to extend either to injure or deface the interior aspect of our churches beyond what was rendered necessary by the destruction and obliteration of matters which had been or might again be perverted to superstitious purposes.' (*British Critic*, No. l. p. 385.) And that to the proceedings which took place at the Reformation 'we cannot with justice attribute the whole extent of mutilation and the melancholy air of desolation and baldness observable in too many of our churches.' (*Markland's Remarks on English Churches*, p. 16, First Edit.) These were the fruits of a subsequent period, that of 'the ascendancy of the puritanic faction under Cromwell, to whose withering influence,' remarks Mr. Pugin, 'half the departures from solemnity and ancient observance, which so degrade the present establishment, are to be traced.' (*Contrasts*, p. 31 *n*., Second Edit.)—EDD. 1848.

FABRICS, ORNAMENTS, ETC. 243

the knees, with such a scraping on the ground, that they Divine Service
cannot hear a good while after, so that the Word is *temp.* Eliz.
hindered; but when any other names of God are
mentioned they make no courtesy at all. . . . We speak
not of ringing when matins is done and other abuses
incident, because we shall be answered that by the book
they are not maintained, only we desire to have a book to
reform it. As for organs and curious singing, though they
be proper to popish dens, I mean to cathedral churches, yet
some others also must have them. The Queen's chapel,
and these churches (which should be spectacles of Christian
reformation), are rather patterns and precedents to the
people of all superstitions.'—*A View of Popish Abuses, etc.,*
pp. 10, 11.

'And herein to deal with every particular error thereof
[the Common Prayer-book], or to meddle with the
patcheries and innumerable trumperies therein, or all
their gross follies, and more than childish, even apish
triflings, or their frivolous constitutions and customs
whereunto they bind and lesson the parish priest to say
his matins and evensong in order, to begin with this confession throughout the year, nay, throughout their life.
Then cometh the priest's general pardon through the
power that his lord Bishop hath committed unto him,
and so he proceeded to his stinted psalms and lessons,
with his certain of Paternosters ever and among; and
of Creeds, their forged patchery commonly called the
Apostles' Creed or Symbol, Athanasius' Creed, the
Nicene Creed, sometimes said in prose, sometimes sung
in metre, on their festivals, their Epistles, their Gospels,
the one to be read with the priest's face towards the west,
the other with his face towards the east; with their
versicles, one to be said by the priest, the other by the
parish clerk or people; with their times when to kneel,
when to sit, when to stand, when to curtsey at the name
of Jesus, when to glory their Lord at the beginning of
their Gospel, or at the end of their Psalms; with their

collects and anthems: this in their ordinary journal, that in their festivals, this at morn, that at eve, &c.'—*A brief Discourse of the False Church*, pp. 75, 76.

Celebration of the Holy Communion

'In their publick Communion, the priest (arrayed in his ministerial vesture) is placed at the north end of the Table, and there is to read his certain. He is there nurtured when to turn to the Table, when to the people, when to stand, when to kneel, what and when to say. The people (after they have offered to the priest) are in their place to kneel down to say and answer the priest at his turns and times, as is prescribed in their Mass-book; where (after Sir priest hath taken a say, and begun to the people) he delivereth unto them (as they kneel) their Maker after the old popish manner, altering the words and form of institution delivered by our Saviour and his Apostles, saying, "The Body of our Lord Jesus Christ, which was given for thee, &c." It were long to set down their preambles and several collects at this their Communion, as at their Christmas-day, Easter-day, Ascension-day, Whitsunday, Trinity-sunday; and how the whole quire, priest and people, glory God with angels and archangels and all the company of heaven, &c. And after they have received the priest's blessing, they are all dismissed with peace.'

'Her Majesty is here counselled, comforted, and assured, even by these men themselves, to resort still to that place for the Sacrament, where she hath found comfort in receiving it. But she hath found comfort in receiving it at the Lord Archbishop Grace's hands, with his rich cope on his shoulders, berayed with all his pontificalibus, the English Mass-book in his hands, yea by your leave with the round wafer.[1] I will not here

---

[1] In the original edition of the *Hierurgia*, several allusions to the use of wafer-bread in Queen Elizabeth's reign are given in this section of the work: these have been transferred to a section dealing with the subject in Volume II. of the present edition.—ED. 1902.

FABRICS, ORNAMENTS, ETC. 245

speak of attiring the chapel and high altar that day, and other court ceremonies.'—*A brief Discourse of the False Church*, pp. 101, 109.

<small>Holy Communion *temp.* Eliz.</small>

Position of the Officiating Minister

* 'The Comunion prayer daily through the yeare though there be no Comunion, is songe at the comunion table standing northe and southe, wheare the high aulter did stande. The Mynyster when there is no comunion vseth a surples onlye, standing on the est side of the table w^t his face towardes the people.

<small>Position of Minister *temp.* Eliz.</small>

The holie Comunyon is mynistred ordinarylie ye fyrste Sondaie of euerie moneth, thorough the yeare, at what tyme the Table is sett Easte and weaste. The preiste which mynistreth. the pystoler and the Gospyler at that time weare Coapes, and non are suffred then to tarrie wi^{t}in that Chauncel but the Communycantes.

ffor the mynistringe of the Communyon we vse (Breade) appoynted by the Quenes highnes Iniunctions.

The Euenynge Prajer in winter is Betwene Three and ffoure, in Sommer betwene fouer and ffyue of the clocke in thafernoone.

At which Praiers; Mr Deane (when he is here) and euery of the Prebendaries are presente euery daie once at the Leaste Apperryled in the Quyer And when they Preache with Surples and Silke Hoodes.

The Preachers beinge at home come to the Common Praier on Sondaies and holie daies wearinge Surplyses & Hoodes.

The Petycannons, the Laye Clerkes and Queristories weare Surplyses in the Quier daylie.

The Scholemaister for Grammer, the vssher and the quenes highnes schollers comme to the Queire on Sondaies and holliedaies in Surplises.

Thirdlie we Certefie, that towchinge the manners vsages and Behauiours, for our selues for ye Preachers,

Position of Minister temp. Eliz.

and other Inferiour mynisters with in our Churche we knowe non that lyueth vnorderlie, or to vse him selfe otherwise then is by order prescribed and permitted. By the quenes highnes Iniunctions.[1]

> Thomas willowghbye
> Willm̃us Darrell
> Johannes Buttler.
> Thomas Beacon
> Theodor Newton
> Henry Goodricke
> Andrew Peerson.'

—*The Certificat of the Vice Deane of the Cathedrall ana Metropoliticall churche of Christe in Canterburye* (circa 1563). Vide *Inventories of Christchurch, Canterbury*, pp. 209, 210.

'There is a third fault which likewise appeareth almost in the whole body of this service and liturgy of England, and that is, that the profit which might have come by it to the people is not reaped. Whereof the cause is, for that he which readeth is not in some places heard, and in the most places not understanded of the people, through the distance of place between the people and the minister; so that a great part of the people cannot of knowledge tell whether he hath cursed them or blessed them, whether he hath read in Latin or in English,—all the which riseth upon the words of the book of service, which are that the minister should stand in the accustomed place: for thereupon the minister in saying morning and evening prayer sitteth in the chancel with his back to the people, as though he had some secret talk with God which the people might not hear. And hereupon it is likewise that after morning prayer, for saying another number of prayers, he climbeth up to the further end of the chancel and runneth as far from the people as the wall will let

---

[1] The foregoing statement, so far as the vestures of the clergy is concerned, is to be compared with the extract from the Advertisements of Queen Elizabeth, of 1564, previously quoted on page 168.—ED. 1902.

FABRICS, ORNAMENTS, ETC. 247

him, as though there were some variance between the people and the minister, or as though he were afraid of some infection of plague. And indeed it reneweth the memory of the Levitical priesthood, which did withdraw himself from the people into the place called the holiest place, where he talked with God, and offered for the sins of the people.

Position of Minister temp. Eliz.

'Likewise for marriage he cometh back again into the body of the church,[1] and for baptism unto the church-door. What comeliness, what decency, what edifying is this? Decency (I say) in running and trudging from place to place: edifying, in standing in that place and after that sort where he can worst be heard and understanded. . . . Now if it be said for the chapters and litany there is commandment given that they should be read in the body of the church, indeed it is true; and thereof is easily perceived this disorder which is in saying the rest of the prayers, partly in the hither end, and partly in the further end, of the chancel: for, seeing that those are read in the body of the church that the people may both hear and understand what is read, what should be the cause why the rest should be read further off, unless it be that either those things are not to be heard of them, or at the least not so necessary for them to be heard as the others which are recited in the body or midst of the church?'—*A Reply to an Answer, &c.*, p. 134.

---

[1] 'At the Reformation, that part of the [marriage] ceremony (and it was the greatest part) which used to be performed at the church-door, was directed to be performed in the body of the church, and at the time of divine service, that the congregation might be witnesses. The *body* of the church occurs in the rubric of our present form; and when I was a stripling I recollect this rule being strictly followed in Lambeth church. Hassocks were placed in the middle aisle [passage] below the reading-desk; the service to the conclusion of the first blessing being there read, there was a remove to the Communion-rails to finish the rest of the office.' (*Letter from Rev. George North, Dec.* 7, 1748. *Illustrations of the Manners and Expences of Antient Times in England*, Appendix, p. 13, 4to, 1797.)—EDD. 1848.

Holy Days, and the Manner of their Celebration

Holy Days temp. Eliz.

'The Sunday is a governing day, and is written in their Calendar with red letters, and ruleth all the days of the week, save certain unruly days and their eves, which will not be governed by it, but challenge to themselves a peculiar worship also : they having their days in the same Calendar written with great letters too, and that which more is, their eves written with red letters. And because they are but strangers and come but once in the year, they look for the more solemn entertainment, that the priest should diligently watch, and the people wait for their coming, and make preparation accordingly. If they come in a clustre, or at some solemn or double feast, then to entertain them with new clothes, clean houses, garnished with green boughs or holly and ivy, with good cheer and much pastime, all work on these their idol days laid aside. Yet though they come but one alone, and that on the week-day, yet that week is not St. Sunday lord of the ascendant ; it is a part of his service to give warning unto the people of the others coming, that they keep his or her eve with fasting and prayer: that upon their day they keep an holy feast, abstain from labour, &c.'—*A brief Discourse of the False Church*, p. 63.

Lent Religiously Observed

Observance of Lent temp. Eliz.

'In the beginning of Lent, this year (1560), was a proclamation issued out, that if any butcher did kill any flesh that time of Lent, he should forfeit £20 for each time he did so.'—*Strype's Annals*, I. i. 368.

'The weekly fasts, the holy time of Lent, the Embring weeks, together with the fast of the Rogation, [were] severely kept by a forbearance of all kind of flesh;—not now by virtue of the Statute, as in the time of king

Edward, but as appointed by the Church in her public Calendar before the Book of Common Prayer. . . . The solemn sermons upon each Wednesday, Friday, and Saturday in the time of Lent, preached by the choicest of the clergy, she [Q. Elizabeth] devoutly heard, attired in black, according to the commendable custom of her predecessors.'—*Heylyn's Hist. of the Reformation*, II. 315, 316.

Observance of Lent temp. Eliz.

'However the observation of the fast of Lent was regarded, yet dispensations also for it were granted upon reasonable causes. This favour the Archbishop [Parker] had formerly shewed to John Fox, the martyrologist, a spare sickly man, whom he permitted for his bad stomach to eat flesh in Lent. And for the like favour that reverend man did now again address to him in a handsome Latin letter. . . .'—*Strype's Life of Parker*, I. 354.

'As for dispensations for eating flesh, they were rarely granted, and this upon the physician's testimonial. And for the most part, the Archbishop remitted part of his fees. And in all these dispensations he refused more than he admitted.'—*Strype's Life of Grindal*, 325.

'And as he [Archbp. Whitgift] was very careful of the laws and constitutions of the Church, so was he also of its rites and observances; as particularly of the keeping of Lent: being also commonly, as it was this year, required by the Queen's command and proclamation, that a consideration might be had towards sick and infirm persons, some few butchers had a licence to kill flesh; and what sort of flesh also might be killed was also prescribed them in the said licence, viz. such as was fit for the sick to eat, and not forbidden by law. Such a licence the Archbishop granted this Lent (1601) to two butchers for his liberties within the city of Canterbury; but it was with much importunity: and two more, for the convenience of the whole city, had licence to kill flesh too; yet little observing the restrictions mentioned in

Observance of Lent temp. Eliz.

their licences; besides the too great quantities by them killed. Of this the Archbishop took notice, and in some displeasure at it wrote to Mr. Bois, his steward, to have it examined and rectified; signifying, "how he was informed of four butchers licensed to kill flesh in Canterbury and the liberties thereof : and of their killing calves by law prohibited; and that in great quantity. He confessed, that through great importunity he had licensed two within his liberties there, the one in Westgate, the other in Stablegate; but that it was expressed in their licence that they should only kill such flesh as was fit for sick persons, and not by law prohibited. That he was the steward of his liberties there; and therefore he charged him to call for their licences, and to read them, and to command the butchers to observe them duly. And that if by order they ought to be bound, to take bonds of them accordingly. And that he would do very well to advise Mr. Mayor to take the like order with such other butchers as were licensed in the town. For I can assure you," added the Archbishop, "that the matter will be very narrowly looked into, and the officers shrewdly censured that shall neglect their office therein. Which advice I do write for the good-will I bear to Mr. Mayor and the officers of that city. And so he committed him to the tuition of Almighty God. From Lambeth, the 25th day of February, 1601."'—*Strype's Life of Whitgift*, II. 456.

Holy Matrimony

Holy Matrimony temp. Eliz.

'They have yet the holy sacrament of marriage solemnly kept in the holy church (for the most part) upon the Lord's day, and an especial liturgy or communion framed to the same. . . . They believe not themselves to be rightly married, except it be done by a priest, after the prescribed manner and in the due seasons also; namely, in the forenoon *at morning prayer* when matins is done, *just before the Communion* (as they

FABRICS, ORNAMENTS, ETC.   251

call it) ; and this not upon any forbidden days (as in *the* holy *time of Lent, &c.*, when men ought to fast) without an especial license from the See of Canterbury, which Popedom hath power both to restrain meats and marriage, and again to permit them, upon grave and weighty considerations, to such as will pay roundly for the same.'—*A brief Discourse of the False Church*, p. 123.

Holy Matrimony *temp.* Eliz.

'Other petty things out of the book we speak not of, as that women, contrary to the rule of the Apostle, come, and are suffered to come, bare-headed, with bagpipes and fiddlers before them, to disturb the congregation, and that they must come in at the great door of the church, or else all is marred. With divers other heathenish toys in sundry countries, as carrying of wheatsheafs on their heads, and casting of corn, with a number of suchlike, whereby they make a May-game of marriage, than a holy institution of God.'—*A View of Popish Abuses, &c.*, pp. 8, 9.

Penance

'That they should not church any unmarried women which hath been gotten with child out of lawful matrimony ; except it were upon a Sunday or holy day ; and except either she, before childbed, had done penance, or at her churching did acknowledge her fault before the congregation.'—*Abp. Grindal's Injunctions.*

Penance *temp.* Eliz.

'*First*, I wish at every public penance a sermon, if it be possible, be had. *Secondly*, In the same sermon the grievousness of the offence is to be opened ; the party to be exhorted to unfeigned repentance, with assurance of God's mercy if they so do ; and doubling of their damnation, if they remain either obstinate, or feign repentance where none is, and so lying to the Holy Ghost. *Thirdly*, Where no sermon is, there let a homily be read, meet for the purpose. *Fourthly*, Let the offender be set directly over against the pulpit during the sermon or homily, and there stand bareheaded with the sheet, or

Penance temp. Eliz.

other accustomed note of difference; and that upon some board, raised a foot and a half at least above the church floor; that they may be *in loco editiore, et eminentiores omni populo*, i.e. in an higher place, and above all the people. *Fifthly, Item.* It is very requisite that the preacher, in some place of his sermon, or the curate after the end of the homily, remaining still in the pulpit, shall publickly interrogate the offenders, whether they do confess their fault, and whether they do truly repent: and that the said offenders or penitents should answer directly, every one after another, (if they be many), much like to this short form following, *mutatis mutandis*.

Preacher. Dost thou not here, before God and this congregation assembled in his name, confess that thou didst commit such an offence, viz. fornication, adultery, incest, &c.?

Penitent. I do confess it before God and this congregation.

Preacher. Dost thou not also confess, that in so doing thou hast not only grievously offended against the majesty of God in breaking his commandment, and so deserved everlasting damnation, but also offended the Church of God by thy wicked example?

Penitent. All this I confess unfeignedly.

Preacher. Art thou truly and heartily sorrowful for this thine offence?

Penitent. I am, from the bottom of my heart.

Preacher. Dost thou ask God and this congregation heartily forgiveness for thy sin and offence: and dost thou faithfully promise from henceforth to live a godly and Christian life, and never to commit the like offence again?

Penitent. I do ask God and this congregation heartily forgiveness for my sin and offence: and do faithfully promise from henceforth to live a godly and Christian life, and never to commit the like offence again.

This done, the preacher or minister may briefly speak what they think meet for the time, place, and person:

FABRICS, ORNAMENTS, ETC. 253

desiring in the end the congregation present to pray to God for the penitent, &c., and the rather, if they see any good signs of repentance in the said penitent.'—*Form of Penance devised by Abp. Grindal. Strype's Life of Grindal,* pp. 387 ff.

<small>Penance *temp.* Eliz.</small>

'That from henceforth there be no commutation of penance, but in rare respects and upon great consideration; and when it shall appear to the Bishop himself, that that shall be the best way for winning and reforming of the offender, and that the penalty be employed either to the relief of the poor of that parish, or to other godly uses, and the same well witnessed and made manifest to the congregation: and yet if the fault be notorious, that the offender make some satisfaction, either in his own person with declarations of his repentance openly in the church, or else that the minister of the church openly in the pulpit signify to his people his submission and declaration of his repentance done before the Ordinary, and also, in token of his repentance, what portion of money he hath given to be employed in the uses above named.' —*Archbp. Whitgift's Articles touching Preachers, &c. Cardwell's Doc. Ann.,* i. 415.

Customs at Funerals

'Likewise also, as these priests visit and housel their sick by this book [of Common Prayer], so do they in like manner bury their dead by the same book. The priest meeting the corpse at the church stile, in white array (his ministering vesture), with a solemn song, or else reading aloud certain of their fragments of Scripture, and so carry the corpse either to the grave, made in their holy cemetery and hallowed churchyard, or else (if he be a rich man) carry his body into the church, each where his dirge and trental[1] is read over him after they have

<small>Funerals *temp.* Eliz.</small>

---

[1] 'Trental,' a series of thirty masses for the dead.—ED. 1902.

Funerals temp. Eliz.

taken off the holy covering cloth[1] and the linen crosses wherewith the corpse is dressed, until it come unto the churchyard or church, into that holy ground (lest sprites in the meantime should carry it away). The priest there pronounceth, that Almighty God hath taken the soul of that their brother or sister unto him, be he heretick, witch, conjurer, and desiring to meet him with joy in the resurrection, &c., who after he hath cast on the first shovel full of earth in his due time, with his due words, committing earth to earth, ashes to ashes, &c., then may they boldly proceed to cover him, whiles the priest also proceedeth to read over his holy gear and say his Paternoster (which fitteth all assaies) and his other prayers over the corpse. That being done, there is for that time no more but to pay the priest and clerk their hire. As for the mortuary, the priest will come home to the house of the dead for that well enough. But now if he be a man of wealth, that he make his grave with the rich in the church, he shall then pay accordingly; for that ground is much more precious and holy than the churchyard, having been consecrated and all sprinkled with holy water. There he shall be sure to lie dry, his grave being cut east and west, and he so laid that he may rise with his face unto the east. Likewise if he have been any hearer of sermons in his lifetime, and have loved them well, he will be at cost to get some learned priest or other to preach over him at his burial; and that shall be much more wholesome for him than a paltry mass. But if he be of any greater degree or but stepped into the gentry, then he hath accordingly his mourners, yea his heralds peradventure, carrying his coat armour and streamers before him with solemn ado and pitching them over his tomb, as if Duke Hector, or Ajax, or Sir

---

[1] Among the benefactions to the Stationers' Company occurs a hearse cloth, of cloth of gold, powdered with blue velvet, and bordered about with black velvet, embroidered and stained with blue, yellow, red, and green. The gift of John Cawood, who died in 1572.' (*Book of Fragments*, p. 210.)—EDD. 1848.

FABRICS, ORNAMENTS, ETC. 255

Lancelot were buried. Then is the corpse brought in with singing and many solemn circumstances that I know not of, and then is mass preacher sure of a mourning gown and a good reward for his pains. . . . Well now the last question is concerning these solemn mourners arrayed in black, many of them with hoods, caps, crosses, and other knacks; where they learned thus to bemourn and lament their dead by I know not how many months? . . . Neither will I trouble them to shew warrant by the word, for the exquisite sculpture and garnishing of their tombs, with engraving their names and achievements, moulding their images and pictures, and to set these up as monuments in their church; which church must also (upon the day of each burials) be solemnly arrayed and hanged with black, that even the very stones may mourn also for company.'—*A brief Discourse of the False Church*,[1] pp. 125, 127.

Funerals temp. Eliz.

'We say nothing of the threefold peal, because that is rather licensed by Injunction than commanded in their

---

[1] The book from whence this and other extracts are made, was written by Henry Barrow, a 'great one' among the early puritans. He is thus alluded to in a song in the *Shepherd's Oracle*, 4to, 1644:

'We'll break the windows which the Whore
Of Babylon hath painted,
And when the popish saints are down,
Then Barrow shall be sainted.'

Not only does he furnish us with interesting information respecting the condition, ornaments, &c. of the churches, cathedral and parochial, in the reign of Elizabeth; he is also a witness to the prevalency of certain catholic or reverent customs during the same period, such as (to place in one view the facts recorded in the text) the observance of church festivals, with religious rites, feasting, sports, merriment, and complete cessation from labour by all classes of people; the position of the officiating priest at the reading of the Gospel; the obeisance made at the name of Jesus; the administration of the blessed Sacrament 'after the old popish manner,' the priest placing the Lord's body in the mouth of the communicant; the presence of the 'whole quire,' and the use of copes and wafers at the holy Eucharist; the celebration of matrimony at the time of matin service just before the Communion, and never during Lent, unless by licence from the See of Canterbury; the solemn obsequies of the dead, with chants, crosses, and banners, the priest himself casting the first earth on the coffin, &c. Barrow, at p. 63, alludes to the custom of saying 'certain psalms and prayers over the corn and grass, and certain Gospels at crossways,' which is still retained by the clergy in some parts of England.—EDD. 1848.

Funerals temp. Eliz.

book; nor of their strange mourning by changing their garments, which, if it be not hypocritical, yet it is superstitious and heathenish, because it is used only of custom; nor of burial sermons, which are put in place of trentals, whereout spring many abuses, and therefore in the best reformed churches are removed. As for the superstitions used both in country and city for the place of burial, which way they must lie, how they must be fetched to church, the minister meeting them at church-stile with surplice, with a company of greedy clerks, that a cross, white or black, must be set upon the dead corpse, that bread must be given to the poor, and offerings in burial time used, and cakes sent abroad to friends, because these are rather used for custom and superstition than by the authority of the book. Small commandment will serve for the accomplishing of such things.'—*A View of Popish Abuses*, p. 9.

'April 2nd, Mr. Crowley, the suspended minister of Cripplegate, seeing a corpse coming to be buried at his church, attended with clerks in their surplices singing before it, threatened to shut the church-doors against them; but the singing-men resisted, resolving to go through with their work, till the alderman's deputy threatened to lay them by the heels for breaking the peace: upon which they shrunk away, but complained to the Archbishop, who sending for Crowley, deprived him of his living, and confined him to his house, for saying he would not suffer the wolf to come to his flock.'—*Neal's History of the Puritans*, i. 181.

'September 8, were celebrated the obsequies of Henry, the French king, in St. Paul's choir; which was all hung with black and arms; and his hearse garnished with thirty dozen of pensils, and fifteen dozen of escutcheons of arms. The hearse was garnished with great escutcheons, bossed with great crowns; and all under feet with black, and a great pall of cloth of gold, and coat-armour, target, sword, and crest. The lord-

FABRICS, ORNAMENTS, ETC. 257

treasurer was chief-mourner ; next the lord-chamberlain . . . and many more mourners, all in black. There were fourteen heralds-of-arms attending in their coat-armour, following after the lords. Then dirge was sung ; and then they repaired to the Bishop's palace to dinner. Thence in the afternoon they came to church again, the heralds before them. And the service was then performed : the Archbishop of Canterbury elect was minister, Scory elect of Hereford preached, the third Bishop was Barlow, elect of Chichester.'—*Strype's Life of Grindal,* 38.

Funerals *temp*. Eliz.

Rogation Processions[1]

'That in the Rogation days of Procession, they sing or say in English, the two psalms beginning, *Benedic anima mea, &c.,* with the litany and suffrages thereunto, with one homily of thanksgiving to God already devised and divided into four parts, without addition of any superstitious ceremonies heretofore used.'—*Articles for Administration of Prayer and Sacraments. Ordinances accorded by the Archbishop of Canterbury.*

Rogation Processions *temp.* Eliz.

'In the Gang week, when the priest in his surplice, singing Gospels and making crosses, rangeth about in many places.'—*A View of Popish Abuses,* p. 14.

'Plain Song,' enjoined in all Churches by Queen Elizabeth

'*Item,* Because in divers collegiate, and also some parish churches heretofore, there hath been livings appointed for the maintenance of men and children to use singing in the church, by means whereof the laudable service of music hath been had in estimation, and preserved in knowledge ; the queen's majesty, neither meaning in anywise the decay of anything, that might

Plain Song *temp.* Eliz.

---

[1] Extracts relating to these processions will be found in full in Vol. II. of this work.—ED. 1902.

Plain Song temp. Eliz.

conveniently tend to the use and continuance of the said service, neither to have the same in any part so abused in the church, that thereby the Common Prayer should be worse understanded of the hearers, willeth and commandeth, that first no alteration be made of such assignments of living, as heretofore hath been appointed to the use of singing or music in the church, but that the same so remain. And that there be a modest and distinct song so used in all parts of the Common Prayers in the church, that the same may be as plainly understanded, as if it were read without singing.'[1]—*Q. Elizabeth's Injunctions of* 1559. *Cardwell, Doc. Ann.*, I. 228.

'Points of Popery' (in the opinion of the Elizabethan Puritans) remaining in the Church of England

'Points of Popery' temp. Eliz.

' 13. The Epistler, that doth read some patch of the Epistle. 14. The Gospeller, that doth read some piece of the Gospel. 15. The Quirister. 16. The Quire or Cage wherein they do separate themselves from the congregation, and cause the word not to be understood of the people. . . . 41. Putting off the caps at the Name

---

[1] By this injunction of Queen Elizabeth it will be seen that a certain mode of saying prayers was commanded at the same time that permission was given for the introduction of metrical psalms. And the whole of the rubrics contained in the Book of Common Prayer prove most clearly that the Offices of the Church were never intended to be delivered 'ore rotundo,' or to be preached to the people. The terms employed were the Ecclesiastico-musical terms of the day, and should of course be interpreted in the manner in which the framers of our Liturgy intended. Now in the sixteenth century, by the term of plain chant was understood a specific recognised chant, which had been appropriated from time immemorial to the reading of the Scriptures, and the other Offices, each having an especial intonation peculiar to itself. When a collect was ordered to be said, the 'cantus collectarum' was used; when the Gospel or Epistle was directed to be read, the 'cantus Evangelii' or the 'cantus Epistolarum' was employed. In short, when the words 'say,' 'read,' or 'sing' occur in the rubrics, they signify the kind of intonation peculiar to each particular Office; and permission is given to 'say,' *i.e.* to use the plain chant in quires where more elaborate music cannot be obtained; or to 'sing,' *i.e.* to employ more ornate chants (known as Services) in cathedral and other establishments where there are 'quires' competent to the performance of the same. It is usual on Festival occasions to 'sing,' and on ordinary occasions to 'say' the Offices.—EDD. 1848.

FABRICS, ORNAMENTS, ETC. 259

of Jesus. 42. Crossing the corpse with linen cloths and such like. 43. Ringing of hand-bells in many places. . . . 46. Ringing of curfew upon hallow evens. . . . 50. Offerings at burials, and the offering of the woman at her churching.'—*A View of Antichrist, his laws and ceremonies in our English Church unreformed. A part of a Register*, pp. 60-63.

<small>'Points of Popery' *temp.* Eliz.</small>

Archbishop Parker's Visitation

'The same year [1570], July the 3rd, he entered upon his ordinary visitation, and visited his church in person. . . . This visitation began with the celebration of the prayers and holy Communion in the chapter-house by one of his chaplains, the dean and clergy present. Which visitation he continued from day to day, until the 22nd day of the same month. And then he gave forth to the clergy and laity of his diocese divers wholesome injunctions, necessary to be observed for several causes. And this was the last session of his visitation, though he prorogued it to the feast of the Purification of the Blessed Virgin.

<small>Archbp. Parker's Visitation *temp.* Eliz.</small>

'The particular method and manner of this visitation, how, first, to be entered upon, for the more regular and orderly proceeding, (as the archbishop delighted to do all his matters in a grave and solemn decency,) was thus appointed:

'*First*, That the service be done in the choir by eight of the clock in the morning.

'*Secondly*, That all they of the choir with the whole foundation, after service done, stand in the body of the church on either side of the middle aisle in due order; and that the dean, prebendaries, and preachers, do come to the palace to wait upon my Lord's Grace, to the church.

'*Item*, At the entry of my Lord's Grace into the church, the choirs to go up before him, singing some anthem.

'*Item*, They being all placed in the choir shall sing the Litany.

'*Item*, That being done, the grammarians and the choir

Archbp. Parker's Visitation temp. Eliz.

to go up into the presbytery, two and two in order ; and so on to the backside of the choir by Bishop Warham's chapel into the chapter-house. The archbishop, dean, prebendaries, and preachers, to meet them at the stairs' head : and they only with the archbishop's officers to be *infra cancellos.* And there and then, before the beginning of the sermon, to sing the hymn *Veni Creator*, and in English. The dean to say the collect following for grace, beginning *Gratias agimus, etc.*, in English.

'*Item*, These things being done, the preacher to proceed to the sermon. Which being done, all the extern laity to be commanded out by the beadle.

'*Item*, The dean or vice-dean to bring in his certificate. And all they of the church being cited, to be called and sworn, and monished to bring in their several presentments in writing in the afternoon between three and four of the clock in the place aforesaid. And then the visitation to be continued.'—*Strype's Life of Archbp. Parker*, II. 21, 22.

* Canterbury Cathedral

Canterbury Cathedral temp. Eliz.

Note y^t thes particulers followinge were only Remaynynge at the first entry of my Lo. of Dov^r into the Roome of the Deanery of this Church an^o 1584.

An Inventary of vtisensellℓ (*sic*) Remanynge in the Revestry & elsewhere aboute the temple of this Church taken the xxiijth of novemb^r an^o xxviij^o RR. Elizabethe by M^r Jo. Bunge Rec' and Jo. Wynt^r treasurer of this Church.

Plate of Sylver

Imprimis two lyvery pottℓ of Sylv^r double gilte weighinge
Item two bazens of Sylv^r parcell gylt weighing
Item one Communion Cuppe wth a Cov^r of Silv^r Double gilt weighinge

Lynnynge clothes for ye Communion table

Item one Clothe wrought wth oylett wholes.
Item iij Clothes of Diaper.
Item one Clothe of holland.
Item iiij olde wyping Clothes.

Canopyes

Item one Canopy of Satten whit & green.
Item a Canopy of Caffay spangd w^t birdes & flowres of golde.

FABRICS, ORNAMENTS, ETC.

Item a Canopy for my Lo. Archbisshop his seat of Reed Caffay spangd wth birdes of golde. Canterbury Cathedral *temp.* Eliz.
An heerse Clothe of blacke Caffay spangd with Golde havinge a whit Crosse thorow the myddest.

Clothes of sylke for the Communion table
Item v Clothes of Crymzon Caffay spangd wth gold birdes.
Item v of green Caffay wth gold birdes.
Item iij Clothes of grenysh silke w^t gold flowres.
An old blewe Clothe of silke for the pulpitt & a Cushion.
One old Clothe of whit silke wth branches.
One old silke Clothe strickd w^t murrye.

Tapettes
Item iiij Clothes of tepestry woorke.
Item iij Carpettes wherof one is Reed.
Item ij Carpettes one blewe thother whit w^t floures.
Item one lytle Carpett of whit.
One olde Carpett in thupper Closett.

Cussions
Item iiij Reed Cussions of Satten wth starres.
Item iiij of whit Satten wth ye Deare & Ringge.
iiij blewe ones spangd wth golde.
vj wth *benedicta sit s^{ta} trinitas*.
ij of mockador green & murrey.
ij thrimmed ones wth spred egles in the myddest.
iij olde ones of gylt lether.
iij thrimmed ones of check^r worke.
one of Carpett worke.
ij whit ones wth blacke Crosses.
one olde one of whit sylke.
one lytle one for the Communion table.
v old ones of Darnex.

Chayers
Item v Chayers of Clothe of tysshue.
iiij iron stooles.
An Iron deske.
A Deske of wodd.
iiij whit Canopy staves.
ij longe Reed staues for tharchbisshop his seat.

Books of Service for the Chore
Item one bible in Englyshe in follio Cov^r gilt.
Item iij other great bibles in follio.
Item v bibles in 4°.
One Communion booke Cov^r green vellett.
iij other Communion bookes.
A number of olde bookes taken oute of the lyberary thinventary wherof.
x old bookes y^t Came from Mr Sympson Custody
ij bookes of martrs one in the body of the Church thother above in the north yle.

Canterbury Cathedral *temp.* **Eliz.**

A great bible in follio lyinge in the north ile aboue by the Chore.
.ij bearers standinge in the Revestry.
.iiij longe Chestes in the Revestry.

In the Chore

Item one Communion Table.
iiij formes.
A tapett under the Communion table.
An Eagle of brasse.
A lytle paire of orgaynes & a great^r paire aboue
Hanginges of Arras roonde about the Chore.
A longe sette of Redd aboue the grates.
A Deske before Mr Deanes seate.
vj Deskes of wainescott befor the prebendes seates.
Item iiij Deskes before the Choresters.
Item a low deske in the myddest of the Chore.
ij formes for the Choresters.
A [ij wood *interlinea*] longe settle [of w *altered to*] in thupper end of the south yle by the Chore.
A lytle Canopy over Mr Dean seat.

In the upper north yle

Item ij Cubberdes of wanescott wth fallinge leaues to shutte.
ij other Cubberdes of wanescott vsed by ye peti canons.

[dd to M ffrench]
A table of the Conversion of St Paule.
Item a longe forme.
Item a table, a long settle & Chare of wanescott for the Commissioners.

In the body of the Church

Item an olde pulpett.
v seates for Mr Dean & the prebend to knele at in tyme of mornynge prayer on the south syd & ij formes.
ix seates & iij formes on the north syde.
A lytle deske for the mynyster to kneele at in prayer.
A Bazon of brasse for Cristenynge with a foote of Iron to stand vpon.
A grave stone of marble by the west dore.
A long lather.

In the Chapter house

A Table.
xxvj formes.

[Added in another hand :]

M^o that the particulers of this Inventorye above mentioned were acknowledged to Remayne as they are above sette downe by the Sexton and Vestrer before Mr Hill Treasorer and Thomas Cockes Chapter Clerke the firste Daye of December 1586 RR Eliz. 29°.

—*Inventories of Christchurch, Canterbury*, p. 240 ff.

FABRICS, ORNAMENTS, ETC. 263

Queen Elizabeth's Maundy

'First, the hall was prepared with a long table on each side, and forms set by them; on the edges of which tables, and under those forms, were laid carpets and cushions, for her Majesty to kneel when she should wash them. There was also another table set across the upper end of the hall. somewhat above the footpace, for the chaplain to stand at. A little beneath the midst whereof, and beneath the said foot-pace, a stool and cushion of estate was pitched for her Majesty to kneel at during the service time. This done, the holy water, basins, alms, and other things being brought into the hall, and the chaplain and poor folks having taken the said places, the laundress, armed with a fair towel, and taking a silver basin filled with warm water and sweet flowers, washed their feet all after one another, and wiped the same with his towel, and so making a cross a little above the toes kissed them. After him within a little while followed the subalmoner, doing likewise, and after him the almoner himself also. Then lastly, her Majesty came into the hall, and after some singing and prayers made, and the gospel of Christ's washing of his disciples' feet read, thirty-nine ladies and gentlewomen (for so many were the poor folks, according to the number of the years complete of her Majesty's age,) addressed themselves with aprons and towels to wait upon her Majesty; and she kneeling down upon the cushions and carpets under the feet of the poor women, first washed one foot of every one of them in so many several basins of warm water and sweet flowers, brought to her severally by the said ladies and gentlewomen, then wiped, crossed, and kissed them, as the almoner and others had done before. When her Majesty had thus gone through the whole number of thirty-nine, (of which twenty sat on the one side of the hall, and nineteen on the other,) she resorted to the first again, and gave to each one certain yards of broadcloth, to

Maundy temp. Eliz.

make a gown, so passing to them all. Thirdly, she began at the first, and gave to each of them a pair of shoes. Fourthly to each of them a wooden platter, wherein was half a side of salmon, as much ling, six red herrings, and cheat [manchet] loaves of bread. Fifthly, she began with the first again, and gave to each of them a white wooden dish with claret wine. Sixthly, she received of each waiting lady and gentlewoman their towel and apron, and gave to each poor woman one of the same; and after this the ladies and gentlewomen waited no longer, nor served as they had done throughout the courses before. But then the treasurer of the chamber (Mr. Hennage) came to her Majesty with thirty-nine small white purses, wherein were also thirty-nine pence, (as they say,) after the number of years to her Majesty's said age, and of him she received and distributed them severally. Which done, she received of him so many leather purses also, each containing twenty shillings, for the redemption of her Majesty's gown, which (as men say) by ancient order she ought to give some of them at her pleasure: but she, to avoid the trouble of suit, which accustomably was made for that preferment, had changed that reward into money, to be equally divided amongst them all, namely, twenty shillings a-piece, and she also delivered particularly to the whole company. And so taking her ease upon the cushion of estate, and hearing the choir a little while, her Majesty withdrew herself, and the company departed: for it was by that time the sun was setting.'—*No.* 6183, *Add. MSS. in the British Museum*, cited in *Hone's Table-Book*, vol. i. pp. 479, 480.

Varia

1565

'But, Bernard, I pray thee tell me of thine honesty, what was the cause that thou hast been in so many

FABRICS, ORNAMENTS, ETC. 265

changes of apparel this forenoon, now black, now white, now in silk and gold, and now at length in this swouping black gown, and this sarcenet flaunting tippet, &c. ?'— *A pleasant Dialogue between a Soldier of Berwick and an English Chaplain, &c.*, qu. Strype, *Annals*, I. ii. 169. <small>Varia temp. Eliz.</small>

1570

'This year (if it were not before) did a brother of this party, Mr. A. G. (Anthony Gilby, I suppose,) write a very hot and bitter letter to several reverend divines, that had been exiles for the gospel, and returned upon Queen Elizabeth's access to the crown; exciting them with all their might against the bishops, for imposing the habits to be worn by ministers in their ministrations; and rather to lay down their ministry than to comply. . . . Where in one place he thus expresseth himself: " I wot not by what devilish cup they [the bishops] do make such a diversity between Christ's word and his sacraments; that they cannot think the word of God to be safely enough preached and honourably enough handled, without cap, cope, or surplice; but that the sacraments, the marrying, the burying, the churching of women, and other church service, as they call it, must needs be declared with crossing, with coping, with surplicing, with kneeling, with pretty wafer cakes, and other knacks of popery." '—*Ibid.* II. i. 8.

1571

'And what sort of popishly affected priests still officiated in the church, the forementioned Northbroke [minister of Redcliff in Bristol] will tell us, in his epistle to a book entitled *A Brief and Pithy Sum of the Christian Faith*. Therein he spake " of certain men, then ministers of the Church, who were papists, and so gave out themselves to be in their discourses. Who subscribed and observed the order of service, wore a side gown, a square cap, a cope and surplice." '—*Ibid.* II. i. 145.

1573

'I would be loth to say . . . that it is not lawful for a man to make of a popish surplice a shirt for himself, or to take the gold of a cope which he hath bought, and convert it to his private use. And herein we do nothing disagree with S. Augustin, which grant that surplices, and copes, and tippets, and caps, may be applied to a good use, either common or private, as they will best serve; but we deny that that use is in distinguishing either the ministers from other men, or the ministers executing their ecclesiastical function from themselves when they do not exercise that office.'

'Although there be [those] which like not this apparel, that think otherwise than either their brethren, or than indeed they ought to do, yet a man may find greater dissent amongst those which are united in surplice and cope, &c., than there is among those that wear them not, rather with themselves, or with them that wear them: for how many there are that wear surplices, which would be gladder to say a mass than to hear a sermon, let the world judge. And of those who do wear this apparel, and be otherwise well minded to the Gospel, are there not which will wear the surplice and not the cap; other that will wear both cap and surplice, but not the tippet; and yet a third sort, that will wear surplice, cap, and tippet, but not the cope?'—*A Reply to an Answer made of M. Doctor Whitgift against the Admonition to the Parliament by T[homas] C[artright]*, pp. 75, 79, 4to (*no date*).

c. 1573

'This is a very slender reason to prove that the Sacrament of the Supper is not sincerely ministered, because there is singing, piping, surplice, and cope: when you shew your reasons against that pomp which is now used in the celebration of that sacrament, you shall hear what I have to say in defence of the same. I think there is nothing used in the administration thereof, that doth in

FABRICS, ORNAMENTS, ETC. 267

any respect contaminate it, or make it impure.'—*Abp. Whitgift's Answer to the Admonition. The Defence of the Answer, &c.*, p. 606, fol. 1574.

Varia *temp.* Eliz.

c. 1573

'They should first prove by the word, that . . . kneeling at Communion, wafer cakes for their bread when they minister it, surplice and cope to do it in . . . are agreeable to the written word of the Almighty.'

'We marvel that they could espy in their last Synod, that a gray amice, which is but a garment of dignity, should be a garment (as they say) defiled with superstition, and yet that copes, caps, surplices, tippets, and such-like baggage, the preaching signs of popish priesthood, the Pope's creatures, kept in the same form to this end to bring dignity and reverence to the ministers and sacraments, should be retained still, and not abolished.'—*A View of Popish Abuses yet remaining in the English Church*, pp. 2, 17.

1577

'Within the church would not the priest's gown suffice [for a note of distinction] without the surplice? his surplice without the cope? his preaching and other ministerial function without them all? For who can he be that doeth these things in the church, but the minister? can there be a fairer white, to know him from all the rest, than these? he that either cannot know, or will not acknowledge him for a minister by these marks, it is not safe that he should know him by the other.'[1]—

---

[1] From this and some of the preceding extracts we may infer that copes were worn in parish churches *temp.* Eliz. They are mentioned (in connexion with the surplice, &c.) as customarily distinguishing the clergy 'from other men,' or 'the ministers executing their ecclesiastical function from themselves when they do not exercise that office.' Had they been confined to cathedrals and private chapels, this could not have been said of them with propriety or truth. The rubric which enjoins their use in all churches at the celebration of the Holy Eucharist, was in force throughout Elizabeth's reign.—EDD. 1848.

The rest of the Second Reply of Thomas Cartright against Master Doctor Whitgift's Second Answer, touching the Church Discipline, &c., p. 252, 4to, 1577.

1586

'A pamphlet was dispersed without doors, entitled "A Request of all true Christians to the Honourable House of Parliament." It prays, "that every parish church may have its preacher, and every city its superintendent, to live honestly but not pompously." And to provide for this, it prays, "that all cathedral churches may be put down, where the service of God is grievously abused by piping with organs, singing, ringing, and trowling of psalms from one side of the choir to another, with the squeaking of chanting choristers, disguised (as are all the rest) in white surplices; some in corner caps and filthy copes, imitating the fashion and manner of antichrist the Pope, that man of sin and child of perdition, with his other rabble of miscreants and shavelings.' *Neal's History of the Puritans*, i. 384.

1588

'The book, commonly called *The Cobler's Book*, comes under this year, or hereabouts . . . The Archbishop, having appointed somebody to look it over, and report it to him, received this account thereof. That he handled these three Articles. I. That the Church of England is not the Church of Christ. II. What opinion is holden of the members thereof. III. That it is contrary to the Scriptures to join with that Church. . . . In this treatise, first he charged the realm to maintain open idolatry, under the name of decency. The idolatry and monuments of idolatry he affirmed to be maintained, were, godfathers, fonts, baptism by women, bishopping of children, standing up at the Gospel, the chancel, bells, organs, &c., wafer cakes, the prescript order of service in the choir, the prescript number of Psalms and Lessons,

FABRICS, ORNAMENTS, ETC. 269

the gang-days, Collects ordinary, surplice, copes, tippets, Wednesdays and Fridays fasts, &c. Adding, that the whole treatise was a mischievous, railing libel against the Queen's Majesty and others.'—*Strype's Life of Whitgift*, I. 565, 8vo, *Oxford*, 1822.

^{Varia temp. Eliz.}

1589

'At his first journey into Kent, which was in July 1589, he rode to Dover, attended with not less than one hundred of his own servants in livery, whereof there were forty gentlemen in chains of gold. The train of gentlemen and clergy in this country and their followers, was above five hundred horse. This grand appearance proved of service to the Church at that time. At his entrance into the town there happily landed an intelligencer from Rome, who wondered to see an archbishop or clergyman in England so reverenced and attended: and being present also the Sunday following at service in the Cathedral in Canterbury, where seeing his Grace attended with his gentlemen and servants, as also the Dean, Prebendaries, and preachers in their surplices and scarlet hoods, and hearing the solemn musick with the voices and organs, cornets and sackbuts, he was struck with amazement and admiration, and declared that " they were led in great blindness at Rome by our own nation, who made the people there believe that there was not in England either archbishop or bishop, or cathedral, or any church or ecclesiastical government, but that all was pulled down to the ground, and that the people heard their ministers in woods and fields, among trees and brute beasts: for his own part he protested, that unless it were in the Pope's chapel, he never saw a more solemn sight, or heard a more heavenly sound."'—*Whitgift, Biog. Brit.*, vol. vi. part II. p. 4255, fol. 1766.

NOTE A. Page 102

In the original edition of *Hierurgia Anglicana*, the following note was appended to a short quotation from *Bishop Cosin's Notes in Nicholls' Commentary on The Book of Common Prayer.*

The weight of this valuable testimony from Bp. Cosin will not be weakened to the thoughtful reader by the unwarrantable suggestion of a late Ritualist, (*How shall we Conform to the Liturgy?* p. 91, 2nd edit.) to the effect that the Bishop *may* have had a cathedral or college chapel in his eye, and not a parish church; or that he *may* have written the note before he was made a Bishop. We are unwilling to let slip this opportunity of considering at large Mr. Robertson's decision against the use of altar-lights.

It is well known that the argument for lights is this: An Injunction of King Edward VI., in 1547, which had the authority of Parliament, orders 'two lights upon the high altar before the Sacrament ... for the signification that Christ is the very true light of the world.' This practice was in force in the second year of King Edward VI., as is shown by the Visitation Articles issued by Cranmer in that year for the Diocese of Canterbury, (*Wilkins' Concilia,* vol. v. p. 23); and is *therefore* enjoined by the present Rubric.

Mr. Robertson, in combating this argument, asserts that the expression in the Injunction, 'two lights upon the high altar *before the Sacrament,*' means the candles attendant upon 'the consecrated wafer, suspended in a pyx over the altar,' (p. 80); and infers that, ' as the lights had been sanctioned only in the character of appendages to the pyx, they were not among the ornaments authorized at the time to which our Rubric refers.'

We believe that Mr. Robertson here makes some confusion between two kindred but distinct practices of the Church, viz. the using lights at the time of the immediate celebration of the Holy Eucharist, and the burning a light continually before the Blessed Sacrament, as reserved for the Communion of the Sick. It is true that he refers to Lyndewode for the first, and speaks more than once of the second practice: but he does not clearly shew that he sees the distinction between them; and by his abrupt reference to the *exposition* of the Blessed Sacrament in his note (p. 80), and his mistake in using the phrase the *exhibition* of the same on the high altar, when he is merely referring to the reservation (p. 82), he seems to shew anything but a clear understanding of the subject.

With respect to the first practice, we may observe that the use of two lights upon the altar at the time of the celebration is one of great antiquity. St. Isidore of Seville (*Orig.* vii. 12) gives the very same symbolical reason for the lights which is assigned in our Injunction—' ut sub typo luminis corporalis illa lux ostendatur de qua in Evangelio legitur, Erat lux vera quæ illuminat omnem hominem.' Mr. Robertson himself quotes Archbishop Reynolds' Constitution in 1322, from Lyndewode, (fol. lxxix. of our edition, *Paris,* 1506,) enjoining the lights at the time of celebration; and the Roman Missal orders them by an express rubric. On the other hand, the number of lights to be burnt before the Blessed Sacrament when reserved, was never *enjoined* to be more than one, and that only in churches possessing considerable means. (*Constitutions of Bishop Walter de Cantilupe*, A.D. 1240, in *Wilkins' Concilia*, vol. i. p. 667.) This light, though it might of course be a candle, was much more generally a lamp; just as the cresset, containing a mere wick floating in oil, is now used abroad for this purpose. The lamp was most common, both for reasons of expense and because it was necessary to watch a candle; for instance, the pasch-light at the Easter Sepulchre was always watched, even if people were paid for doing so, as we know from many records. Now this light was to burn night and day; 'continuè lampas ardet die videlicet et nocte,' (*Wilkins* as above); and so in the Rubric in the *Rituale Romanum, De Sanctissimo Eucharistiæ Sacramento*, ' die noctuque perpetuo colluceat.' Thus the practices were widely different: the one requiring wax candles to be burnt on the altar at the time of celebration; the other enjoining a lamp or light to be kept burning continually before the Blessed Sacrament.

Now against Mr. Robertson's view that the two lights ordered by our Injunction had reference to the latter custom, we may argue that it is scarcely to be conceived that *two* lights should have been ordered by Edw. VI. in 1547, to be burnt *continually*, while in earlier times one only was enjoined when a church possessed 'amplas facultates'; particularly since Cardinal Pole, when reviving the reservation of the Blessed Sacrament and its light, in his Legatine Constitutions, 1555, enjoins, to cite Mr. Robertson's own italics and quotation, '*where it can be afforded* " ut perpetuo lampas vel cereus coram sanctissimo hoc sacramento ardeat,"' (p. 84). But so confirmed is Mr. Robertson's mistake that he proceeds to remark, ' Pole's order leads me to observe, that lamps may satisfy the Injunction of 1547 as well as wax lights '; apparently forgetting the symbolical meaning of the *wax* lights on the altar, which in another place he himself quotes from Lyndewode, (p. 314).

It is true that in England the Blessed Sacrament was generally reserved in a hanging pyx over the high altar, rather than in a tabernacle, or than in an aumbrye, as was usual in other countries, and as is recommended in preference to the high altar in the Rubric from the *Rituale* before referred to.[1] This of course partly explains the difficulty felt by Mr. Robertson. The cresset must have hung, in this case, over or before the altar continually: the altar-candles were a distinct ornament, and were only lighted at the celebration. We may observe also, that even candles, if used instead of the more usual *lamps* before the pyx, were suspended; as in the great abbey of Durham, (*Antiquities of Durham Abbey*, p. 14, 8vo, 1767).

Having thus distinguished between the practices of burning two candles upon the altar at the time of celebration, and of keeping a light continually burning before the reserved Sacrament, our readers will be able to examine the force of Mr. Robertson's reasoning.

In 1536, Cromwell, as Vicar-General, by an ordinance abolished the use of all lights ' afore any image or picture,' excepting two or three specified *single* lights; one of which was ' the light before the sacrament of the altar '; which of course means that before the pyx. The proclamation of Henry VIII. in

---

[1] The Editors of 1848 have misunderstood the rubric in the *Rituale*, which recommends the use of a tabernacle over a side altar, in preference to the tabernacle over the high altar.

With the possible exceptions of two doubtful cases, no instance of an altar tabernacle, properly so-called, is known to have existed in England before the time of Queen Mary, when Cardinal Pole attempted to introduce the arrangement from abroad. The hanging pyx was general in England, as in France, but in some places the aumbry in the north wall of the chancel seems to have been used, as was usual in the north and east of Scotland.—ED. 1902.

1538, authorizes the setting up of candles 'on Easter-day before the Corpus Christi,' (*Wilkins*, iii. 842); and his Injunction of 1539 (*Wilkins*, iii. 847) repeats the order in the same words. Mr. Robertson, omitting to quote the words 'on Easter-day,' infers that these ordinances made a reduction of the number of lights before allowed, and were connected with the practices now under consideration; while they refer in truth to a special and distinct ceremony. Proceeding onwards to 1547, we find Edward's Injunction ordering 'two lights,' upon which all this question depends.

Now (1) this, if supposed (with Mr. Robertson) to refer to the reserved Sacrament, deliberately increased instead of reducing the number of lights burnt before the pyx; a conclusion which he would himself surely be the last to welcome. Again (2), the Injunction orders the two lights to *remain*: which is intelligible upon the view that the altar-lights at the time of celebration are alluded to, because Cromwell's ordinance referred only to lights set 'afore any image or picture,' a point passed over by Mr. Robertson. If we compare the two we find that Cromwell forbids more than *one* light, the Injunction allows two lights to remain: either then we must suppose that the latter speaks of what had been legally removed as still remaining, which is absurd; or else that it refers to a different practice, namely, the burning of two lights at the consecration of the Holy Eucharist; and that Cromwell's order does not allude to this observance at all, either by way of permission or of prohibition. This view is confirmed also by the following considerations. First, if Cromwell meant to allude at all to the lights at the celebration, he must have intended to forbid them, as they are not among the single lights specifically allowed. Secondly, that he did not mean to allude to them may be inferred from the fact, that the altar-lights were not removed in consequence of his order, but were in use eleven years after it, at the time when Edward's Injunctions ('evidently formed from it,' Mr. Robertson says incorrectly, p. 81,) appeared and prescribed them; and continued in use afterwards. It is further plain that the altar-lights were not removed, because it is impossible to conceive that the light before the pyx was permitted to remain, and that candles were allowed to be set up before the Corpus Christi on Easter-day, and carried on Candlemas-day; and yet that the use of the altar-lights at the celebration of the Holy Eucharist (which we have seen was considered a very important part of the ceremonial) should have been omitted. That the altar-lights remained in 1547, may be further shewn by the fact, that Cranmer's Communion Office, put forth in that year, (*Wilkins' Concil.*, vol. iv. p. 12,) orders that 'the time of the Communion shall be immediately after that the priest himself hath received the Sacrament, *without the varying of any other rite or ceremony in the Mass*, (until other orders shall be provided).' Cranmer's Articles also, issued in the next year, mention the 'two lights on the high altar' which had just been ordered by the Royal Injunctions. It remains only to shew that altar-lights were used *subsequently* to the Injunctions; which appears from their being forbidden, together with the other ceremonial of the Mass, by the later Injunctions of 1549, (*Cardwell, Doc. Annals*, i. 63, 4,) and by Ridley's Injunctions, founded upon the last, in 1550. We have shewn then by these considerations, that Cromwell could not have meant to allude to altar-lights in his ordinance of 1536; and it would seem to follow, that the Royal Injunction of 1547 refers to a subject quite distinct from Cromwell's order, namely, to two lights burning, not before the reserved Sacrament, but on the altar at the time of celebration.

Again, we shall find, by examining the 'Articles' of 1549, that the lights mentioned in the former Injunctions, to which reference is made in the 1st Article, meant candles, and not a lamp; from the circumstance, that the clergy are ordered to 'omit in the reading of the Injunctions, all such as make mention of . . . candles upon the altar,' (*Cardwell, Doc. Aun.*, vol. i. p. 63); and the second Article distinctly connects these candles with the ceremonial of the Mass, without any reference to the reservation. Ridley also, in his above-quoted Injunction in 1550, connects in like manner the altar-lights and the celebration; as is inadvertently admitted by Mr. Robertson (p. 84) in the words, 'This last sentence relates not to the use of lights as allowed in 1547'—that is, according to Mr. Robertson's interpretation—'but to candles lighted at consecration.'

Another point in confirmation of this view is the following. Lyndewode (lib. iii. folio lxxii.) says, 'Note that the candles to be burnt at the celebration of the Mass must be of wax, rather than of any other material. For the candle, *sic ardens*, signifieth Christ Himself, who is the brightness of eternal light.' It is fair to conclude that the *sic ardens* must have been in the view of those who drew up the Injunction of 1547, which gives the same symbolical reason.

It might also be argued against Mr. Robertson's interpretation of the Injunction, that Cranmer, in 1547, when following up and enforcing its provisions, omits the words 'before the Sacrament' altogether, and commands the use of 'only two lights on the high altar.'

To all which may be added, the argument derived from the constant practice of the Anglican Church in retaining candles upon the altar. According to Mr. Robertson's view, the pyx, for which alone these candles were enjoined, was itself forbidden within a very short time after the appearance of the Injunction. But the candles, instead of sharing the fate of the pyx, to which Mr. Robertson would attach them, survived, as he himself admits, at least in cathedrals, and royal and collegiate chapels. The Injunction of 1547 was understood in the way for which we now contend, in opposition to Mr. Robertson, by Bishop Cosin, (quoted at length *ante* p. 86,) and was obeyed as binding in this way by Bishop Andrewes and his followers.

We hope that it has been satisfactorily shewn that Mr. Robertson has no grounds for interpreting the Injunction as referring to the pyx and its lights. But even if he had proved this connection, we should by no means allow his inference that 'they were not among the ornaments authorized at the time to which our Rubric refers,' (p. 83). For that they were *in use* at that time has been shewn, and is all that is necessary to bring them within the letter of the present Rubric. And it is not conceivable that so general a reference should have been made to the ornaments then in use, if the most striking of all the ornaments were meant to be excepted from the renewed Injunction. Here again the fact that the words 'ornaments of the *church*' were *added* to the Rubric in 1662, is of the greatest importance and significance.—EDD. 1848.

NOTE B. Page 136.

Letter from Lord Halifax in *The Guardian* of Feb. 2, 1881, in reference to the disuse of the Chasuble and the comparative survival of the Cope.

SIR,—There is one point having an important bearing on the interpretation of the Ornaments' Rubric which has not, I think, been sufficiently noticed in your columns, and yet it is one which deserves notice, because it clears up, as it seems to me, some of the difficulties which have prevented eminent persons amongst us from acknowledging, what at first sight certainly appears to be, the obvious meaning of that Rubric.

Those difficulties, it will be admitted, are, to a great extent at least, derived from a single source—how to suppose that the apparently unambiguous words of the Rubric have the force which seems to attach to them, in face of the actual disuse of the vestments which they profess to prescribe?

Now the point I would press is this—that a perfectly simple solution of all the difficulties that have been recently developed in connection with the Ornaments' Rubric is to be found in the Rubrics of the Communion Office of the First Prayer Book of Edward VI.

The general Rubric prefixed to that service prescribes that the Priest who is to execute his Office—I omit other matters—is to wear a vestment or cope. The Rubrics which conclude the Office, with the object of discouraging Masses at which the celebrant alone communicated, after forbidding the celebration of Holy Communion except there were some to communicate with the Priest, provide that on Wednesdays and Fridays after the Litany, and on other days when the people are accustomed to pray in church, the minister, if there were none to communicate with him, shall, *vested in a cope*, read the Communion Service as far as the Offertory, and there stop.

That is, to put it shortly, the Rubrics of the Communion Office of the First Book of Edward prescribe, under certain circumstances, the use of a portion only of that Service, and provide, when the Office is so curtailed, the use of a particular vestment—*i.e.* the cope. Nothing could be more natural than such an arrangement, since the Litany, which had been substituted for the procession at High Mass, and as such, in its original intention, was intended as an introduction to the Communion Service (in some of the Injunctions, Orders, etc., it is called the 'Litany of the High Mass'), would, like the 'Procession' itself, so far as the chief officiant be concerned, have been sung in a cope, and the Priest was merely told not to change it for the chasuble, when he began the Communion Office, as he would have done according to existing usage, unless the Holy Communion were going to be actually celebrated.

The meaning of the Rubric, then, is this, not that the cope was to be used indifferently with the chasuble, but that the use of the chasuble was to be limited to actual celebrations of the Holy Communion; the use of the cope to 'Table Prayers.'[1]

The light this throws upon the disuse of the chasuble and the comparative survival of the cope, as well as upon the real meaning of the Canons, is obvious. The chasuble fell almost entirely into disuse for the simple reason that, in the ecclesiastical anarchy of Elizabeth's reign, the Holy Communion itself was, in many places, so seldom celebrated. Communicants are not to be created at once. The Puritans—and the prevailing Calvinism of the time must be borne in mind—were profoundly indifferent on the subject. Celebrations of Holy Communion dwindled to three or four times a year, if so often. On the rare occasions when it was celebrated, those who refused to wear even a surplice were not likely to wear a chasuble, while 'Table Prayers,' if they were said at all, were often said in the reading desk. Under such circumstances the fact of the disuse of the chasuble is explained at once.

In Cathedrals and Collegiate Churches, however, such a total disregard of the law was more difficult. The actual celebrations of Holy Communion

---

[1] See, however, the reply of the chapter of Canterbury, quoted on p. 245, previously.—ED. 1902.

were, perhaps, not more frequent, at all events, till the reaction in a Catholic direction under Andrewes, by which time most of the chasubles would have disappeared; but the reading of 'Table Prayers' in the chancel would be insisted upon, and would carry with it, in some places at least, the continued use of the cope. Hence the survival of the cope as compared with the chasuble.

In the light of these facts the real object of the Canons is also clear. That object was not to substitute the cope for the chasuble, or to bring the ritual of the Church into harmony with the supposed 'other order;' but it was to insist, at least in Cathedrals, which were understood to be the models for the diocese, upon the ornaments prescribed by the rubrics for what, having regard to the rarity of actual celebrations of Holy Communion, was practically the ordinary service on Sundays and Saints' days. That the Canons should mention only the surplice in reference to parish churches, in view of the disuse of Holy Communion, and the determination of the Puritans to wear only the Geneva gown, is entirely in harmony with the facts above mentioned.

In conclusion, it is worth while noticing how completely such a view of the case fits in with the objections taken by the Puritans to the Ornaments' Rubric, and with the reply of the Bishops at the Savoy Conference. The former, having regard to the actual practice which had grown up in the Church, objected to the Rubric as seeming to enforce the vestments. The Bishops, who neither wished to enforce the vestments nor to lower the standard of the Church, merely replied, the question at the moment not being a practical one, by referring the Puritans to the general reasons they had already given why ceremonies should be retained; while, at the same time, they refused to alter a rubric which maintained intact what had all along been the actual law of the Church. No one wishes to-day, any more than in 1662, to enforce the vestments. What is claimed, and what without the grossest injustice cannot be refused, is the extension of the same toleration to those who wish to observe the Church's law as, now for so many years, has been accorded to that party who in this, as in so many other points, have persistently disregarded it.

CHARLES L. WOOD.

10 BELGRAVE SQUARE, *January 28th*, 1881.

NOTE C. Page 199.

Mr. Robertson (*How shall we conform to the Liturgy?* 2nd edit. pp. 101-2,) concludes his quotations on the subject of copes with an argument intended to shew that we are bound at the present time by the LVIII. Canon rather than by the first Rubric. That is to say: whereas the Rubric enjoins the retention of the cope as being one of the 'ornaments' in use 'in this Church of England by the authority of Parliament in the second year of the reign of King Edward the Sixth,' while on the other hand the Canon orders the use of a surplice 'where the Prayer-book,' to use Mr. Robertson's words, 'in strictness prescribed a cope'; we are to obey the latter in preference to the former. The argument by which Mr. Robertson supports the inference appears to be this. The general Rubric respecting ornaments corresponded with the Act of Uniformity, 1 Eliz. But to the latter was attached a provision that the ornaments should be retained 'until other order' should be taken. Now Burn (*Eccles. Law*, iii. 437, quoted by Mr. R.) contends that no such other order ever having been taken the Rubric remains in force, and consequently the LVIII. Canon, which contradicts it, is null and void. We may add that Bp. Cosin (Notes in *Nicholls' Commentary*, p. 17, quoted at length *ante* p. 192, and *ibid*. p. 18), Gibson (Codex I. 363, quoted *ante* p. 150 *n*.,) and Bp. Overall (*Nicholls' Comm*. p. 18, quoted *ante* p. 183,) decide in the same way. But Mr. Robertson wishes to believe that the Advertisements of 1564-5, (though he cannot assert that they were issued in the way provided for by the Act, yet) 'fulfilled the condition of the Act, and consequently have the full authority of law.' Then the Canons of 1604 (which it must be admitted refer in Canon LVIII. to the said Advertisements) must, as agreeing with these Advertisements, supersede the Rubric. This discrepancy and the virtual abrogation of the Rubric, Mr. Robertson would have us believe, continue to the present day, in spite of the enactment of the Rubric in 1662, and the want of any additional sanction to the Canons since 1604. Now on the other hand we would urge that the Advertisements of 1564-5, which confessedly were not made in accordance with the method prescribed by the Act, could not supersede the Rubric. Even if they superseded the Rubric in practice, they could not do so in point of law. We are not concerned to deny the fact, that these Advertisements and the subsequent Canons cannot be reconciled, upon this point, with the Rubric. The difficulty to the Clergy of that period was not greater than that under which we labour, when we promise to obey injunctions which are next to impossible to be observed. However, in 1662, whichever way the balance may have seemed likely to incline before, the deliberate re-enactment of the Rubric surely confirmed anew its provisions, and so superseded the Canon. To us then the case is not difficult; since even on other grounds it may be shewn, and is generally acknowledged, that in any point of disagreement the Canons must yield precedence to the Rubric. That the Divines in 1662 re-enacted this Rubric with deliberation is shewn by the fact, that they introduced certain alterations in its terms, which made its provisions more general; and by the important circumstance that this was done in spite of the remonstrance of the Presbyterians, to the effect that this Rubric would seem to enjoin copes, albs, &c. We may safely conclude then, that it was the intention of the Bishops not to lower the standard in respect to ornaments and ceremonies: and this is at least as good an argument in reference to intention as that urged by Mr. Robertson. But in truth we have little to do with the intention of any parties, while the fact remains that we are bound by the plain words of the present Rubric.—EDD. 1848.

INDEX

TO THE PRINCIPAL MATTERS

A hyphen between two page-numbers signifies that the subject is mentioned on each of the intervening pages also.

ALBE, 135, 136, 144, 145, 148, 154, 155, 162, 164, 165, 174, 177, 183, 192, 196, 199, 200, 203, 205, 206, 225, 226.
Almuce, 151, 156, 157, 174, 176, 213, 267.
Altar, 27-131.
—— consecration of, 39-42.
—— coverings of, 29, 36, 37, 42-56, 71, 72, 88, 95, 98, 102, 105, 143-145, 150, 153, 157, 162, 171, 173, 179, 188, 190, 194, 196, 241, 260, 261.
—— material of, 27-37, 190.
—— ornaments and furniture of, 56-114.
—— position of, 27-37, 90, 245.
Altar-book. *See* Textus.
Altar-cushion, 39, 44, 46, 51, 52, 66, 69, 78, 85, 87, 93, 103, 105, 107, 109, 150, 157, 161, 173, 198, 261.
Altar-lights, 48, 56, 57, 63-68 and *note*, 69, 71, 73-78, 80, 82, 86-88, 90, 93, 99-114, 138, 146, 154, 155, 165, 178, 181, 185, 192, 196, 198, 199, 201.
—— two in number, 57, 63, 65-68, 74, 76-78, 82, 86, 93, 99-105, 107-110, 112, 138, 192.
Altar-plate, 41, 48, 58-60, 62, 71-75, 78-84, 87, 91, 96, 102, 104, 105, 108-112, 149, 160, 161, 176, 178, 260.
—— consecration of, 80 ff, 84, 86, 103, 107, 115-122.
—— display of, 38, 48, 63, 64, 67, 68, 77 and *note*, 89, 90 and *note*, 92, 99, 101, 109, 112, 182, 208.
Altar-rails, 30, 31, 34, 39, 49, 77, 78, 88-91, 95, 100, 109, 112, 193, 198.
Altar-shelf, 53 *note*, 68.
Altars, overthrow of, 37.
Amice, 154, 155, 164, 165, 177.
Ampulla, 59, 165.

BANDS, 232.
Banners, 178, 214, 231, 233.
Banner-cloths, 161.
Banner-staves, 178.
Bells, 138, 144, 155, 173, 178, 259.
Buskyns, 167.

CANDLESTICKS. *See* Altar-lights.
Canopy, 88, 143, 149, 153, 161, 177, 188, 214, 260, 261.
Cap, 69, 74, 174, 176, 194, 216-218, 265-268.
Censer, 122-127, 138, 155.
Chancel, 13-24, 240, 245, 246.
Chasuble, 162, 163, 225. *See* 'Vestment.'
Chasuble and Cope, note on, 178 *note*.
Choir-stalls, 23, 89.
Chrismatory, 62, 155, 161, 167. *See* Ampulla.
Churching-veil, 153, 219-222.
Communion-table. *See* Altar.
Cope, 41, 71, 74, 97, 135-141, 145, 146, 151, 152, 154-156, 162-164,

166-170, 175-177, 180-203, 205, 206, 245, 266-269.
Cope at coronations, 208-212.
—— at funerals, 212-215.
—— in parish churches, 77, 135, 146-148, 152, 155, 157, 171-174, 176-178, 182, 193.
'Cornetes,' 154.
Corporal, 73, 87, 89, 105, 144, 145, 161, 173.
Corporax-case, 144, 145, 154, 161, 173.
Credence, 78, 91, 94, 113, 184, 185.
Cross, 58, 62, 63, 65-68, 138, 154, 155, 165-167.
Cross-banner, 173, 177.
Cross-cloth, 161.
Crucifix, 58, 64-66, 69, 73, 75, 77, 88, 89, 100, 191, 194, 196.
Cruets, 57, 59, 62, 67, 97, 106, 124, 138, 161.
Curtains, 88, 89, 143, 145, 162, 171, 173.

DORSAL or upper frontal, 42, 43, 45, 48, 51, 67, 74, 76, 78, 79, 85, 87, 91, 95, 98, 102, 105, 188.

FALDSTOOL, 96.
Font, 3-10, 72, 240, 262.
—— consecration of, 9.
—— material of, 5, 7-10.
—— position of, 3-9.
Font-canopy, 3, 4, 7, 162.
Font-cloth, 3, 4, 7, 8, 10, 46, 128, 173.
Font-cover, 4, 6-10, 72.
Font-drain, 8, 10.
Funeral-lights, 230.

GLOVES, 60, 167, 226.
Gown, 204, 206, 207, 215-218, 231, 234, 265, 267.

HEARSE-CLOTH, 143, 149, 153, 157, 161, 165, 173, 176, 178, 214, 228, 230, 232, 254 *note*, 261.
Holy-water stoup, 154, 155, 165, 167.
Hood, 74, 135, 136, 151, 168, 174, 181, 183, 190, 193, 194, 198, 202, 213, 218, 231, 234, 245, 269.
Hour-glass, 179.

Houseling-cloth, 127-131.

IMAGES, 21, 22, 58, 64, 75, 194, 196.
Incense, 122 *note*.
Inventories (*the principal quoted*) Bodmin, 172-174; Bristol, 170, 171, 178, 179; Canterbury, 160-177, 260-262; Chapel of Bp. Andrewes, 95-97; St. George's Chapel, Windsor, 80, 97, 104; St. Paul's, London, 58-62, 110, 111, 138-144, 148, 149, 224; Wycombe, 145.

KNIFE, 78.

LACE, 22 and *note*.
Lamp, 173.
'Layres,' 101.
Lectern, 72, 97, 101, 166, 262.
'Leires,' 68.
Lent-cloth or veil, 57, 155, 161, 162.
Litany-desk, 101, 105, 262.

MACE, 228.
Mitre, 167, 194, 223-235.
Monstrance, 166.

'PASTE,' 157.
Pastoral-staff, 136, 137, 192, 196, 209, 223-235.
Pax, 61, 67, 154.
'Pectorell,' 161.
'Pontifical,' 60, 166, 226.
Processional-cross, 161, 165, 167, 224, 226.
Processional-lights, 151, 215.
Pyx, 58, 155.

RING, 167.
Rochet, 74, 76, 136, 147, 150, 171, 173, 192, 194, 198, 205, 208, 226, 228, 233.
Rood-screen, 13-24, 240.

SANDALS, 166.
Sepulchre-cloth, 143.
Ship (*for incense*), 122-126, 155.
Shoes, 167.
Spoon, 59, 123, 124, 166, 167.
Streamers, 146, 157, 161.
Surplice, 71, 74, 135-137, 146, 147, 149, 151, 152, 154, 168, 171, 173, 174, 177-181, 183, 184, 187,

INDEX

190, 192-194, 196-198, 200, 202-208, 211, 213, 214, 217, 232, 245, 265, 266-269.

TEXTUS, 39, 61-63, 74, 76, 82 and *note*, 85, 87, 92, 99, 103, 105, 106, 109, 149, 261.

Tippet, 38, 74, 174, 176, 194, 215 and *note*, 217, 218, 265-267, 269.

Tunicle, 135, 136, 141, 142, 148, 153, 155, 164, 166-168, 196.

VESTMENTS, 66, 135-235.
'Vestment,' 135, 138, 141-143, 145, 146, 148, 152-155, 157, 166, 167, 170, 171, 173, 177, 178, 183, 205, 206.

WAFER-BREAD, 244 *note*.

www.ingramcontent.com/pod-product-compliance
Lightning Source LLC
Chambersburg PA
CBHW071956220426
43662CB00009B/1150